The Rise and Fall of Natural Law

Friedrich Julius Stahl

THE PHILOSOPHY OF LAW

The Rise and Fall of Natural Law

Volume 1A of the Philosophy of Law:
The History of Legal Philosophy

Friedrich Julius Stahl

Translated, edited, and prefaced by
Ruben Alvarado

WordBridge
PUBLISHING
εν αρχη ην ο λογος
AALTEN, THE NETHERLANDS

WORDBRIDGE PUBLISHING
Aalten, the Netherlands
www.wordbridge.net
info@wordbridge.net

German original: Friedrich Julius Stahl, *Die Philosophie des Rechts: Erster Band: Geschichte der Rechtsphilosophie.* Fifth unchanged edition. Tübingen and Leipzig: J. C. B. Mohr, 1878.

ISBN 978-90-76660-56-1

COVER ILLUSTRATION: "Moses Breaks the Tables of the Law" by Gustav Doré (1866). This photographic reproduction is in the public domain.

TABLE OF CONTENTS

PREFACE

It is obvious to even the most casual observer that our age is in thrall to radical subjectivism. Which is to say: the individual and his or her[1] conviction is the driving force in the determination and assessment of social, cultural, political, and juridical mores, standards, values, and goals. There is no overarching standard that transcends individuals and what they, each in and for themselves, determine to be right and wrong, good and evil, worthy of praise or of opprobrium. As a result, there is no shared set of values by which individual self-determination can be guided or restrained; instead, what passes for a shared set of values is simply the aggregation of individual legislations pitted against similarly aggregated yet opposed legislations, whereby the winners impose their aggregated mass of particular interests on the entirety.

It used to be that such a result was accepted until the next election. But nowadays even that threadbare concession to objectivity has been jettisoned, at least by the subjectivist vanguard. If their approach ends up triumphing, the end result will be the termination of the experiment and the imposition of the permanent reign of whoever is able to secure and maintain power. Such does seem to be the next stage in our lengthy downward trajectory.

It is to such straits that we have been reduced; and it is rather a chore to have to trace out the origins, seeing as how there is so little prospect of redressing this catastrophic farce of a public order so as to restore it on sound foundations. But this is our calling, and we will not shirk it. Thankfully, there are not a few witnesses past and present, who have chronicled the career of the debacle the final stages of which we now are privileged (or condemned) to observe on a daily basis. One of them is presented in his own words, in the book you have before you.

Friedrich Julius Stahl (1802–1861) was a leading statesman and legal scholar in 19th century pre-Bismarck Germany. He was one of the century's great parliamentary orators, but because he labored in favor of a Christian-historical order of things, his work has fallen into oblivion. This is no fault of his, but of the

---

[1] That even these qualifiers have become problematic as being insufficiently inclusive, is symptomatic of the phenomenon.

turn toward the catastrophic we have noted; for his words are full of wisdom and caution, all which have gone unheeded. But regardless, they are well worth recovering and exploring, for they make clear the depth of depravity to which we have sunk, and how we have gotten there.

This book, which contains over half of Stahl's *History of Legal Philosophy,* traces out the history of one of the major contributing factors to our modern age. That would be natural law, something which hardly anyone talks about, or even knows about. This was not always the case; once upon a time, natural law was the vehicle of choice to propound all manner of systems of law and order. The leading idea in all of them being that in natural law we have a standard by which to judge all existing, "positive" (i.e., man-made) legal systems.

A fine aspiration, one would think. But the devil is in the details. And not even the details: it is in the starting point. For the methodology of natural law already contained in itself the seeds of natural law's destruction. And Stahl here traces out that course with masterly hand.

Before we proceed any further, we need to ask the question: whence cometh this thing we call natural law? How did it ever become such a central element in learned discourse in ethics, law, politics, and constitutionalism?

Stahl provides a clue when he remarks in passing that natural law is an "expression inherited from the Romans" (p. 179 below). Roman law is of course the primary constituent of the Western legal tradition, and its various rather cursory explorations of the concept mediated its reception in theology and philosophy. But the matter reaches farther back than that, and Stahl accordingly begins his exposition with the Greeks, Plato and Aristotle. Here he is concerned to describe their contribution to "the science of the just" (p. 1), which is his definition of legal philosophy. What he finds is that they contributed essential building blocks for the development of a doctrine of natural law, but without advancing it, without allowing it to run its course. The same is true for the Romans, who incorporate the idea of natural law into their legal philosophy, such as it was; but they, instead of developing it, focused on practice, in order to develop the real-world legal system they inherited.

Opposed to the natural-law philosophy introduced by the pagans was the conception of the will of the personal-infinite God being the source of the ethic and thus of law, characterized by Stahl variously as Jewish, Judeo-Christian, or Christian (pp. 31ff., 34ff., 8off.). Working from Christian revelation, Augustine mediated the conflict between Plato and Aristotle by introducing the concept of the Fall of Man, "the middle term which alone can unite Plato and Aristotle." In this manner, "the contradiction between the absolute moral task of the human race, which imbues Plato, and the laws of nature and the natural constitution of man, which Aristotle makes into a standard, is solved" (p. 45). Hence, natural law as absolute unattainable standard (Plato) is reconciled with natural law as inherent life force (Aristotle); but the reconciliation comes at a price, recognition of the living God.

Thus from the start, Christianity had within it the resources to develop a higher law answering to the science of the just. But instead of developing this insight further, it took over the natural-law building blocks of antiquity and merely juxtaposed them with the Augustinian understanding of God and the world, thus without transforming them. This was the system of scholasticism, and its preeminent developer was Thomas Aquinas (pp. 47ff.). To accomplish this, Aquinas adopted the concepts of an eternal law (*lex aeterna*) and the natural law. Eternal law is "the world-ordering reason in the Divine Spirit" which in itself is of the nature of art, an example, an idea – *artis vel exemplaris vel ideae* – but which with regard to human action has the form of a law. Natural law is participation in eternal law without being equivalent to it, being limited especially by man's fallen state (p. 47).

The problem here lies precisely in the ambivalent concept of the *lex aeterna*. For Aquinas makes a far-reaching distinction with regard to how God Himself relates to it. In itself, the will of God is not subject to this *lex aeterna* – but with regard to the creature, the will of God *is* subject to it. "In and of itself, therefore, the divine will is one with reason, but in relation to the creation and rule of the world, it is subordinated to the standard of reason" (p. 47). The upshot of this arrangement is to divorce God's will from the reasonable eternal law, and thus from the reasonable natural law. God's will becomes a subordinate category; and *a fortiori*, His revealed will does as well. Therefore,

> regardless of how deeply and truly the source of all moral commandment is acknowledged to be in the divine reason and wisdom, as is likewise the unity of the divine will with the divine reason and wisdom, an unacceptable divide is introduced here between the divine will-substance and the divine counsels, which in its further development leads, and actually did lead, to the will-

substance or the eternal law in God manifesting itself as mere supreme rule, as something given, apart from any decision (pp. 47f.).

This was a fatal move, for it delivered the higher law over into the hands of autonomous reason. From this point, natural law could, and eventually would, take on a life of its own. Initially, the Christian scientific endeavor continued in the train of a juxtaposition of Greek, in particular Aristotelian, thought with Augustinian doctrine (pp. 51ff.). Then came the twin movements of Renaissance and Reformation, bringing a new element into play, the subjective: "The principle of subjectivity was first unleashed" (p. 62). For the first time, the thinking subject became the central factor in scientific analysis. And in its subsequent development, this principle of subjectivity came to express itself in terms of a new demand: the right, without acknowledging any authority or receiving any given content, to access and develop knowledge, hence, the right of autonomy. The science of natural law followed ineluctably in its wake. "The philosophy that only recognizes what follows from reason cannot very well look elsewhere for this source of the ethic than in reason. In this consists natural law" in its now-purified form (p. 93).

To be sure, scholasticism had already prepared the way for this development. In the *lex aeterna* it had devised a way to sidestep the personal-infinite God and His will; indeed, to do so was "the precondition, the first step that natural law had to take to clear space for itself" (p. 94). The *lex aeterna* "abolished freedom of decision and determination in God" (p. 95), making way for Grotius' – the father of modern natural law (p. 139) – famous adage that reasonable right and wrong would be what it is even if God did not exist. Grotius was not the first to enunciate this principle, for it was already expressed in medieval times – another indication of the preparation provided by scholasticism for modern natural law. At most, God could be considered the author of natural law in the sense that He caused it to reside in man's heart; but His will was relegated to the category of divine positive law, a subordinate and dependent category.

Grotius, the legal-philosophical counterpart to René Descartes, pioneered modern natural law. Natural law's first, Grotian, iteration was in the form of "sociabilism," with its starting point placed in the sociable nature of man. Hobbes turned this on its head, placing the starting point in fear and insecurity, but this was a side track. Thomasius took things a step further, introducing the pursuit of happiness (cf. pp. 139ff.).

But what lay at the heart of natural law was the centrality of autonomous reason. Wolff realized this and dropped the notion of a starting point in this or that drive of human nature altogether; rather, he zeroed in on the rationalist principle at the heart of natural law, making it itself the starting point. Taken on their own merits, his efforts were rather feeble, but they at least had this positive result: they constituted "an impetus for Kant to take the rationalist principle seriously" (p. 159). Following through on this principle, Immanuel Kant laid bare the basic conundrum faced by the doctrine of natural law: the conflict between two concepts, a timeless unchanging law of reason, on the one hand, and a world of concrete things, acting subjects, on the other. Try as he might, he could not reconcile the two, because "he contemplates reason as a static form, and consequently as a thing. A thing and another thing that is set over against it, will always remain apart." Fichte proffered the solution: "It was therefore necessary to regard reason as active; not as the determinations of thought and laws, but as the *activity of thought*. This was the precondition for explaining this connection" (p. 174).

In taking reason to be an active thing, as activity of thought, Fichte brought the natural-law tradition to its terminus, enthroning the subjective principle over the supposed objective, eternal, unchanging law of reason. Even more than this: he accorded exclusive existence to subjectivity, and denied the existence of an objective world outside of consciousness. Unpalatable though it might be, this was the inevitable conclusion to the subjective-rationalist train of thought. But the more practical issue of Fichte's philosophy has been the triumph of the principle of subjectivity in the area of law. With Fichte, the individual becomes the source of law and as such an absolute legislator. "Law has no power over people; its realization depends on their arbitrary will" (p. 198). How can such a sovereign individual coexist with others, you may ask? Fichte had no convincing answer. Without an overarching law to restrain individuals, what is left is power relations. "If you can, make yourself into the ruler of the world. Freedom of the individual as the principle of the doctrine of law necessarily leads to this end" (p. 201). The principle even extends to education, whereby Fichte purged education of received learning, "burdening the pupil with the production of the entire future fund of knowledge from out of his own pure thought-activity" (p. 193).

With Fichte we have arrived squarely in our own world. The radical subjective principle has taken over every area of thought and practice. Each individual has become a legislating god pronouncing his or her "LET THERE BE ..." and woe to whoever stands in the way of every particular "AND THERE WAS ...."

How do we escape this descent into the maelstrom? Although his major positive contributions are contained in Volume II,[2] Stahl already provides some answers here.

The core problem with natural law, having hitched its wagon to reason, converts reason from an instrument to discover truth into a, indeed the, source of truth. Thus, we look to reason, not to revelation or divine authority to discover the truth. But this is to put the cart before the horse. "The true, the just are therefore that at which reason in its activity arrives, not what it is; they are what is discovered *through it*, not *from it*. It sees the light and testifies of the light, but it is not the light and did not make the light. This is precisely what is wrong with rationalism: it turns the organ of truth into truth itself, and because of this, it thinks that by dismantling and examining this organ it has obtained the content of the true, which this organ was supposed to convey" (p. 216). To view reason as the source of knowledge and truth is akin to believing "that the corporeal instruments through which we receive and distribute food, actually *are* our food. Such a conception corresponds with rationalism's procedure" (p. 217).

This point of departure leads natural law, as we saw, to attempt to reconcile an eternal unchanging law of reason with human freedom. This supposed antinomy is a problem of its own making. For "the contradiction arises only from the fact that human freedom is founded on a concept. If it is deployed by the free will of God and as part of His specific moral order, then all difficulties are smoothed away: it reaches as far as it wishes to, it has its limits in how far it may alienate itself in the determination that He gave it; but within this boundary it has its truly free, change-effecting movement, because God, unlike reason, brings forth more than what is only logically necessary" (p. 130).

The missing link is the personal-infinite God of the Bible. Only He can unite law and personality, and only in His creative act can these both be brought

---

[2] The volume as a whole is entitled *The Doctrine of Law and State on the Basis of the Christian World-View*, comprising the subvolumes *Philosophical Presuppositions*, *Principles of Law*, *Private Law*, and *The Doctrine of State and the Principles of State Law*.

forth, into a world of manifold complexity which cannot be reduced to the forms of logic, to mere negative knowledge. Rationalism provides negative knowledge; God provides positive knowledge.

> What is found from reason (*a priori*) is, according to Schelling's deeply significant expression, not "being," but only "not-capable-of-not-being." Thus, for example, that a triangle has three angles that together add up to two right angles, or that, as Wolff deduces, "seeing is the property of an animal with eyes" (thus a seeing animal), is only a negative knowledge; on the other hand, that the earth is round and not triangular, that there are plants and animals, this is positive knowledge. Another would not be unthinkable. Positive, and the object of positive knowledge, is, if I may put it in an absolute and exhaustive manner, the person, what is specifically primordially determined for him (i.e., holiness, the love of God, etc.), his act, and the product of his act. Therefore, it is merely negative knowledge that there is a being, a power, a ground, by which the world exists, because the opposite would be contrary to logical concepts; on the other hand, it is positive knowledge that there is a God in the true sense, a personal, self-conscious creator; likewise, that this God is gracious and merciful. It is positive knowledge when we consider the world to be the act and creation of God, and only negative knowledge when we consider it to be the eternally necessary consequence of reason. Philosophy which derives all knowledge from reason, can have no other than negative knowledge (p. 81).

This personal-infinite, creating God produces positive knowledge and therefore also events, new occurrences, history; and His purpose in history is constitutive to law properly conceived, and thus legal philosophy. This understanding of history, Stahl avers, was lacking to the Reformation, as part of an overreaction to the Catholic emphasis on the authority of human tradition. We may dispute the details,[3] but we cannot argue with the fact that the emphasis on

---

[3] In particular with regard to the shortcomings in Stahl's treatment of Calvinism. His accusation that Calvinism completely ignored the historical dimension is overdrawn. His Lutheran predilections lurk behind the curt dismissal of Calvinist theology and ecclesiology as thoroughly ahistorical (p. 64). And his post-Revolution monarchist

history as a crucial determinant of a proper ethic and legal philosophy has arisen in the meantime, largely in response to the ostensible timelessness of the rationalist philosophy. As Stahl remarks, "These latest scientific endeavors should not merely scientifically give shape to the inherent drive, the principle of the Reformation according to its true, full, positive aspect, but at the same time revive an aspect which even the Reformation left to one side. That would be the ethical significance of world history as the work and manifestation of the World Power" (p. 64).

The Christian-*historical* approach, then, alone reconciles law and freedom:

[T]he historical view is the one by which something has happened and is happening, according to which there is a free act. Schelling called the Christian view of the world the historical as opposed to the logical view of modern philosophy. For the latter would have it that the world and all particular things are necessarily contained in the essence of God, while the former says it only arose (came about) through His voluntary creation. I have referred to the Judeo-Christian view of ethics as historical for the reason that it views law as law because God willed it so. Thus, man had the ethic before any incident of his own; but he has it only by the act of God; it does not exist by itself, with the concept of its existence or of being in general. And the past is not the higher, the present is; and the highest is the future, because God leads the world and law to it (p. 80).

Likewise, it alone maintains a true ethic:

According to the *Jewish* conception, it is the personal God, not limited by anything, who according to His free will rules the destinies of the world, and who prescribes to men their end. Ethical precepts have no foundation apart from His will. All establishments and regulations bear the imprint of His omnipotence:

---

sympathies cloud his judgment of the Calvinist Monarchomachs (pp. 238ff.). Stahl was not acquainted with the work of Althusius, which was rediscovered by Gierke only after Stahl's death. If he had been, he would have had to modify his conclusions, especially regarding the scientific nature of Calvinist political theology. Both of these issues – Calvinism's historical dimension and its political theology – are treated in Alvarado, *Calvin and the Whigs* and *The Debate that Changed the West.*

"Ye shall not deal falsely one to another, *I am the Lord your God*" [cf. Leviticus 19: 11.] Good and evil exist only because He willed it or forbade it, for His alone is the glory.... *History is only the work of an agent....* In Judaism, not only do human destinies have a history, but the disposing power over them does as well. In events, everything is foresight, preparation for a future destination, everything is the result of interaction of the free act of people vis-à-vis God and the no less free act of God vis-à-vis people. The Judeo-Christian narrative as a whole turns out to be a great stage play, the archetype of all tragedy, because it is the divine tragedy. The ethical commandments themselves are a history. There is no ideal closed off in itself as the norm for the manifold relationships that develop outside of it, but He who alone is the source of the ethic, for each event, when it happens, at the same time imparts the law, because nothing happens that was not present in His will (pp. 31f.).

And furthermore:

An ethic that creates the norm while simultaneously generating the conditions and circumstances, which itself moves in an uninterrupted ascent to its final form, and therefore may be something else for a different time and different incident, without contradiction – an *historical ethic* can have its basis only in the free and omnipresent will of a personal God. Thus in Greek philosophy, although it recognizes a positive and meaningful principle of things, yet already has the beginning of the unhistorical view, since the cause of the world and the ethic appears as unfree, *thallos*, something merely existing. This view reaches its extreme in modern, abstract philosophy and certifies here more clearly the untruth thereof, whence it is also necessary for philosophy to return to that ancient historical view, the *Judeo-Christian*, which has never ceased being valid in life (p. 34).

Given its abstract character, natural law lacks this historical dimension. Not only that, it also, its rationalist point of departure deprives it of concrete content. It cannot take life relations and elevate them; rather, it must eliminate them in order to create a new order of things. We are experiencing the inexorable logic of this rationalist subjectivism in our day, whereby every activist movement believes it can remake human nature after its own image.

Stahl laid bare natural law's ultimately anti-natural character, pointing out its inability to take created realities into account. Instead of accepting God-given verities, it determines to overthrow them and recreate reality in terms of its abstractions. This becomes evident in its treatment of social structures and the inherent purposes they contain.

> The innermost untruth of natural law, which must strike every unprejudiced observer as soon as it is stated, is that it completely disregards the *inherent purpose of life relations*. Every human life relation bears within it its own particular purpose and thereby lays upon people a vocation to fulfill it accordingly, to give shape to it. This is the basis for the moral requirements that pertain to it, and also the requirements of its legal arrangement. For instance, the inherent purpose of marriage (the union of spouses for full life community), and not the reciprocal relinquishment of freedom among spouses, is that from which the entire legal formation of marriage proceeds: the obligation of faithfulness and community for better or worse, the prohibition on polygamy, incest, arbitrary divorce; the purpose of parental relations from which proceeds on the one hand paternal power, on the other the sustentation of children. The same holds true for every other human relation: property transactions, occupational groups, political groups, local community, state, church. This purpose of life relations is the principle of both ethics and law. All actual law indeed aims for this, and law is rational to the degree that it is shaped in accordance with these relations.... This purpose of life relations is the ground on which true legal philosophy takes its stand in opposition to the false philosophy of natural law (pp. 229f.).

What impelled the career of natural law was the effort to discover a common ground for all right-thinking persons beyond the dividing lines of sectarian religion. If our times have taught us one thing, it is the absolute untenability of the notion of a such a natural law accessible to people of "good faith," regardless of conviction, on the basis of a common ground in shared nature, human or otherwise. The gradual elimination of all such shared bases, brought about by the inexorable march of logical consistency on the basis of contradictory presuppositions, regardless of how flawed they might be in themselves, should by now have disabused us of this fata morgana. Stahl had already anticipated such a turn of events nearly two centuries ago. As he wrote in the introduction to

Volume II of this work, "Every philosophical system of whatever name in the final analysis rests on a foundational presupposition that is nothing more than faith, no matter what claim it may make to so-called scientific certainty. Even unbelief is a faith – one cannot reason from naked doubt. We have no immediate or homogeneous view of the highest principles of things and thus no absolute certainty; therefore for philosophical systems a purely objective knowledge independent of all personal judgment, such as mathematics, the natural sciences, or even the positive sciences, is ruled out."[4] Modernism is not based on neutral science but on specific presuppositions enthroning autonomous reason, which, consistently applied, end up destroying life.

How do we avoid this fate? Generally speaking, we need to recover a Christian-historical understanding of life, the world, eternity. But in terms of systematics, Stahl proposes a novel solution. He notes that every system, however ultimately illogical, is based on some aspect of reality which serves as a presupposition from which all else is deduced. "All of these doctrinal systems in their ready-made manifestations are closed, self-sustaining worlds. But they are still created in the one real world, and if their movement of *thought* begins and ceases within themselves, they do have a *factual* ground, outside themselves" (p. 3). Intellectually, these systems are carried out in lopsided fashion because they focus on a specific human interest which in itself is legitimate and finds its basis in reality. "The various systems do not at all allow themselves to be united, because true and false cannot be united, and there is no community between opposing basic assumptions. But with regard to the interest that is specific to each philosophy, it is impossible to say in advance that one such would by nature exclude another. On the contrary, we might reason that each in itself, because it is human, is a true one, and that history desired its satisfaction, but is untrue in the product which it brought about in separation from the rest" (p. 4). Stahl's method is to deconstruct these philosophical systems in terms of the human interest which spawned each of them and which serves as its particular point of departure, and reintegrate them by joining these disparate interests into a comprehensive system embracing them all. Such is only possible through a comprehension of the whole man, of his true and original nature, because only his nature combines these interests. The knowledge of this, in turn, can only come

---

[4] *Principles of Law*, p. 4.

from his Creator.

And so, having passed through the subjectivist phase, finally turning away from his rationalist autonomy, there is only one alternative for modern man. "And when at last he sees himself compelled to turn back to the recognition of independent existence outside himself, he no longer can consider it in the Greek fashion, as held together by the idea or the laws of nature, but as the work of the freely acting God" (p. 38).

NOTES ON THE TRANSLATION

The usual translating conventions are followed. Square brackets [like this] are used either to show the original text in cases in which the translation is not straightforward or unambiguous, or to provide interpolations for better understanding, or to provide supplementary material.

A note about the notoriously difficult words "Recht" and "Gesetz": as is well known, English has no direct counterpart to them; they both refer to "law." Often they are used synonymously, but just as often they are not. This is similar to the Latin words "jus" and "lex," which confront the translator with the same ambiguity. Now then, there are three cases of contradiction referred to by these words. In one case, "Recht" refers to law in the more elevated, transcendent sense, while "Gesetz" refers to law in the positive, man-made sense. This is usually referred to as the contradistinction between natural law and positive law. But this is not the only kind of contradistinction they may denote. There is, in addition, the distinction between moral and juridical law, a distinction which plays a large role in the discussion of this book. In order to set juridical law apart from moral law, Stahl combines the words into one, using the term "Rechtsgesetz" for law which functions exclusively in the juridical sphere, and it is here translated that way. Yet another contradistinction is that between law and rights. Here, it is English which is unambiguous, German and Latin which are ambiguous. "Recht" in the singular I have almost always translated as "law" except where it was obvious from the context that "rights" were meant (e.g., p. 111); the plural, "Rechten," always refers to "rights," and it is here so translated.

Einleitung.

Rechtsphilosophie ist die Wissenschaft des Gerechten. Der Erwartungen sind nun verschiedene, welche man von einer Wissenschaft des Gerechten hegen kann. Man kann sich unter ihr ein System wirklicher Entscheidungen denken, ein höheres Gesetzbuch, oder nur eine Richtschnur des Urtheils über bestehende Gesetze. Das aber ist unbestreitbar: das Gerechte muß unabhängig von seiner Anerkennung unter den Menschen sein Daseyn und seine Tugend haben, und die Kenntniß desselben daher eine andere seyn als die des geltenden Rechts, eine solche, an welcher dieses selbst gerade allein zu messen und zu erproben ist. Manche sind wohl auch dahin gekommen, alle Einrichtungen für sittlich gleichgültig zu halten, oder zu läugnen, daß dem Menschen die Kunde des Wahren und Gerechten vergönnt sey. Es ist aber ein heiliger Glaube der Menschheit, daß eine Gerechtigkeit ist, und daß wir ein Wissen, sey es auch ein beschränktes, von ihr haben. Wo aber ein Wissen ist, da muß auch irgend eine Einheit, ein Zusammenhang in ihm seyn und ausfindig gemacht werden können, da muß es also auch eine Wissenschaft, in was immer für einer Art, geben.

I.   1

INTRODUCTION

Legal philosophy is the science of the just. Expectations may differ regarding such a science. One can envision a system of legal decisions, a code of higher law, or merely a rule by which to judge existing laws. But one thing is undeniable: the just must have its being and its virtue independently of its recognition among men, which means that the knowledge of it must be something else than the standing law; in fact, standing law can only be measured and tested against it. Some have even come to hold all institutions to be morally indifferent or to deny that the knowledge of the true and just is vouchsafed to men. But it is a sacred belief of mankind that there is a justice, and that we have a knowledge of it, limited though it may be. But where there is a knowledge, there must also be some sort of unity and coherence to it, which can be identified, for which reason there must also be a science, of whatever sort it might be.

If one truly wishes to get on with such a science, the thought arises that the same thing has already been tried by others, in various ways, with various results. These previous attempts cannot be ignored, because it is human nature that we only be convinced and believe ourselves to be on the right track when we are aware of being in command of any conflicting belief. This puts us directly in the midst of the aspirations of our time. And even if the investigations into the just must have the same goal at all times, in each particular one a special way may be mapped depending on the state of the science which is found in it. But this means that our science will require quite a distinct approach. For not only is opinion divided and vacillating regarding individual institutions, it is so even regarding the standard by which their justice is to be assessed. Our legal philosophy cannot escape the total uncertainty of all knowledge and thought which is the fruit of the rapid succession of destructive systems of philosophy, while it also faces harrowing developments in its own field.

When at the end of the last century a long-held orientation broke into the open, it was the prideful freedom of human action and thought that led scientific efforts. Seeking sole dominion, like any new motive force, it expressed itself in the destruction of everything it encountered. The multiplicity of particular relations, the entire structure of the moral world would be torn down so that nothing would exist but what pure reason finds and brings forth out of itself. This orientation retained vitality until it used up its fuel and manifested its inability to provide a new world for the fallen one. At that point, the Higher Power once again was recognized and revered which, hidden to us, brings the human condition to shape and maturity. Once again the value of each individual life, each peculiarly formed institution, was asserted. And the law no longer appeared to be a product of the laws of thought, but a living member connected with all the relations of life of the peoples and the movement of history.

And so, this orientation was overturned, but mainly by virtue of a mere natural reaction. As in that case there was a hatred of all that exists, so in this case there was a hatred of all free reflection. Governments should maintain the existing condition; lawyers should know of the institutions of the present and their historical derivation, not judge them. In this manner, the fight against the philosophy of the times became a rejection of philosophy altogether. The power of life, the further development of relationships, which require examination and judgment, then also made this one-sidedness palpable; and in the Historical School[5] the need once again became manifest for a standard of the just, but without a specific view as to where it should betake itself.

Meanwhile, a new treatment of the philosophy of law arose in the philosophical system of Hegel. It not only opposes the other two orientations but generally demands a previously unheard-of way of thinking. We observe these three opposing scientific schools in the field of our legal philosophy. Next to them, partly based on them, partly independently, are writers who pursue practical interests without general scientific exhaustiveness. These are the representatives of countless political confessions.

So this is the ground on which the investigation of the just currently finds itself as it embarks on its course. It might take a course opposed to all of these viewpoints, or it might link up with one of them; whatever it does, it will encounter the opposition of the others. It therefore requires at the start a justification against them, namely one which they themselves must recognize. This would then constitute a grounded judgment over them. Without this scientific

---

[5] [The Historical School of jurisprudence as represented chiefly by Friedrich Karl von Savigny. It will be discussed in detail in Volume I B of this work.]

justification, any investigation incurs the charge of arbitrariness. It cannot convict the opponent and therefore cannot consider itself to be secured. The same task also extends to the views of yesteryear, because our historical teaching transplants them to the present, and we cannot excuse ourselves from taking up a certain position vis-à-vis them.

But the difficulty of this task becomes evident already in advance. If a decision is to be made between opponents, it will not be possible otherwise than by they themselves recognizing common ground by which to measure themselves. Now then, every system which is to be secured contains in itself a supreme principle of law, in fact in part even a supreme law of thought and knowledge, thus the supreme thing against which everything else is measured; and it acknowledges this to be nowhere outside itself. Everything must be conceded to it, if one submits to its test of what is truthful. If, however, one denies this and chooses another, it can demand no further concessions. But this test of the truth, against what can it itself be tested? Whatever is established as a rule of justice, or as a logical law according to which things are decided and proven, is still only a new system placed alongside the previous one, equally isolated, rejecting and being rejected. It could not acquire authority over other ways of thinking, each of which is like a circular line moving around its own center, returned to its starting point, a self-sufficient closed world. But if one wishes to select what is true from among all of this, he must presuppose something that should be the result of his investigation – a standard. In so doing, he loses the recognition of all, and retains only a colorful composition, without unity and internal stability.

Hence, a community of the various views, each assured of its own rightness, seems impossible even before one begins.

All of these doctrinal systems in their ready-made manifestations are closed, self-sustaining worlds. But they are still created in the one real world, and if their movement of *thought* begins and ceases within themselves, they do have a *factual* ground, outside themselves. No system forms itself: it is formed by people. There must, therefore, be some drive, some interest in human nature, by which it is produced and gains its existence in an enduring manner. Its basic assumption cannot, by its very nature, be obtained by conclusions which it presupposes; rather, it is nothing else than precisely the interest that the thinker finds in his own innermost being, which he cannot give up. But the scientific method is always determined by the basic assumption – the manner of assuming, of deciding, of demonstrating, hence the entire system. The systems have therefore varied as the progress of history has brought forth a different character of the human mind and its various motives.

The interest that generates and maintains a philosophy is something higher than the philosophy itself, because the existence of the latter depends upon the existence of the former. The measure of philosophy is therefore likewise the measure that must be applicable to the interest that generated it. But its measure can only be a factual one. For example, that the good is good and evil is evil, cannot be demonstrated logically, but is true only while the primary source of good at the same time possesses omnipotence. Could humanity indeed break free from these ideas and the power that they contain, then the distinction between them would have to fall away in science as well. The historical progression, the real nature of man is the judgment over all motives of philosophy, and thus even over this. Science, as with the legends of the saints, must seek out the strongest lord.

The various systems do not at all allow themselves to be united, because true and false cannot be united, and there is no community between opposing basic assumptions. But with regard to the interest that is specific to each philosophy, it is impossible to say in advance that one such would by nature exclude another. On the contrary, we might reason that each in itself, because it is human, is a true one, and that history desired its satisfaction, but is untrue in the product which it brought about in separation from the rest. Now should it find a deeper, fuller interest that would contain all these interests in itself and alone generate them, then it would be satisfied through the satisfaction of all the others. The philosophy that exacted this would be the secure one. It would unite all the others; not their claims, but their true drives, by which alone both their false results and their true ones could become reality, the vital acting element in each one. This total interest with its rich content would be nothing other than the true and original nature of man, from which have emanated all conditions and motives, and to which they purpose to return. A view is certain not merely if it is grounded and agreed within itself, but if it satisfies the whole man, and also provides insight into how the others could arise; for no other position grants full overview of the others than the highest.

The task is therefore to present our philosophical knowledge genetically. The knowledge of the historical succession of philosophical views will not suffice here; instead, their own origin and inner gestation, the driving force in the human being that they produced, has to be revealed. Therefore, completeness of writers and their opinions cannot be the goal, but only the completeness of the scientific pathways; and with every system, the question is not so much which institutions it declares to be just, but what for it *is* the just, and whence it draws the knowledge thereof.

In this manner, the consideration of the past should lead to new results.

BOOK I: IDEAL AND EMPIRICAL LEGAL PHILOSOPHY (THE GREEKS)

PART I: PLATO

The Idea and Its Knowledge

Our eye receives the light and reflects the light, but it is not the light and did not make the light. Rather, Helios radiates the light; he gives things color and visibility, and our eyes the ability to see them. In the same way, the idea is the cause of good. She is the queen of the world of spirit, as the sun is of the world of sense. Indeed she even brought the latter forth, and set the light and the sun as her image in that world. Only through her is there a distinction of good and evil, of truth and falsehood, as the difference of color comes through light. Our spirit bears witness to the idea, but is not the idea; but by her it has received its ability to detect these differences. And were she to retire from the world, it also would no longer know good and evil, as when the sun goes down, the eye no longer distinguishes between colors and objects, although the power of distinguishing seemingly lies in itself.

This is Plato's parable.[6]

So the idea has an existence and therefore a quality, a determinateness other than the capacity in ourselves that, by its aid, sees its effects. And it must also be recognized as an independent entity in this way. Just as now no one investigates the eye in order to observe the sun and the light or to prove their existence, so Plato does not infer and find the essence of goodness from reason; but it itself is the first and original that there is, and of which the mind [Geist] has knowledge; not that it has to be there because some ground in ourselves made it necessary. The laws and the organization of the eye in themselves are nothing; the power and activity in it are stirred only by the light which ensures vision. Only through the idea is the power stirred that sees good and evil – the *vision of the spirit* [Anschauung des Geistes]. It is not placidly there, as sight is not placidly there in the eye, and does not have its possession in itself. Rather, it simply is, while it absorbs the object, like the rays of light, outside itself. If light and color are nothing other than what already lies in the organization of vision, from whence should it have its peculiar luster and the joy that it infuses in the

---

[6] *The Republic,* Book VI.

viewers? Now, if the idea is something outside of the laws and determinations of the mind, why should it be restricted to the paucity thereof, why should the good and righteous be merely formal, an epitome of general rules without special content? The idea in fact works according to its own nature, and nothing stands in the way of its having inward splendor and immense wealth, like the sun, with its rays breaking into manifold colors.

Influence on the Doctrine of State

With Plato, therefore, justice is no rule or system of rules, but a full display of manifold, quite determinate activity. Hence his republic is the pattern of concrete usage. He shows us his citizens in the full activity of their lives, how they meet their needs, what their employment is, what their spiritual aspirations are, how they are educated and informed, what they think to be good and estimable, bad and shameful. The constitution and form of the state appears in indissoluble unity with this particular life. These can as little be transferred to other citizens as its citizens could live under a different constitution. It is impossible to distinguish and delineate what in this state is the eternal, the ideal, and what is of accidental appearance. For if we were to abstract a principle from it and hold to it as the self-contained true and eternal, we would by no means hit Plato's meaning. It is not, e.g., the bare surrender of the individual to the whole that appears to him to be the true and magnificent; what matters is only the specific manner of surrender, the specific manner of activity, as it is conducted through all the diversity of human activity.

The ideal is so determinate and individual, determinate even for the moment in which it is presented, that it contains, as an essential element, even the mind and the worth of the ruling persons, who in fact change while the general principles of the constitution remain. Wise people are worth more than wise laws, this is what every simple man thinks: this judgment now makes its appearance in a scientific work, and it pertains to the idea of this state, that the wise (philosophers) govern it. In fact, for the mutual relations of its citizens there should be no rules at all. The sure judgment of well-bred men will decide in the particular case.

Hence, the notion that the general principles professed in its laws by the state, and presented in its constitution, contain the just, is quite far from the mark. The just does not aim for this stasis, the architecture of public life; rather, the just is a living condition, it consists in the particular action of the moment.

The scientific course followed by Plato, by which he discovers, tests, proves institutions, is nothing like *logical deduction*, by which, from given premises, others arise of necessity. He tests their *actual result* by assessing whether a situation arises that he desires for the whole. If the idea of the good and the just is something other than the organization of the mind, who then would require it always to desire a conclusion which of necessity follows from two premises, rather than from what the *whole* freely wills with a *single* will, regardless of how many components it might have? In a logical deduction, the connection is similar to a building, where the lower always carries the upper, without being carried by it; but contemplation [Anschauung] which is aroused by the idea is like a living body in which each member both holds and carries the other and is held and carried at the same time. The analogy that Plato uses between the unity of the people and the state makes it apparent that he does not seek the unity of the concept, but of the living. His picture of the state emerges in one step at the same time in all parts, complete, in the world, like wisdom from the head of Zeus.

Plato's facsimile from his archetype, or, in turn, others' facsimiles of his republic, is therefore completely different from those done according to abstract concepts and the more recent doctrines of state. The latter can be called the facsimile of stasis, the former the facsimile of the act. The facsimile of stasis is subsumption: juxtaposing rules having no intrinsic content and therefore lying ready at hand for any content – for example, equal freedom – with material otherwise indifferent, given apart from it – landholding, commerce, or whatever it might be. But Plato's facsimile does not impart a disconnected rule to the original which it only needs to take up; and no material is sufficient for it that was not already thoroughly shaped according to the idea. Any logical mind could therefore choose to introduce the justice of Kant or Hegel into a country, but whoever would undertake the formation of a state according to Plato, or a legal philosophy developed in the same sense, would have to be equipped with creative power.

Therefore, the facsimile of stasis must also mimic the image of stasis. To wit, actual institutions must mathematically satisfy the general principles of justice, and these must be amenable of realization. But the facsimile of act must mimic the original model of the act. The same spirit, the same effect must prevail in the facsimile as in the original. And so the painter's image of man cannot and ought not be equal in terms of ruler and compass, but should have the same effect as the original, i.e., the painting should bring forth the same perception in the viewer as the person painted. The question of feasibility is therefore the most incongruous measure one can apply to the republic of Plato. For the meaning is not that these laws are to be literally implemented in a state as he designed it, but that a real state bear the same spirit within itself, engender the same mind in its citizens, and through its institutions exercise the same impression on the beholders as upon him who designed it. It is this which is feasible, and if it cannot be achieved to that extent, at least nothing stands in the way of states making their institutions so as to approach it. And yet, in fact, this idea of the Platonic state is none other than what really moved the Greek states; in the period of their luster and their excellence, they together imitated it with greater or lesser success.

It has become prevalent in recent times to look at the real shape of things as the sole representation of the good and the just; and, while not admitting the existence of things apart from the idea, certainly not the idea apart from things. It has even been attempted to attach the Platonic ideas to this relation. But according to Plato, although the idea did bring about all things, its own existence is not conditioned by that which it produced; it is not just an aspect, foundation, form, or motive power of the product, but has a real independent existence, like the sun, which would still be the sun even if there were no objects for it to illuminate, no growth for it to unfold, and no eye to look upon it. To Plato the dissatisfaction of every great mind with earthly things is obvious. His ideal is nowhere in the world, as even his own visualizations could not show how things stood to his mind's eye. The reality that does not contain it, should first only strive to form itself in accordance with it. His knowledge is therefore not the same as that of a knowledge that is in the existing order, but of one that is currently outside of it, that only in the future perhaps will be in it – it is therefore a *preview*.

The Republic

This image of the state in Plato's mind's eye is the abundance of manifold forces corresponding to the human community, each fully unfolded in its own way, and all, in the entirety of all their activities, oriented to a goal, gained from an ordering sense in proper measure. "Justice" (we could more correct translate: perfection) for the state is precisely what it is for the individual. The first requirement is, that each develop his innate aptitude undisturbed, so that no force remains hidden, and all the wealth placed in the nature of man unfolds itself. The second is that each person be referred to his proper place and ambulate therein. The last, finally, is that these cheek-by-jowl, diverse aspirations and achievements all be mastered by a single will and interest – that the state also be *one* state.

Accordingly, citizens are divided into two main classes, one for the lower functions of material needs (the farmer, belt-cutter, potter, etc.), the other for the higher functions of military protection and spiritual leadership – the "Guardians." The separation occurs in an equitable manner if each is allocated the position to which he is called by his nature. Accordingly, even in the lower class, employment is not left to individual choice but according to aptitude and capacity, thus ensuring that each activity is brought to perfection. Equally, citizens are classified in the higher or lower class according to their higher or lower nature, their moral and intellectual gifts. For some souls by nature have gold mixed in them, others silver, others a baser metal. But the distribution in the two classes is hereditary because only a noble line yields noble offspring, and here still, precautions are taken against degeneration. However, this does not rule out members of the higher class becoming demoted if they degenerate, while members of the lower, if they ennoble themselves, become elevated to the higher. The lower class is further left out of consideration. It forms, according to the Greek manner, the base layer that is lowered into the enveloping earth in order for the splendor of the building to rise above it. The ruling class of Guardians alone is actually the state; in it alone is represented the perfection of human common life. Its members are relieved of any common concern and employment; the state meets the need. From childhood on they receive the most thought-out education; gymnastics and music bring all their physical and intellectual aptitudes to maturity, every great mind is nourished in them, every disturbing impression is kept away. Thus, imitative poetry itself is excluded because it endangers truthfulness and dignity.

The full development of the forces and the resulting proper distribution thereof has impressed upon it the seal of perfection by the *unity of the goal* that they serve. Everything is to be directed to the whole, to the state, not to any personal (private) interest. Citizens are not ends in themselves but merely a means for the state. In particular, the higher class of the Guardians, in which the perfect state is represented, imposing this utter self-renunciation and unconditional surrender on the whole – they are absolutely not allowed to have any particular interest. They are not allowed to travel on their own business, are not to make use of gold and silver, are to have no personal wealth. Even the bond of family is abolished among them. Marriages are holy, says Plato, but the most holy are those most beneficial to the state. Therefore the community of women and children should be introduced so that one should not have any greater concern and desire for those that concern him alone, rather than all others. No one is supposed to know who is his father, who is his son; one is to consider everyone to be father and son, so that a family love pervades the entire community. Only then will the state really be *one* state; all actual states did not deserve the name, because in each one there are several states, especially two, a state of the rich and of the poor, but actually there are countless, namely as many as there are individuals.

Therefore this state, preferably in its truest elements, the class of Guardians, is to contain all the noble powers, bravery, wisdom, gentleness, love of country, etc. But each of them has to attain the position which that they are appointed by nature to assume, and maintain it. Insight has to make the decisions, bravery has to execute them, strength that is determined by the idea of lordship must decree, those destined to serve must obey, and care is to be taken that none overstep one's own area into another's. Herein lies justice in the strict specific sense. But if this measure is kept, and if the scattered activities are to remain focused on a goal, it is necessary that the wise men stand at the head of the state – those who are not determined by the desire for money and delights, fear of death, but, equipped with strength of mind, with memory and mind are focused on the knowledge and execution of the good, who therefore do not look to appearance, but to the truth, above the changing and transient, and only strive after what is permanent and eternal. These, imbued with the greatness of the ideal and incapable of selfish volition, will share in the entire intricate motion of the animating rhythm. In them the summit of the Platonic state is reached, as it were in an unrelenting enthusiastic devotion, with which the people worship the idea of the good in the glory of the state which they form and which they present.

Assessment

What Plato calls the justice of the state is rather only the beauty thereof. Because what distinguishes the just from the beautiful is this: in the beautiful, the fullness of manifold existence is unconsciously united and without satisfying the parts; but the just grants every being its own existence, satisfaction and independent movement, so that it itself, as a whole, may freely engage the larger whole. But this is not found in the state of Plato. He sacrifices the human being, his happiness, his freedom, even his moral perfection. For this state exists only for the sake of itself, for the glory of its appearance; and the citizen is only destined as a ministering member to fit himself into the beauty of its structure. So it has a pictorial character. It is a work of art that seems to be there less for its own parts than for the spectator.

But an eternal law has it that even true aspiration, if pursued in isolation, when it injures another, at the same time destroys itself. Plato is prevented from attaining what for him is overriding – the inner harmony of the state – by the very fact that he disregards the interests of the individual.

Plato would even like his state to represent a higher harmony than nature, indeed the highest. But it can only do so by existing likewise as a realm of freedom, so that the beauty of its structure is not merely there, like nature, but is created in every moment anew by those who desire it and are enthusiastic about it. But this is made impossible by the institutions themselves. Nowhere is a right and a choice granted to the citizens; everyone has a position he must, rather than should, fill. There is no protection of the person but only of the abilities which he possesses, even against his will, so that here as well, it is not he who is protected but the archetype for which those abilities are used. In fact, it is not even intended, nor is any care taken, that he himself become a participant in the knowledge of the greatness which he represents. Everything that is an object of human control, possession, and desire is taken away from the class of rulers, so that even the possibility of devoting themselves to the state is taken from them. It makes of them a destitute rather than noble people. Harmony, as Aristotle interposes, does not refer to the same tone always being struck, but to many notes being struck in unison. Thus, the state must not merely be *one*, as Plato would like, but at the same time also *many*, in order to achieve beauty and harmony. It must consist of men who freely choose to act of their own will. Because Plato gives this up, he even pushes his state below the level of natural beauty.

When he does not take the happiness of its citizens into account, for example does not worry whether the class of Guardians will be satisfied with the position he allots them, indeed when he allows the infirm who are unable to serve the state to die, and banishes the doctors who would eke out a useless life for them – for he even believes a justification for life to be required – the intactness of the whole will of itself bring about the happiness of individuals, and it does not matter whether this or that class is taken care of, but only whether the state corresponds to its archetype. But the existence of the happiness of the people, and of a particular concern to that end as an end in itself and not a means to some other end, also pertains to the complete picture of the state. Such rigors as those do not adorn that picture. The forces of nature may go about destroying living existence and still remain sublime and beautiful, but human institution cannot imitate their relentless passage without violating their purport. Aristotle criticizes Plato for educating his warriors like dogs, to be mild to locals, rough and hostile to strangers, because an ungentle disposition is nowhere befitting. In itself, this institution holds no interest for us; but in it the great question comes to a head, whether the perfection of man or of the state takes precedence. Plato is not concerned with the human perfection of the warrior, but with the development of military power in the state. He promotes the inconsistency of a disposition of natural hatred against non-citizens because the human mind tends to gain greater strength in the direction that it unilaterally pursues. More disturbing than this is the education of women to male activity, to war and national defense. One is not permitted to become what he should be as human by nature, but only that by which the state has the greatest profit. Not only is the consummation of the individual sacrificed to the state; so also is the consummation of human relations and aspirations, for it holds true for these no less than for the state, that they fulfill that which nature has determined for them.

The bond of family is abolished so as to avoid any special interest. Poetry is banished, because, while it imitates the humble as well as the exalted, it does not promote the purity and lawfulness of the soul, which this state requires. The unity and cohesion of the state is no atonement for the fact that in itself high aspirations are lacking and sacred relations are desecrated. The Platonic state would have achieved a higher beauty if Plato had sought not merely beauty and enthusiasm, but also freedom and humanity. For the good, even according to Plato, must be of an even higher beauty than even the beautiful.

A sublime spirit runs through all these institutions of public life, the demand of unconditional boundless devotion without regard for self. However, with the state being made the object of this devotion, an unconscious structure is set over the people which cannot reciprocate, nor even feel, this devotion. How much truer and friendlier is the saying: "Man is not there for the sake of law, but law for the sake of men!"

Plato's doctrine is not free of the error that, while he pursues the *idea*, he insensibly imputes the *ideal* to it. Ideal, namely, is the perfection thought up by man by contrast with the perfection intended by God's command and purpose. The ideal therefore does have a trace of exaltation over reality, with all the bad and the common that adheres thereto; but it also has a trace of conflict with and violation of the natural order and thus true perfection, whereby it even falls short of reality. In this way, Plato fashions by human thoughts a perfection through devotion to and renunciation in favor of the state, which, while elevated over selfishness, nevertheless violates the right of personality and the vocation of sex and the bond of family as ordained by God's law.

Despite all this, Plato's doctrine of the state remains a model and an upbraiding teacher for subsequent times through its true goals, which are absent from subsequent science – the positive development of forces, the beauty of the design, and the inner spirit and enthusiasm which it recognizes as demands of public life.

PART II: ARISTOTLE

Standpoint

The Platonic idea of the good illuminates a future, and only a preview that it itself grants puts the mind in a position to recognize it. This preview, the special gift of Plato, is absent in Aristotle, who therefore must derive his knowledge of the just from what exists, what is observed with certainty, without enthusiastic intuition. His basis is the world as it is, and the laws that visibly receive and govern their existence. For him, the cause and measure of the just is not a freely designed shape that floats over reality futuristically, unattained and perhaps unattainable; but nature itself, the drive of which acts in unconscious things and the relations of men.

That institution which follows this drive is just. Aristotle's motto is "nothing can be good and noble that is against nature." So he derives the ethical law from the natural. The content is one and the same to him, only that with the former, freely-choosing beings *implement* it.

This assumption seems already to harbor a contradiction in itself. Nature, namely, acts with irresistible power, so that wherever it expresses its drive, no choice, therefore no ethical law is conceivable. Where, however, there is choice and resolution, hence room for ethical prescription, there also nature has retreated and accords no standard. Furthermore, nature arouses conflicting drives. Both selfishness and self-sacrificing love are its work, and it is certain that the ethic [ethos] usually enjoins precisely that a natural drive be overcome. If, therefore, a choice is made among these conflicting things, one would think that a different measure than the law [Gesetz] of nature would have to be found lurking in the background, a peculiar ethical law, from which the decision comes.

But Aristotle has no need of such. These contradictions have a basis only if one pays attention to individual effects. But for Aristotle the measure of the just is nature and its intention as a whole. An activity runs through the whole of creation which, while in appearance and in detail eliciting opposites, when taken as a whole acts in agreement. Unconscious nature everywhere manifests a creative drive, a drive seeking after preservation, propagation, increase of existence, through which creatures exist and multiply. It also displays the sphere of spiritual beings. It uses necessary wants to push people to combine, links them instinctively together, and so generates the various social relationships. Nature desires absolutely the richer, the manifold, the developed, even if, rebelling against its own goal, it here and there seems to wish to destroy existence and dissolve its creations into simple matter. It is therefore in accordance with nature that barriers of organic plant life restrain the raw elements; it is in accordance with nature that the reign of the drive to sociability and its constructions in the spiritual world be secured against outbreaks of selfishness. It is a natural drive by which man seeks the constant expansion of wealth, of luxury, since each activity is directed to its enlargement; but the general drive of nature sets a limit to him by showing that wealth is to be used only for one's own preservation, for the family and the state.[7]

So Aristotle requires no other measure beyond reality; instead, reality provides this measure to him, for he finds the universal in it and recognizes it for what it truly wishes, and should be. It does not necessitate irresistibly; rather, whether or not it will be obeyed in detail is an open question. It is not conflicting in itself; the conflicting drives are not the ones which run through it universally. And it is clear that its requirements are not to be overcome by the ethic, but rather correspond to what is recognized as ethical.

Aristotle's standard is thus the *purpose of nature* (τέλος). This is something quite different from what one usually understands by the concept of purpose (teleology). It is a purpose that lies in the thing itself (objectively), not arbitrarily set by man (subjectively), and it is ever already an effective and fulfilled purpose in natural or social formations, not one lying outside of them, by which therefore nothing is but a mere means, hence valueless in itself. Accordingly, Aristotle's method is *observation*. He traces the phenomena of nature in order to discover, through analysis and comparison, the intention and the inner aspirations of nature in those phenomena. By this course and in this manner he examines human life relations, beginning with the simplest and climbing to the richer, more developed; and this leads to his doctrine of the state.

Principle and Course of His Politics

The first human life relation effectuated by nature is the union of man and

---

[7] In *Politics,* Book I.

woman, the purpose of which is the propagation of the race. To this attaches the parental relation and the lordship relation (i.e., between masters and slaves); these differ essentially from each other in that the parental relation is for the benefit of both parts, the obeying as well as the ruling, while the lordship relation only serves to benefit the ruling part. Nature leads to other ties, to villages, hamlets, finally to the *state* (taking city and state in the Greek manner as equivalent).

The state is the supreme relation, it is the fulfillment of that which nature aimed at in those preceding relations, because it alone has self-sufficiency (αὐτάρχεια), while those others always require another and higher connection that receives or protects them. That is why the state is the final purpose of nature, and man is a creature destined for the state (πολιτικὸν ζῷον). He who wishes to live without the state, would have to be a being of a higher or lower nature than man. The state is therefore for the people, that is, the state is that which nature, already in the individual, aims at as its final purpose, as it everywhere refers the part to the whole, and in the part pursues the whole.

But the purpose of the state is first and foremost the *life* [Erhaltung] (ζῆν) of its citizens, thereafter the *good life* [Wohlerhaltung] (εὖ ζῆν). The latter requires many external circumstances (good soil, convenient location and the like), but above all it requires *virtue*, for it is in virtue, not in external goods, that satisfaction and well-being consist, and the education of the citizens to virtue therefore also manifests itself in Aristotle as the first task of the state.

Speaking of the constitution of the state, the first and general requirement, in accordance with this purpose, is that it, like the parental power, be oriented as much toward the benefit of the subjects as the rulers, and not like the lordly power, exclusively for the benefit of the rulers. Accordingly, in each of the three basic forms – monarchy, aristocracy, and democracy – we distinguish between a true representation and a degeneracy (παρέκβασις) of the same, depending on whether it meets that requirement or not. It is necessary to distinguish *kingship* (βασιλεία) from *tyranny*, depending on whether the monarch is restricted by laws to the welfare of his subjects or not; *aristocracy* from *oligarchy* depending on the whether the meritorious are appointed to positions of rule for the general benefit, or simply the rich for their own benefit; *polity* from *democracy*, depending on whether the rule, which belongs to the whole, is really for the benefit of all or merely for the benefit of the poor, who constitute the majority. The polity – which Aristotle considered to be the most perfect form of government – is to be achieved through a combination of oligarchic and democratic aspects, not simply through an organic expansion and arrangement of both classes, but rather by an intermediate path between the two principles, e.g., applying the oligarchic means of punishing the rich with fines for absenting themselves from the popular assembly, together with the democratic means of rewarding the appearance of the poor in the assembly with donations, with access to the popular assembly linked to a moderate income, and offices allocated not by lot or turn-taking (in the manner of Greek democracy), but by election with reference to competence.

Taking that general requirement – orientation toward the common utility – as given, the first standard of the constitution for each state is the *relative* one, i.e., the consideration as to which constitution is the most appropriate to its particular condition and the elements existing in it. Where by birth, wealth, education the citizens are equal to each other, the democratic form exists; where a smaller number predominate, the aristocratic form does; where one protrudes above all others, the monarchical form does. A constitution that would be generally and unconditionally commanded and just does not exist, because none of them can realize the purpose of nature in the state – the good life, education for virtue – in all circumstances, or at any rate in the best way.

Nevertheless, there is also an *absolute* standard of the constitution, namely that constitution – provided its appropriateness in terms of the given elements – that in itself approaches achieving that purpose most nearly, or one could also say, that constitution corresponding to the elements that are best for that purpose. This is precisely what the *polity* is, because in his *Ethics* Aristotle refers to the virtue which indeed is the purpose of the state as being a mean between two vices, e.g., between greed and waste, cowardice and foolhardiness. That is why the condition of achieving the purpose of the state is most favorable where the middle class predominates, because, without the temptations of wealth or poverty, it is most likely to go the middle way everywhere. Such a condition of hegemony on the part of the middle class corresponds to the polity.

Position vis-à-vis Plato

Accordingly, Aristotle shared with Plato the procedure of deriving knowledge from *objects* rather than from human *reason*. As the idea was for

Plato, purpose in nature is for Aristotle that which has content in itself that can be discovered, not by examining [logical] thought determinations, but only by an activity of mind directed to the object, i.e., observation, vision. Of course, Aristotle cannot find the purpose of nature by *direct vision,* as with Plato and the ethical ideal; he needs *abstraction.* For inwardly in the spirit Plato sees a future, and this vision is sufficient in itself to recognize what is just, because its content is precisely that which is contained in the idea, perfection; Aristotle, on the other hand, sees only what is real, which as such cannot be the measure of the just; he must therefore compare the manifold manifestations of what is real; he must discover the universal from the particulars. But this abstraction of Aristotle's has its proper use, which is the negative function of limiting, ordering, maintaining. It by no means itself provides him with the content; this he also derives from observation, which he engages in with every step. Currently, it is unjustly claimed of Aristotle that he understood pure thought free from sense-derived particularity, the logical law, to be the essence and the truth of things. But neither he nor Plato attempted to disregard actual things and infer the necessity of any existence from a thought. For him as well, justice is not a system of rules, but a condition of men. And legal institutions have their measure and their valuation not in consistency, but in the actual effects they exert on circumstances and the opinion of men.

The undertone is also the same for both: the state comes first, and people are subordinate to the purpose of its existence. On the face of it, Aristotle approaches to the modern point of view, especially in view of his objections to Plato. Since he blames Plato for rendering it impossible for his Guardians to exercise charity and moderation because of their enforced poverty, and for sacrificing the happiness and perfection of man to the state, he seems to desire personal freedom and satisfaction. But on closer inspection, Aristotle shows that at bottom he does not differ from Plato. He likewise, by virtue of that pronouncement that the state is prior to the people (i.e., that the state is the purpose of nature in man), considered man in all his existence to be a mere subordinate member and agent of the state without a higher relation independent of the state, because it is the absolute end. Similarly, the will of the people is not the purpose of the institutions, nor is it their cause. The noblest must rule whether the others like it or not, for otherwise, he says, they would only concede equal rights even to Zeus himself if he lived among them. In his constitutional doctrine as well, the idea of a personal claim to dominion or freedom, of an acquired right on the part of a prince or a state or nation, can nowhere be found; the crucial consideration is only ability, qualities [Eigenschaftung] to achieve success that will redound to the whole. Thus in terms of type, Aristotle shared with Plato this trait of the subsumption of men in the state, although in lesser degree and thus less conspicuously.

Aristotle is however opposed to Plato in this: Plato recognizes a purpose beyond all that the real world with its phenomena has to offer, even, it would seem, out of its reach. Aristotle recognizes no ought, no purpose (τέλος) of things other than what nature manifests to be its will, that it either already has attained or at least provides the means to attain. His opposition to Plato therefore does not carry the usual meaning: "these designs are certainly just and noble, but not capable of implementation," but "they contradict the preconditions of nature, wherefore they are not what the source of the ethic desires and pursues, they are untrue and unjust." Added to this is the uniform difference of character and treatment.

Aristotle requires the investigation of all that nature has hitherto formed, which is everywhere evident in changing and repeating forms. The diverse social conditions, the differences among people, their activities, earthly possessions, talents, their relations determined by preceding events, their desires and motives, the functions of state – judiciary, government, the armed forces, the possibility of their distribution, mixture, complementary position, whence the infinite variety of constitutions – all this, how it is produced, and what it in turn effects, Aristotle finds necessary to examine to find out what maintains itself, therefore what is in accordance with nature, what is just. He is therefore the creator of actual political science, i.e., the science of the natural action and reaction of the institutions that everywhere are found in the same or similar manner, and which relates to the living aspirations of every time and nation in the same manner as mechanical laws to individual organic beings. This knowledge, which is essential to the statesman for him to choose the means for his purpose, Aristotle requires, in accordance with his standpoint, in order to discover the ultimate goal.

So this is the basis and the path of his investigation. In this he limits himself to reality, and discovers the result from many isolated observations. But for all the acuteness of this investigation and the truth of individual observations, the final shape that ought to arise – the state, which fully conforms to the purpose of nature – is not at all clear. The investigation is like a stream which after a magnificent course loses itself in the sand. Plato, by contrast, does not require all of these investigations to discover the just. It is given to him directly, something more glorious than any comparisons of the real could grant. Filled by his archetype, he creates new forms, he aims only at the one single state, the perfect; he sees it all at once and outlines it with the clarity of real life. If in details, in which Aristotle is so trenchant, he often considers the unseemly, what is contrary to nature, nevertheless around the whole there hovers a halo of moral elevation that pertains to an entirely different world than the natural strength and safety of the Aristotelian institutions.

With such opposite starting points, these two also certainly must come to conflicting results. But it is one and the same power that effectuates the natural conditions and drives and also provides the purpose for which man and his chosen ties are to strive. This explains the relation between nature and ethic, which reality illustrates, and thus also the relation between Plato and Aristotle.

Relation between Nature and the Ethic in General

The conditions wrought by nature are the necessary *substratum* of the ethic. Marriage, parental authority are based on the natural drive of procreation, the helplessness of children, etc. But as such they not only receive a law from the ethic, they also lay down a law for it, only in a different way. The ethic prevails over nature through its act (actual [aktuell]), by what it positively wants, ordering nature in terms of its purposes, analogous to the master over the servant. In this manner it shapes natural copulation into the thoroughly ethical institution of marriage. But nature gives a law to the ethic by its character (substantial [substantiell]), by what it is, analogous to the servant vis-à-vis the master. Though something is demanded of him, nothing can be demanded that he is not able to accomplish. For example, a law could not effect the power of children over adults, even if it were absurd enough to wish it. Hence, true moral demands hereby run up against a barrier in the incapacity of earthly nature, and they become untrue, like nonsensical laws of that sort, if they do not take this restriction into consideration, but instead try to evade it.

But natural conditions are also the *prelude* to the ethical. They then form the first link in the great chain which forms the historical progress in the ethic itself. Already in the instinct of animals, in the insensate drive of the plant, there is that which, as morality, prompts men in ever more exalted form in the various epochs. This is Aristotle's justification. He can reason from the efforts of unconscious things to the ought of conscious beings, pursuing the uninterrupted climax.

Finally – besides the fact that nature is the substance of the ethic, and the less developed representation of the shapes thereof – nature has this in common with the ethic, that it leads to the same *outcome* in ethical relations, independently of the ethic. The natural drive is set up in such a manner that, purely in accordance with its own nature, it becomes a determinant in meeting requirements that do not share its same root. If people wished to isolate themselves, the natural need for aid would drive them to the state; and yet, the peculiar significance of the state is not this aid. The want of security calls for public punishment to deter crime; and yet, it is this public punishment as just retribution that is grounded in the higher order of the ethical world.

This is the basis of the community of Plato and Aristotle, through which they, pursuing opposites, on the whole not desiring similar results, still arrive at them. Plato requires a multiplicity of forces and their fulfilled formation for the rich harmony of his depiction; this leads him to the gradation of classes [Ständen]. Aristotle requires this gradation and shows the natural need of it, and this leads him to the fulfilled formation like Plato's. Plato has his state seek after the idea of the just, and as a result, happiness follows. Aristotle merely has it seek happiness, and this also results in virtue. It is a comparison of two architects, one of whom, by seeking merely to answer the purpose of the building, unintentionally makes a work of art, while the other wishes to answer all the demands of beauty, and so as a matter of course cannot leave unsatisfied any of the building's requirements.

Value of the Ideal View and of the Empirical

Both also recognize the *single spirit* that rules throughout all creation; but Plato believes he can see it immediately at a higher level than everything that exists, and can behold it without the aid of what exists; Aristotle wishes to recognize it in its expression in the lower levels, and thus be certain of the higher. This also portrays the only two true human ways of knowledge, ideal vision and empirical investigation.[8]

They also are inseparable. For Plato, the examination of reality always promotes elevation towards its primordial image [Urbilds], and if Aristotle were not already filled in advance with a harmonious vision, he would not have arrived at these results. Yet with each of them, the one or the other is repressed. Both approaches therefore are clearly presented right at the beginning of philosophy, thus guaranteeing the unity of its object – but no less its own inadequacy. The empirical way appears safe and all-attaining, mediating the law of its progress from the antecedent course to its climax and thereby determining its future stages. But progress in nature is not like a straight line in which two points determine a third, but is like the vibrant growth of a plant, whereby its flower and the fruit cannot simply be extrapolated from its seed and stem. So he who understands the significance of the beginning, would have to know the end. But just as true and apt is that which corresponds: we do not understand the importance of the beginning, because the end is hidden from us.

From this comes the continuous uncertainty and often the error of the Aristotelian analogy. "Every whole of nature is greater than the parts." From which he concludes: "The state is also higher than man." But with any natural whole, the invigorating drive proceeds from that whole and not from the parts; but in the state, it is people, not the state, that put people in motion. And who can guarantee that the highest vocation is not the perfection of man without the state, whereby, as Aristotle himself says, he becomes like the gods? While for every activity nature provides a tool which is not for itself, but for someone else, Aristotle deems slavery justified as a tool for the family and its care. But whether or not the higher sphere of free beings tolerates the existence of a mere tool like the lower sphere does, is something which that comparison cannot reveal.

Here, then, is the seat of the error which is the basis of the much-discussed defense of slavery. Although this institution is no longer recognized, the rationale from what nature enjoins is still held by many to be infallible. The higher level always has a law of an entirely new sort, if only because it is the higher. Wealth contains poverty, but poverty does not contain wealth. The observation of what precedes, and of the process itself, can only direct, determine the

---

[8] It hardly needs mentioning that empiricism here is not meant in the ordinary sense of a mere passive registration lacking the control and penetration of mind.

selection, confirm, but cannot of itself [für sich selbst] provide right knowledge. Therefore, in order to know what is known or ought to be known, an immediate perception is necessary, because this is what makes the preceding intelligible; it is not given in the preceding. This constitutes the ideal vision. But it is a special gift, and it promises, in accordance with its nature, only a limited knowledge. If the eye only sees by the sun, it will only see what Helios wills more or less to illuminate for it. So also, when the mind receives the power to recognize the good through the idea, which it itself is not, its knowledge is dependent on how far this Helios sends its rays into the world and to its eye. And so far it has not granted to mortals all the splendor of its light. Plato himself, who to this day is held to have the glory of the sublimest mind that has applied itself to philosophy, is likewise only struck by a ray of it. After him, history engendered higher thoughts, a life of nobler and deeper meaning than he imagined, and he could not even keep his likeness free of untrue, obfuscating features.

If empiricism and the vision of the ideal interpenetrate, knowledge will probably increase in degree, but deficient knowledge will not be made into perfect knowledge.

Explanation of the Conflict between Plato and Aristotle

Now the question arises: from whence does it come that these two paths here appear divided, indeed hostile to each other? Why does Plato not inquire into the real and concrete activities of nature; why even design the state partly contrary to its conditions; and even more so, why does Aristotle close his eyes to what is higher, and remain content with the imperfect world? The only explanation is the lack of *historical character* in Greek philosophy. They both assume the existence of a drive which is working towards a conclusion in simultaneous progressions from the lowest stages of unconscious nature to the highest stages of men and philosophers. But the same sequence of stages in time, the progress of generations and world epochs, and beyond that, the future transformation of conditions to which men are subjected on earth – these are things they do not take into account. So, the union of the given condition and its imperfection with the advanced condition and its perfection is wanting, and onesidedness of one form or another is inevitable. Plato steadfastly maintains that the perfect ought to exist. But he finds no relation of it to reality, and this lack appears to him to be accidental, or at any rate unaccounted for: and yet he cannot learn anything from it, nor is there a reason to consider it. Aristotle on the other hand steadfastly maintains that the real does not allow for perfection. Therefore what seems to him to be the highest, in fact the final object, is precisely the imperfect. So he falls into the contradiction: nature strives after perfection, and yet it contains in itself the law that it cannot attain perfection.

PART III: THE ETHIC OF THE GREEKS

The common characters of the philosophy of Plato and of Aristotle have been revealed: the cause of the ethic, existing in itself and extrinsic to human reason – the lack of historical principle – the predominance of the state over man, whose happiness, freedom, moral perfection is sacrificed to it. Already what these two thinkers have in common, and the opposition they form, in part to older, in part to newer ideas, goes to prove that these characteristics of their doctrine are not the result of a particular line of reasoning, but a particular quality of their spirit – the culture [Bildung] of their nation.

Religious Standpoint of the Greeks – Unhistorical View of the World – Ethic Thereof

If the causes that are manifested in different ways in the various activities of a people are to be traced back to their common origin, one need look no farther than the highest conceptions of that people, in the consciousness of its relation to the deity. Now for the Greeks, the gods, endowed with personality as they are, are not in any manner the supreme rulers of things; blind fate dominates them and produces events. But the ethical world is under the sway of ideas, the highest thoughts or forms of the good, the beautiful, the sublime. Fate and the ideas, themselves without self-consciousness, determined neither by others nor by themselves, set everything in motion and wield the scepter over gods and men.

This manner of thinking is certainly not the oldest of all, nor humanity's original one. Allow us to compare it with another which has been preserved in the most ancient documents and handed down to the new world in a more elevated form, which is still the content of public faith among us, perhaps even among those who do not believe in its divine origin, and which can lay claim to consideration as the prototype of man.

According to the *Jewish* conception, it is the personal God, not limited by anything, who according to His free will rules the destinies of the world, and who prescribes to men their end. Ethical precepts have no foundation apart from His will. All establishments and regulations bear the imprint of His omnipotence: "Ye shall not deal falsely one to another, *I am the Lord your God*" [cf. Leviticus 19: 11.] Good and evil exist only because He willed it or forbade it, for His alone is the glory. Now among the Greeks this belief was converted absolutely into its opposite, as expressed decisively in Plato's *Euthyphro:* "The holy is not the holy because the gods love it, but the gods love it, because it is the holy" [cf. 10e]. This is to separate the divine essence in a different way than polytheism does. That is to say, not only is it divided into different gods, but personality itself, the willing and the contents of its will, the thing willed, are two powers entirely separated from each other, and these, the mere products, are set over their producers. For what appears to the Greeks to be fate, to be the idea over God, in reality is only that upon which they had decided upon, that which they put forward as task and goal.

The Supreme Being [das höchste Dasein] has thereby ceased to be a free and conscious entity; He has been diminished. But man, in the midst of these separated powers, has been elevated, made freer. He does not fear destiny, because it cannot do him any harm, as little as it can avert harm. It can as little pity the man as it can rage against him. But the gods are faced with the same necessity as man, and the hero is encouraged to undertake dangerous deeds of glory, because gods and heroes must fulfill their lot. Gods and men are subject to the same moral laws, and the extent to which the Greek recognizes them as his own, he also dares to apply to his gods. Thus, according to Herodotus,[9] a prominent Cymian overcomes a god who gave to his hometown the vile advice that it should hand guests over, by flushing the protégés of the gods, the birds nesting in the forest. This gives rise to the greatness of man, who with his free act overcomes unfree destiny, even the haughty greatness of Prometheus, who rebels against the immortal gods, a character in which the East sees only the abomination, and not the greatness.

Because an unconscious power is placed above the gods, the historical principle is automatically given up. *History is only the work of an agent.* Fate and the ideas merely *exist* from everlasting to everlasting, in them there is no decision, no act, no progress. In Judaism, not only do human destinies have a history, but the disposing power over them does as well. In events, everything is foresight, preparation for a future destination, everything is the result of interaction of

---

[9] *The Histories,* I.159.

the free act of people vis-à-vis God and the no less free act of God vis-à-vis people. The Judeo-Christian narrative as a whole turns out to be a great stage play, the archetype of all tragedy, because it is the divine tragedy. The ethical commandments themselves are a history. There is no ideal closed off in itself as the norm for the manifold relationships that develop outside of it, but He who alone is the source of the ethic, for each event, when it happens, at the same time imparts the law, because nothing happens that was not present in His will. Yahweh Himself ordains whereto destruction, whereto protection. The refusal of the incomprehensible – inhumane, as one would have it lately – commandment also meets with the divine wrath. And despite the existence of enduring institution and legislation, the Jewish ethic is still not exhausted; indeed, what is most essential in it would not be described if the individual commandments that run through all of history and form that history, were lacking in it. Therefore, like any history, it can only be depicted by narrative. Finally, in redemption all events attain their fulfillment, and law attains its transformation, its new, previously hidden shape. Free guidance and predestination rescind the contradiction of the inequality between beginning and end, and nevertheless the proclaimer of the truth, because He founded a new kingdom, said: "I am not come to destroy, but to fulfill."

The Greek view, however, sees their events go on without leading toward a goal; hence, an eternally recurring change of things. The archetypes, and with them the moral requirements, are the same at the start as they are further on. Always in the same way, man strives for them, and is unable to reach them. It is the contradiction that cannot be explained: the ideas had from the start to make the world in accordance with themselves, if they have power over it, and if the ideas are perfect, so would the world be. Therefore Aristotle diminishes their own content. He is perhaps the first philosopher gloomily to be resigned to the inevitable limitations of present nature as something eternal. A greater momentum elevates Plato over his nation; his lively aspiring mind could not do without the self-conscious creator and the final consummation of all things. So he closes the *Republic* with the prospect of an otherworldly future, which alone for him resolves the contradiction. But in terms of scientific application, he stands on the same line with Aristotle. Both ignore progress in history as a means to infer the content of the idea. In both cases the ethic is a form prepared from eternity to eternity; actions, which lie outside it, either comply with it or contradict it.

And God cannot be stirred by prayers, says Plato, because He cannot deviate from the idea of justice.

An ethic that creates the norm while simultaneously generating the conditions and circumstances, which itself moves in an uninterrupted ascent to its final form, and therefore may be something else for a different time and different incident, without contradiction – an *historical ethic* can have its basis only in the free and omnipresent will of a personal God. Thus in Greek philosophy, although it recognizes a positive and meaningful principle of things, yet already has the beginning of the unhistorical view, since the cause of the world and the ethic appears as unfree, *thallos*, something merely existing. This view reaches its extreme in modern, abstract philosophy and certifies here more clearly the untruth thereof, whence it is also necessary for philosophy to return to that ancient historical view, the *Judeo-Christian*, which has never ceased being valid in life.

Absence of Charity

Charity [Carität] is the peculiar characteristic of the Orient. It is the end of all the Jewish commandments, excluding those based on the historical relationship of the people to God, such as the exodus from Egypt, the promulgation of laws, etc. The divine love extends to all living things, from animals up to slaves, from strangers to the sons of the chosen people. But charity is only from person to person. Fate and the ideas are without sensation. Even the jealous God of the Old Covenant restricts the penalty to the fourth generation, while He blesses the thousandth. But the Greek avenger of morals [der Sitte] strides relentlessly across the earth. An intervening god may liberate after extended agony, but only rarely. The greatness of heroes is only elevated over the Nemesis through the atonement of a freely chosen downfall. Here then, charity ceases to be the driving force, the ideas cannot require it; they cannot reciprocate, because it is not their essence. They do not disappear; but they become something other than they originally and peculiarly were. Namely, not the person himself, whether God or man, is its innermost motive, but the beauty of their actions. This explains the hardness of Plato, the inhumanity of Spartan institutions, and generally the lack in Greece of laws with the welfare of the people as their final and energetic intention. This is perhaps the contrast generally between Oriental and Occidental virtue. The former has its ultimate source and its final goal only in a personality; the latter waxes enthusiastic about the highness of a thought, law, state, art, honor, so that even pride or stubborn assertion of one's own claims can be held to be duties.

The Greek life, one might say, is the initial astonishment of mankind when the Lord took from it the fear of His face, and it beholds, free and awakened, the immense splendor of the world. Mankind is set outside of himself and immersed in the world. To depict this beauty in the spiritual world, as it is expressed in the physical, is the task of people and of states. Here for the first time an occupation is bestowed on man, here first is there free state formation. He separates himself from the divinely given forms of life (the theocratic constitution) to create anew in accordance with divine models. In place of blind passive obedience comes man's own free reproduction. "Thou shalt not blur the boundaries of the things I drew, the sequence of stages in the whole of nature, but keep them holy!" is the idea manifested in a series of Jewish statutes: "Thou shalt not let thy cattle gender with a diverse kind: thou shalt not sow thy field with mingled seed: neither shall a garment mingled of linen and woollen come upon thee" [Leviticus 19: 19]. This order is not limited to unconscious nature, it also proceeds among the people, separates priest and Levite, and forms the structure of caste which is represented in the whole of the Orient. The same idea now is what causes Plato to consider the development of manifold forces, their measure and their delimitation, to be the justice of the state. But with the former, it is God's created beauty that is found and kept holy; with the latter, it is the creation of something new which is demanded by those models. Therefore, it is not regard in nature but in self-formed human relations, distribution according to ability, a separation and reconnection which man comprehends because he himself undertook it. With the former, the unity of the delimited elements is given by the divine purpose in all of creation; with the latter, man himself must first create them – *he finds them in the state.*

The state of Plato, in which this is the moral of the story, is proven here to be the same model pursued by all the Greek states. Thus, the Spartan state represents a vibrant body animated by a spirit, which as with a *single* will strains every sinew for the struggle. Athens developed a richer life. Art, philosophy, family connection, commerce, shipping, trade, all spheres of human activity are encountered here, and each is assured its own existence, as its nature requires. An abundance of magistrates and courts, each of which is assigned the care of a certain entity, spreads across the state. In the diversity of their education, their celebrations, the buildings for their assemblies, and finally, the leading interest of their object, they provide a rich picture, but they receive their proper boundaries from a shield under which they all repose, the supreme court of the Areopagus.

This rapture does not leave room to maintain a separate existence. Man only perceives himself as a part of the whole, from which he cannot separate himself, neither in fact, nor in thought. An irresistible urge propels him to intervene in its rhythm.

The ethic does not arise as a task of the individual but of the whole; it is something general (objective), directed to the world; man encounters it only as a member thereof. It therefore calls not for his actions (considered individually), but rather the existence of the moral order as a whole, the purity of the spiritual world. For this reason the Nemesis also pursues the involuntary act. And for those caught in the struggle of conflicting obligations, destruction is inevitable. However he chooses – Orestes may leave the father unavenged, or murder the mother – through him there arises either a gap or a discord in the moral world, and it must expel him. In this manner, in time out of mind the ancient royal houses fell, and in this manner within historical memory Timoleon falls into mental derangement, the punishment for murder despite its inevitability.

Even the state does not require the ethic from individuals, for them to give shape to it, but from the world, that it exist. It shall be, and shall represent a specific shape. Only from this do the duties of citizens issue, and not vice versa, the shape of the state from the duties of citizens. Therefore, there are ethical requirements that no human being, considered in himself, could recognize as his own, for example, the formation of classes [Ständen], and the perfection of the state is the first thing that is to be, and only then that of people. For it itself taken as a whole is the subject of the ethic. This explains the unnatural calling of women in Plato, the banishment of poetry, and the like.

Of law in our sense, according to which someone may do as he will within a certain sphere , there is here no conception. Nowhere does the Greek set his foot outside the world to which he belongs, his state. Greek liberty is not like Roman – protection of free disposition over a certain delimited object – but an ideal share in the actions of the state. It follows automatically that individual freedom is abolished in the Platonic state, in Sparta. Attic law could not leave off having standards appropriate to private pursuits, given its bustling trade and commerce. But nevertheless, it did not regulate them according to the principle of private law, that is, by the will of men, but sought to apply its own inherent ideas in an appropriate shape, as is readily demonstrated. The absolutely alien nature of the concept of personal entitlement to the Greeks is shown most clearly by a point in the first book of the *Republic* of Plato. Among all the possible determinations of the just which are to be assessed here, he comes also to the one in which "each is to be given his due." Here we think we have discovered the Roman *suum cuique tribue*, and thus law and entitlement in our sense. But he who studies this statement of Plato's accurately, finds in it that friends are to be treated well, but enemies badly. Under what is due (προσῆκον, *suum*) is not meant something that someone can dispose of at will, either to acquire or to leave aside, but something that applies to him with necessity according to a different standard than his will, even in opposition to his will. To suffer evil can be no enemies' *right;* nor can receiving good be understood to be a friend's *right.* This provision does not denote justice that protects individuals [schirmende], like the Roman legal principle does, but justice that visits retribution [vergeltende].

This is the objective character of the Greek constitution [des griechischen Wesens]: the ethic goes forth into the objective world and requires its perfection, not the individual human being's, and nowhere is action to be determined merely by one's own will, but everywhere by the order over him. The same character runs through science. Just as here the general question regarding the cause and the end of things urges itself, so does the investigator at no time look into himself, closed off to everything external, in order to find the answer. His thought always moves among the major objects of the world that surround him, which he in unprejudiced contemplation absorbs. The investigation pursues coherence in the things themselves, the sense [Verstand] that expresses itself in them. It does not have the obligation, nor even the permission, to seek a solution without taking into account what is to be solved. Therefore, Greek philosophy is [characterized by] free treatment, full of life. It draws on all the wealth of creation, it takes hold of development and growth, change and decay in all variety and tumultuousness, as life itself presents it. From this world, which it recognizes apart from the reason of the beholder, it had to arrive at a principle thereof which exists apart from his reason, an objective principle – water, fire, the natural purpose, the idea. To the degree that it considers this necessary to explain the world, it attributes to these a peculiar quality and effectiveness. Thought, on the other hand, only needs to refer to its own essence to do this, without taking the world into consideration.

In modern philosophy, the thinker withdraws into himself; he stands by the subjective principle, his reason. Hence the formalism. But he also finds freedom and personality in himself. And when at last he sees himself compelled to turn back to the recognition of independent existence outside himself, he no longer can consider it in the Greek fashion, as held together by the idea or the laws of nature, but as the work of the freely acting God.

APPENDIX TO BOOK I: THE ROMANS

The Roman world epoch embodies a major advance in legal and political consciousness: both the idea of the purely legal order which, while determined by ethical ideas, ought not be deflected by ethical motives in individual cases, and the idea of entitlement (law in the subjective sense) which here is not thought of in the way it is in our time, as a notion of human rights (either in the true or the false sense of the word), but manifests itself merely as a notion of the acquired right of the person, of a right warranted by the legal order.

And yet, the Roman world epoch embodies no advance in the awareness of the deeper reasons and ideas of law, no progress in the philosophy of law. In this, the Romans merely appropriated the products of Greek culture. Cicero, the main writer in this field, borrowed all his terms and principles from Plato and Aristotle, without any significant new thoughts. He does not even bring that which lived in the national consciousness – subjective entitlement – to scientific cognizance, and is not even aware of its opposition to the Greeks. The studies contained in his jurisprudential and political writings[10] revolve broadly around two issues: the existence of a natural moral law, and the best state constitution. He asserts the existence of a natural law (*lex aeterna*), as did the Greeks, especially with respect to the denial of Carneades; but he stops short at the general notion that morality [die Sitte] is true and independent, by no means a product of prudence; he does not concern himself any farther than this, in particular with the existence of a natural juridical law [natürlichen Rechtsgesetzes], which so recommended itself to the Romans. His investigations into the Roman constitution rest on the foundation of Greek political science, with the difference that, in accordance with patriotic sentiment, he comes to the conclusion that the mixed constitution, which he holds the Roman to be, is declared the most perfect. Even Stoic ethics retained with the Romans a peculiar strength of operation rather than a specifically scientific implementation, with more concern for the aspect of morality than the ordering of the social condition, than jurisprudential or political problems. Only the element in it of common humanity can be emphasized, which spread in the mind

---

[10] In particular, the *Republic* and *Laws*.

especially later (e.g., Seneca, Marcus Aurelius); but this did not give shape to legal and governmental institutions, neither in life, nor in their own teaching.

Much more important for the world-historical progress of legal ideas than the philosophical and political writers among the Romans, therefore, were the legal arrangements themselves, in part the conceptualization thereof by jurists of positive law. This has been dealt with in detail in other places of this work, particularly in the appendix to the volume on private law.[11] Therefore we may here proceed directly to the following period, which really does provide new scientific ideas, the legal philosophy of the Middle Ages.

---

[11] Stahl, *Private Law*, appendix: "Regarding the Value of Roman Private Law."

BOOK II: THEOCRATIC LEGAL PHILOSOPHY
(THE MIDDLE AGES)

PART I: AUGUSTINE

Among the Church Fathers, it is Augustine in particular who asserted Christianity in terms of a scientific philosophical presentation over against classical philosophy; he is the primary founder of Christian speculation, and he became decisive for the entire Middle Ages both in science and life [Lebensgestaltung].

Speculative Conceptualization of World History

The basic idea of his book *Of the City of God* (*De Civitate Dei*) is the antithesis between a heavenly state (*civitas Dei, civitas coelestis*) and an earthly state (*civitas terrena*), founded on the biblical contrast of God's children and the children of the world, albeit in a speculative formation. To wit, it conceives this opposition as a world-historical economy rather than as the mere nature of individual human beings, as the opposition of two coherent organized areas of sentiments, aspirations, tasks, but also institutions, destinies, world designs, running right through earthly life. It is, if one wishes to use a more modern term, a construction of world history. It begins the demonstration of this opposition at Cain and Abel, and conducts it on the one hand through secular history, the empires of the Assyrians, Persians, Greeks, Romans, and on the other hand through the sacred history of the Patriarchs, the Jewish judges, kings, prophets, up until the appearance of Christ and the Christian church. The end is the eternal glorification of the God-state and the downfall and the destruction of the earthly state.

The term *state* (*civitas*) is used symbolically in both relations, and therefore the question is, how does the real state on earth, the civic organization, relate to these two states? The expressions of Augustine on this score are not clear, in details perhaps even contradictory; nevertheless, the thoughts that form his total conception can be identified with certitude.

View of the State

The civil state is it not the same to him as the "earthly state" (*civitas terrena*), although he alternately uses the term *civitas terrena* for the realm of secular, and for the state. For he recognizes that the purpose of the state, earthly peace (as opposed to eternal peace), in itself is not blameworthy, and that Christians should wish for that peace and make use of it as long as mortality continues; precisely for this reason they also owe the state obedience, and to this end are to have community with the earthly-minded.[12] Accordingly, it cannot be something absolutely evil, as is worldly-mindedness; and that which is spoken of regarding the "earthly city" – that it will fall under eternal judgment with the devil – cannot refer to it.[13]

But yet he brings the state into the closest connection with the earthly kingdoms. For him the state, and not merely the current condition of the state, but the existence of a state generally, is simply the consequence of sin,[14] and therefore also a mere emergency institution, an arena of the passions and the oppression of the weak by the powerful. Accordingly, he considers interest in the state as something purely secular. Therefore the establishment of states everywhere proceeds from the earthly-minded; the heavenly-minded do not concern themselves with it. In this manner, the first state was founded by Cain, the original representative of the earthly kingdom – "he built a city" [Genesis 4: 17] – while Abel was a stranger on earth and an exile.[15] Likewise, the Roman state was the state κατ᾿ ἐξοχήν [par excellence], founded by Romulus, who, earthly-minded, also murdered his brother, and is a type of Cain. While the classical view considers the state to be the highest thing in human life, for Augustine it occupied the extreme opposite position, as something deeply subordinate for the true man. The degree to which the practice or allowance of pagan worship, which Augustine experienced in reality, influenced his judgment in this should not be left out of account.[16]

Nonetheless, he energetically asserts that only Divine Providence determines the formation of states and their destinies,[17] and he even takes it upon himself partly to show the moral motivations of this Providence in the governance of world destinies. In particular, he conducts a comprehensive discussion

---

[12] *City of God,* Bk. XV ch. 4, Bk. XIX chs. 14, 16, 17.

[13] "Aeternum supplicium subire cum diabolo" [eternal punishment with the devil], Bk. XV, chs. 1 and 4.

[14] Bk. XIX ch. 15.

[15] Bk. XV ch. 1.

[16] Cf. Bk. XI ch. 1 and Bk. XIX ch. 21.

[17] Bk. IV ch. 31.

of how the Romans were allotted the empire by God for the sake of their civic virtues.[18]

Practical Political Tendency

In accordance with such an assessment of the state, Augustine pays scant attention to its actual political tasks and allocates its main function only to the *protection of the church*. That and only that appears to him to be the truly ethical significance of the state, understandably so because in this way it enters into the service of the celestial empire (*civitas coelestis*). The practical goal in Augustine's doctrine of the state is therefore the maintenance of ecclesiastical prescriptions and the restriction and punishment of heretics by the external power of the authorities; that is the idea which most vividly fills Augustine and the one by which he became so decisive to the subsequent shape of Christianity.[19]

Verdict

Running through this whole conceptualization is the true insight, given with the Christian revelation, that the state, like the entire human condition, is estranged from its true eternal form, that an act changed the original condition of human existence, and that an act will one day again restore it. To the Greeks, this insight was absent; it is the middle term which alone can unite Plato and Aristotle. From it, the contradiction between the absolute moral task of the human race, which imbues Plato, and the laws of nature and the natural constitution of man, which Aristotle makes into a standard, is solved. On this basis, one neither needs, like Plato, to require an arrangement of human coexistence, of which man is incapable, for the sake of its ethical truth, nor, because of this human incapacity, does one, like Aristotle, need to tone down the moral requirement on the individual and the whole, and to hold the mere (negative) midpoint between two vices to be the nature of virtue, instead of recognizing the positive and infinite content thereof. As a result, the absolute devotion of the people, which Plato requires for the state, is referred to another realm than this ephemeral and tenuous one.

---

[18] Bk. V ch. 15.

[19] This notion is particularly implemented in a few of his letters: cf. epist. 93 ad Vincent., epist. 185 ad Bonifac.

Herein Augustine, by virtue of Christian enlightenment, extended moral- and legal-philosophical knowledge infinitely beyond classical wisdom. He gave it its true center. But he failed to recognize the independent and divine significance that earthly life relations, and thus, above all, the state, still have, even in their present turbid condition. Rather than penetrate the secular sphere with the recovered truth, he flees from it. The idea of the state as state, heroism, justice, wisdom, like the arrangements and tasks of well-ordered, properly structured public life, lie beyond his attention; they are not in themselves divine and worthy of Christian interest, and the significance which he concedes to one of the two great institutions of God, the state, is not that it solves its own problem, but only that it come to the aid of the other, the church, regarding the church's tasks. Basically then, for Christianity only the church can remain, and it makes use of the state to realize its rules externally – thus forcibly. Therein lies the origin of the hierarchical idea, according to which the church erects itself as a state, as a theocratic empire, and maintains the faith as a civil law, so that heresy, as the supreme civil crime, commands the death penalty. The state, as Augustine conceives it, is either completely unnecessary and worthless for Christianity, or the church must truly and fully use it. This is the result when the state is denied its own importance, and the protection of the church is acknowledged as its sole task. On the other hand, if one presupposes the independent importance of the state, then its connection with the church, which Augustine expressed, is an indestructible truth which has been tested from that hour to this among the Christian nations, and is being challenged at this time only because the peoples are no longer imbued with the same liveliness of the Christian faith. For the separation of church and state, today's solution, is only taught by those who either share this lack of faith, or cannot envision a different public condition than the one with which they are surrounded.

PART II: THE GERMANIC WRITERS[20]

Thomas Aquinas' Outline of the Ethical Sphere

The scientific ethics of the Middle Ages, if the *Summa* of Thomas Aquinas is representative, recognized, in accordance with its Christian basis, the living God as ultimate principle. For this purpose, it took over the traditional concept of a law of nature from antiquity, notably the Romans, and brought it into connection with that ultimate principle.

Accordingly, Thomas initially differentiated between the eternal law (*lex aeterna*) and the natural law (*lex naturalis*). The eternal law is the world-ordering reason in the Divine Spirit (*ratio gubernativa totius universi in mente divina existens*). This governing reason, in itself and with respect to the creation, has the nature of art, of an example, of an idea (*artis vel exemplaris vel ideae*), similarly to how an artist has an advance idea of his artwork (understood of the technical, not the aesthetic aspect); but respecting human action, which it impels to the same end, it has the nature of a law [eines Gesetzes]. The natural law then is nothing but the "participation" of people in this eternal law, as regards the distinction between good and evil, or the "impression" of the divine light in us. But it is not equivalent to that eternal law, because governing reason behaves differently in the regulator (God) than in the regulated (people); rather, it is imprinted in people only to a limited extent and scope, especially in man's fallen state. Yet everything that man, by nature, has of moral knowledge and requirement, is only the effect of that eternal law in God.

This now leads to the question: how does God relate to this eternal law in Him? Thomas answered with a distinction: the will of God in itself and in terms of its substance is not subject to the eternal law, but is one and the same with it. But the will of God in terms of what He wishes with regard to creatures (*circa creaturas*), is subject to the eternal law, insofar as the reason for what He wills lies in divine wisdom. In and of itself, therefore, the divine will is one with reason, but in relation to the creation and rule of the world, it is subordinated to the standard of reason (*rationabilis*). And yet, regardless of how deeply and truly

---

[20] [Subjects of the Holy Roman Empire of the German Nation, hence both Germany and Italy broadly speaking.]

the source of all moral commandment is acknowledged to be in the divine reason and wisdom, as is likewise the unity of the divine will with the divine reason and wisdom, an unacceptable divide is introduced here between the divine will-substance and the divine counsels, which in its further development leads, and actually did lead, to the will-substance or the eternal law in God manifesting itself as mere supreme rule, as something given, apart from any decision. Philosophically this is all the less well-founded because Thomas here did not even characterize this eternal law or divine will-substance as the eternal essence and holiness of God, but as His world plan.[21] In this manner we approach to a diminution of the inner freedom of the divine decree, binding it absolutely to reasons [Gründe] (*ratio*), while, as we shall see below, people are subjected to the will of God or His vicar [Statthalter], as the case may be, as to something apart from reason [grundlosen].

It is evident that, in this presentation, what is meant by natural law is not the legal sphere but, as with Cicero, the ethical sphere in general – in fact, only the moral sphere. But here the moral law, insofar as it inheres in human nature, is opposed to the law that is eternal in God and comes to man by way of revelation.[22] Therefore Thomas adds a third category: *human law (lex humana)*. This now encompasses the legal sphere, but only in its character as *positive* law. Accordingly, with Thomas the legal sphere is only understood in terms of the aspect of its positivity, human sanction; and only this aspect, not the aspect of a particular content, a particular life-sphere [Lebenssphäre], sets it off against the moral sphere. A relation of positive law to natural law in our sense is not in question and, in accordance with this, cannot be; it is only the question of the relation of positive law to natural *ethical* commands [Sittengebote], and that is how it is construed: all positive law (*lex humana*) is only the outflow of the natural moral law (*secundum quam in particulari disponuntur, quae in lege naturae continentur*)[23] and only insofar as this is the case, is it justified. But on the other

---

[21] For a more detailed elucidation of the question itself, cf. vol. II, book I [*Philosophical Presuppositions*] of this work.

[22] In the book *De Regimine Principum* [On the Government of Princes] as well, book I, ch. 15, it can be seen that a distinction is not yet made between law and virtue.

[23] [See *Summa Theologica,* Benziger edition, II.I. 91, art. 3 conclusion: "It is from the

hand, the positive law (*lex humana*) cannot exhaust the full extent of the natural law (*non omnia vitia prohibere potest*),[24] because it pertains to the class of imperfect virtue. So there is no distinction between an idea of law and of morality; but positive law is nothing else than a partial sanction of moral law by means of human authority and penal administration.

Thus while the distinction between ethics and law [Recht] in relation to statute [Gesetz] and life-sphere (i.e., in terms of the objective side) entirely evades Thomas, he nevertheless has some, albeit very vague, notion of this distinction in relation to human virtue and the specifics of entitlement (i.e., in terms of the subjective side). He lists *justice* among the human virtues, and indeed a particularly excellent one, which for him consists in giving to each *his right* according to proportion (*aequalitas*). This virtue of justice is distinguished from the other virtues (*proprium inter alias virtutes*) in that it comprehends only action vis-à-vis other subjects (*ad alterum*), not action against itself; it therefore is not concerned with attitude (*non considerato, qualiter ab agente fiat*), and has only outward acts as its object, not inward, hence not the mastery of desires; all of this obviously has the character of the sphere of law [Rechtsgebietes]. Thus he takes law [Recht] into consideration merely as an object of virtue, that is, the moral character of the individual, not as a specific law [Gesetz] ruling human life, or as a sphere in its own right. He declares the just and the law (*justum* and *jus*) to be one and the same. It is in this sense that he conceives of the distinction between natural law and positive law, namely as that which is due to someone by the nature of the case versus that which is due according to the particular determination of the parties or of the people. This indicates that for him, the concept of natural right [Rechts] (*jus naturale*) does not even stand in the remotest connection to the concept of natural law [Gesetzes] (*lex naturalis*), which was discussed above. He does not even consider the judiciary (*judicium*) to be an element of a higher order, an institution, but rather a product of the virtue of justice.

But even in the sphere of (subjective) virtues, this virtue of justice, for

---

precepts of the natural law, as from general and indemonstrable principles, that the human reason needs to proceed to the more particular determination of certain matters."]

[24] [*Ibid.,* 96, art. 2, reply to objection 3: "Human law does not prohibit everything that is forbidden by the natural law."]

Thomas, does not always exactly correspond with the just in terms of object and character. Its more detailed description, namely, is this: as justice regulates man's actions with other men, it refers either to the whole of the human common condition, and orders actions for the common good (*bonum commune*), or it relates to other individual persons, and orders actions such that each is granted his right. The former is general (*universalis*) justice, the latter particular (*particularis*). General justice now is at the same time the general virtue for all earthly virtues, which does not mean that it contains all of them or is the same as them in terms of concept and essence (*essentia*), but that it determines all of them as cause (*causaliter*), namely, it orders them for the common good, which is the ultimate goal of all earthly virtue. It is therefore also to be named law-fulfilling justice (*justitia legalis*) since (earthly) law also seeks nothing else than the common good. Similarly, love is the universal virtue of the heavenly virtues, since their final goal is the heavenly good. Particular justice, which apportions to each individual his right, is again divided into *commutative* which, assuming the equality of persons, regards only things and processes respecting things as the measure of what is due to each, e.g., in purchase and exchange, and *distributive*, which regards the people themselves, their divergent worth and the merit of their personal actions, as the measure, e.g., the wise or the rich are entitled to a greater share in rule.

Accordingly, in this entire doctrine of justice, only commutative justice pertains by object and character to the sphere of law[Rechtsgebiet]. General justice includes all earthly virtue, and distributive justice, although it also intervenes in the sphere of law, is still not determined by a fixed external order, but by the reasonableness of contingent [jeweiligen], often merely internal relations. What imbues the basic conception of Thomas is the separation of heavenly and earthly virtue, while the separation of the moral and the legal order in earthly life itself escapes him; and it is the mingling of the (subjective) virtue of justice with the (objective) life-order of law which, since the characters of the latter make themselves felt in [outward] experience, brings him to consider the attitude of the actor to be a matter of indifference to the virtue of justice.

This is the outline of the system of ethics in the Middle Ages as portrayed by its most celebrated master.[25]

The Political Doctrine of the Middle Ages: Aristotelian Element

But with regard to the doctrine of state and (philosophical) state law in particular, the writers of the Germanic Middle Ages – Thomas, Dante, Occam, Marsilio, Andlo, etc.[26] – composed their teaching mainly of two elements, the philosophy of Aristotle and the Christian conception of the state, the latter especially after the example of Augustine, but each modified according to the standpoint and consciousness of time and nation. Essentially the same thoughts and the same manner of reasoning and presentation run equally through all of these writers. The legal-philosophical temper [Bildung] of the Middle Ages had more of a traditional than a successive and developing character. Now Dante, as far as philosophical deduction is concerned, was peculiar in the highest degree, emancipated even from Aristotle, just as he surpassed all other political writers in deep philosophical conception;[27] but precisely because of his

---

[25] With regard to all of this, cf. Thomas Aquinas, *Summa Theologia,* in particular *prima secundae quaest.* 91–96, *secunda secundae quaest.* 57–59.

[26] Thomas Aquinas (†1274), *Summa Theologia, loc. cit. Idem, De Regimine Principum* (the question regarding the partial or entire inauthenticity of this writing does not affect the argument here, in that it is in any case a document of the educated thinking [Bildung] of the Middle Ages – on the other hand, Thomas's commentary on Aristotle's *Politics* is of no significance to us, in that it only elucidates, and provides none of the commentator's own insights). – Dante Alighieri (†1321), *De Monarchia.* – William of Occam (†1347) *Dialogus.* – Marsilius of Padua (†1328), *Defensio Pacis* – (in Goldast, *Monarchia St. Rom. Imper.*), Petrus de Andlo (†1480), *De Imperio Romano* 1460.

[27] So, for example, Dante declares it to be the goal of the state (i.e., the Christian empire) that the human race as a whole engage the entire force of possible intelligence (*actuare semper totam potentiam intellectus possibilis*) initially for knowledge, and then for action, Book I, ch. 3. Like Kant, he distinguishes between freedom of the will and arbitrary will [Willkür], Book I, ch. 12. Sinning for him is nothing other than *progredi ab uno spreto ad multa* [to proceed from despised unity to multiplicity], Book I, ch. 15. Then: "Ex iis liquet, quod jus cum sit bonum, proprius in mente Dei est, et cum omne, quod in mente Dei est, sit Deus (juxta illud: quod factum est in ipso vita erat) et Deus maxime se ipsum

peculiarity, he had no effect on the further development of science.

Medieval political science took first and foremost from Aristotle the philosophical concepts and categories in general, e.g., the three categories of *ens, motus,* and *finis,* and the proposition that a mover must be above the moved, to prove that all rule is from God[28] – furthermore, those general propositions of natural observation applicable to politics, for example, that the whole is greater than the parts, that nature everywhere seeks for perfection – finally, however, in particular the lessons and propositions of politics itself, namely the derivation of the state from the social nature (πολιτικὸν ζῷον – *sociale animal*) of man, the doctrine that the purpose of the state is the good life (εὖ ζῆν, *bene vivere*), that this consists in virtue, that the distinction between true and false constitutions is drawn simply according to whether the rulers or the ruled are the goal, the classification of forms of state in *regnum, politia,* etc.[29] All this can be found equally in all writers.

Christian Speculative Element

In the same way, the Christian speculative conception of the state in the Middle Ages is based on the thought of Augustine, whereby the civil order is the result of sin, states are established by divine providence, two kingdoms run through earthly history, the Romans possess world rule because of their virtue

---

velit: sequitur, quod jus a Deo, prout in eo est, sit volitum. Et cum voluntas et volitum in Deo sit idem, sequitur ulterius, quod divina voluntas sit ipsum jus" [From these things it is clear that the right is a good, it is God's own, in the mind, and with all that in the mind of God, He is God (as it is said that what was in him was life;) and since God principally wills himself: it follows that the right from God, inasmuch as He is, belongs to the thing willed. And when he had the will and the thing willed in God is the same, it follows further that the divine will is the right itself]. These examples are sufficient to give an idea of Dante's speculative treatment. [Translations are from the Henry edition.]

[28] Thomas *De Regimine Principum,* Book III, chs. 1–3. Similarly Marsilius, Andlo.

[29] Thomas's investigations (*De Regimine Principum,* Book II) into the material conditions and material goals of the state (situation, climate, means of subsistence, highways) can also be viewed as a copy [Nachbild] of Aristotelian treatment, albeit a completely free facsimile [Nachbildung].

(also used as a justification of the Germanic empire, which indeed was viewed as one with the Roman), etc.[30] But there is nevertheless an essential, profound difference between the medieval conception, founded on the Germanic view of life, and that of Augustine. If with Augustine the state appears as a mere work and interest of the earthly kingdom (the worldly-minded), here it is the realization of God's kingdom in accordance with one of its aspects. Hence, in place of that contempt of the state, there emerges here an apotheosis of the state, i.e., of the Germanic-Christian imperial state which maintains justice and peace in the Christian world, by order of God. But nevertheless, here as well this recognition of the state is always due to its relationship with the church.

According to the famous doctrine of the Middle Ages which runs through all these writers, God set two swords over Christianity, the spiritual and the secular, the former in the hands of the pope, the latter in those of the emperor. They are directly ordained and vouchsafed by Him; He rules on earth through them, and every Christian – yea, because the true God also has power over those not yet recognizing Him, every person – is subject to both. Therefore, the legitimate supremacy of the pope and the emperor is asserted even over newly discovered and still unconverted princes and peoples, and in Christendom itself, division into several completely independent kingdoms instead of one empire is held to be as illicit as, in the church, its breakup into bishoprics rather than the papal primacy (Lampugnano). The dispute between the papal and the imperial party is only about the reciprocal relationship between these two swords. The teaching of the former, which was the first to be developed scientifically, is that the papal power is the higher,[31] because the spiritual and eternal stand above the worldly and earthly, just as, of the two lights, the sun stands over the moon; just as Levi and Aaron stand over Judah; even more, while the emperor receives his temporal power first through the pope, only the papal power comes directly from God, again by analogy with the election and dismissal of Saul by Samuel, and the offering of the three wise men (kings) before Christ. The pope was therefore the head of Christendom, the kings the arms, for which reason

---

[30] Thomas, *De Regimine Principum,* Book III, chs. 4–6.

[31] Thomas, *De Regimine Principum,* Book III, ch. 10. See also Dante's counterargument, *De Monarchia,* Book III, ch. 9.

only the pope is anointed on the head, the princes on the arms.[32] The further implementation is then: Christ conferred both swords on Peter and his successor, the spiritual for his own use, the worldly only as a sort of deposit until the future conversion of the Gentiles and of the state. For this reason Pope Sylvester reissued this sword to Constantine after he converted, on behalf of God. Under Charlemagne, however, the Pope as vicegerent of God transferred world empire from the Greeks to the German nation. This was the basis for its legitimacy.

The primacy of the spiritual over the secular seemed so evident that for a long time it captivated the mind of the Germanic peoples. Finally, though, the temporal power also acquired its scientific arsenal. It was countered that the spiritual and secular are two different spheres which are independent of one another without any relation of domination and subordination. This idea, so simple and so familiar to us now, was lacking then; and the imperial power had suffered from it. The shift took place in a decisive way with William of Occam. Dante separated church and state by the two purposes of human nature, corruptible and incorruptible, but he nevertheless acknowledged that the state receives the power of grace from the spiritual kingdom, which the papal blessing infuses in him,[33] and accordingly did not wish the independence of the secular power to be understood so strictly (*stricte*) that the emperor would not be subject to the pope (*in aliquo non subjaceat*); rather the emperor owes homage to the pope like the first-born son owes it to his father. Partly, public awareness was still too much in thrall to papal supremacy, and partly Dante was too profound to maintain a complete separation of the two spheres, like the defenders of Louis of Bavaria did. But the proper distinction, differentiating the spiritual

---

[32] *Decretales Gregorii IX*, I. 15, *de sacra unctione*.

[33] "Si ergo dico, quod regnum temporale non recipit ease a spirituali, nec virtutem (quae est ejus auctoritas) nec etiam operationem simpliciter; sed bene ab eo recipit ut virtuosius operetur per lucem gratiae, quam in coelo et in terra benedictio summi pontificis infundit illi" [In like manner, I say, the temporal power receives from the spiritual neither its existence, nor its strength, which is its authority, nor even its function taken absolutely. But well for her does she receive therefrom, through the light of grace which the benediction of the Chief Pontiff sheds upon it in heaven and on earth, strength to fulfill her function more perfectly]. *De Monarchia of Dante Alighieri*, Book III, ch. IV.11.

kingdom and the external church power, which already was intimated in the standpoint of Dante's, was, in terms of its fullest insight, only the work of the Reformation. Similarly, it was denied, albeit not entirely accurately in terms of history, that the papal coronation made Charles the Great into the emperor – rather, this supposedly took place by the will of the people (*acclamatio populi*). Finally, the independence of the secular authority, and its direct ordination by God, was set out in the great acts of state of the nations.

How the Two Cohere – The Theocratic Principle as Foundational Characteristic of the Medieval Conceptualization

Although the argument about the precedence of the two swords was conducted in this manner, still everyone was agreed on the idea that this dual sword, the papal-imperial empire, was based on immediate divine institution and had absolute prestige. It was thus a power erected for external earthly things as well as for faith and conscience, to which every Christian owed unlimited obedience. To this was attached Daniel's prophecy of the five world empires,[34] in that the last empire, which puts an end to every other one and endures into eternity, points not to the otherworldly kingdom of God (which, however, had already begun here on earth with Christ's appearance, but only as an inward, not yet revealed kingdom), but to the Holy Roman Empire of the German Nation, under pope and emperor. This was therefore regarded as identical with the kingdom of God, and usually thought to be an uninterrupted connection and future segue between the two.

This conception is found in the most exhaustive but also most glaring way with Petrus de Andlo. In his presentation, the Augustinian economy of the heavenly (heavenly-minded) empire is transformed into a formal dynastic succession. From the hand of God there first reigned Adam, Abel, the Patriarchs, judges, the kings and priests of Judah until Christ, and since then, again from God and in Christ's place, there reign Pope and Emperor, whom the Pope handed the secular power. The last emperor will lay down the trappings of his kingdom in the church, and there they will be taken up by Christ. Thus, from the creation until the resurrection not even the gap of an interregnum between

---

[34] Thomas, *De Regimine Principum*, Book III, chs. 12–16.

the divinely authorized rulers was left.[35]

Apart from this theocratic foundation of the state and its authority, the political theory of the Middle Ages also had another peculiar, although subordinate element, the analogy according to divine relations. Augustine, as did other Fathers, loved to conceive of the natural creation blatantly allegorically in order to explain ethical-religious relations. In similar manner, the scholastics and the political writers of the Middle Ages sought the solution of the question of state arrangement often in comparison with divine models. In this manner, the monarchical form of government was established by analogy with the unity of divine dominion;[36] similarly, the obligations of the sovereign and other things.

Both the theocratic element and this symbolizing one now everywhere appear much more emphatically among the representatives of the spiritual power. The supporters of the secular power are much more sober, and come closer to our present way of thinking [Bildung].

The writers of that time could not have been unaware that the doctrine of Aristotle, which they venerated, was not consistent with their Christian-ecclesiastical life valuation. They sometimes permitted themselves a different judgment than Aristotle's in specific cases, especially on the worth of the forms of government, where they almost unanimously declare not Aristotelian polity but, according to Christian-Germanic custom, monarchy,[37] usually elective

---

[35] Petrus de Andlo, *De Imperio Romano Regis et Augusti Creatione* [The Creation of the Imperial Roman Monarchy], Book I, ch. 1, ch. 13–15, and Book II, ch. 8 (pp. 11, 12, 45, 55, 65), finally in particular the conclusion: "de Romani imperii exitu et ejus finali consummatione" [Of the Issue and Final Consummation of the Roman Empire] (p. 140).

[36] Petrus de Andlo, p. 34. Thomas Aquinas, *De Regimine Principum,* I, 12. Dante (*De Monarchia,* Book I, ch. 15), according to whom it is not the rule of the state that approaches divine rule; the human race itself through unity (which yields it dominion) approaches God.

[37] Thomas nevertheless was able to reconcile this by characterizing the appropriate form as polity for the city (*civitas*) and monarchy for the territory [Land] (*provincia*). In the *Summa* he declares the mixed form generally to be the best. But it is traditionally the case in the medieval conceptualization that the concept of monarchy rules out

monarchy after the model of the German emperorship, to be the best form of government. On the whole, however, they seek to reconcile the contradiction of the two elements which they include in their teachings by distinguishing the spheres , attributing the secular to Aristotle, the spiritual to the Christian idea. The "Philosophus" (i.e., Aristotle) could have known nothing about the entire extent of revelation and grace, therefore also nothing of the priesthood, the spiritual regiment, hence the entire ecclesial side; but for matters for which no revelation exists, and which pertain to what man can attain with his natural capacity, the Philosophus is and remains the authority, and to this pertains in particular the arrangement of the secular regiment. The same distinction is applied to the purpose of the state, which is placed, in accordance with Aristotle's procedure, in the good, i.e., the virtuous life. Here also a distinction is made between, on the one hand, *earthly virtue*, recognized by reason and attainable by man in his own strength, as well as, in conjunction herewith, his earthly well-being – all of this forms the scope of the state (*regnum*) – and on the other hand, the virtue that can only be known through revelation and attained only by divine grace and the means of salvation, and corresponding to this, eternal well-being; this forms the sphere of the church (*sacerdotium*). This explanation is found in Thomas Aquinas[38] and others, but at its clearest and most complete in Dante,[39] although with him it does not serve to ground the relationship to Aristotle, but the relationship between emperor and pope. From this angle, inappropriate though it is to grace and revelation, is thus derived the task which was lacking

---

subordination to the laws [Gesetze]. Thus Thomas, *De Regimine Principum*, p. 300; Andlo, p. 32.

[38] Thomas, *De Regimine Principum*, I, ch. 15. Likewise Marsilius in Goldast, II, pp. 157–164.

[39] Dante, *op. cit.,* Book III, ch. 16.6, where among other things the following statement is found: "Propter quod opus fuit homini duplici directivo secundum duplicem finem: scilicet summo Pontifice, qui secundum revelata humanum genus produceret ad vitam aeternam, et Imperatore, qui secundum philosophica documenta genus humanum ad temporalem felicitatem derigeret" [Wherefore a twofold directive agent was necessary to man, in accordance with the twofold end; the Supreme Pontiff to lead the human race to life eternal by means of revelation, and the Emperor to guide it to temporal felicity by means of philosophic instruction (Henry translation)].

in Aristotle, that the state is to provide for worship.

Indeed, such a delimitation of the two spheres by no means eliminates the opposition between these two elements, in that the Christian idea also finds its application in the secular sphere ; and such is also found among these expositors. For this reason, throughout their entire presentation the contradiction remains unresolved. For instance, it is contradictory when in accordance with Aristotle they base the state on the socializing nature or the mutual need of man (*humana indigentia*),[40] but at the same time view it theocratically as God's representative; or when they in accordance with Aristotle's guidance investigate the worth of different forms of government, yet also teach that God has set monarchical power, and indeed a single one, over all of Christendom. For this lacks the coherence, for instance, of the application of Aristotelian notions to demonstrate the rationale of divine action, or that God established states because people need each other (which in fact was not entirely applicable), etc.; instead, these two run without connection alongside each other. Therefore, a dualism runs through the legal philosophy of the Middle Ages, there being two elements without penetration, without a unifying principle.

Similarly, they are also unaware of how the Aristotelian conception, which is derived from Greek life, is so dissimilar to the state of the Germanic Middle Ages, in which they lived and to which they were attached. Hence this intruding ancient mentality [Bildung] already contains the first seeds of the breakup of the medieval condition, and the furnishing of the European countries with a character approximating the ancients, such as they have at the present day. But even more than that: In their Germanic appropriation, the lessons drawn from Aristotle lack the Greeks' emphasis of the objective – the consideration of the state as a given, higher whole, in which the individual is subsumed. Therefore, where the Christian element, the positive divine sanction, recedes, the state will no longer manifest itself as a given power over the people, but rather, in the

---

[40] Thomas (*De Regimine Principum,* Book II, ch. 2) admittedly deduces the necessity of the state not merely on physical mutual need but also on the requirement of the community for intellectual need and the exercise of some virtues (particularly, justice and friendship). But entirely independently of this he teaches (Book III, ch. 9) a God-ordained hierarchy of authorities: men over animals and things, princes over men, the church over princes. Likewise Andlo, p. 12, cf. p. 11.

principle of subjectivity, as the work and the mere object of people.

In this manner the traces of today's doctrine of popular sovereignty are here and there already found in the medieval writers. This is very decided and well-developed in the case of Marsilius of Padua, who, of course, lived in the midst of alternative viewpoints. According to him, the people – i.e., the totality of the citizens or their *valentior pars* [stronger part] – is the legislator, or the first and actual efficient cause of the law. The same is likewise also the cause of the princely power (*principatus*) and also has the competence to punish the princes in cases of grosser violations of the law (*corrigendi*). The doctrine of Aristotle, whereby genuine state constitutions are those in which the government at the same time is directed to the goal of [serving] the subjects (the people), Marsilius conceives in this manner, that government must be conducted according to the will and the agreement of citizens (*voluntas et consensus civium*). He declares that for this reason elective monarchy is a more adequate form of government than hereditary monarchy.[41] All of this is indeed no longer specifically medieval, but already constitutes the transition to the modern political view.

But there emerges through these specifically medieval ideas a completely new principle in the philosophy of law: the *personal will of God*, which is nowhere to be found in ancient times, at least not as a scientific principle. Accordingly, the state not only has the ideal sanction of the good and the beautiful as with the Greeks, but also the reality of divine institution. Likewise, world history emerges under an ethical principle: the divine will. Among the Greeks, an ethical power is to determine the way in which states are to be constructed; but how they really are constructed is an affair of accidental human decisions and accidental events. Here, however, the real nature of states, the historical leading of their destinies, is determined by ethical power (the divine will). World empires and the contemporary construction of states manifest themselves as its work. The divine sway in history is here recognized, and also becomes one aspect, in fact the most important, of scientific conceptualization.

---

[41] Cf. Goldast, *Monarch.* II, pp. 169, 175, 185, 163, 165. When in opposition to this, Dante (*De Monarchia,* Book I, ch. 12) says of the king (emperor), "qui minister omnium procul dubio habendus est" [without doubt the Monarch must be held the chief servant of all] (with an expression similar to Frederick the Great later on), this has an entirely different, innocuous meaning [translation from the Henry edition].

This principle, which is true in itself, appears here in crude, external shape – as the *theocratic principle*. That is, it assumes everywhere a direct manifestation of God's will; accordingly, God ordained the authorities in church and state through a visible personal act (while Christ in person constituted the pope and through him the emperor), and their regard or majesty [Ansehen] is founded in this specific ordination, not simply in a general divine commandment.[42] Similarly, the events of world history are the direct expression of His will, and constitutional questions are decided according to His pronouncement. That God assigned world rule to the Romans because of their virtue, and the pope in the name of God conferred it on the Germans, is the ethical and legal basis on which science established the reputation of the supreme power of that time, and with regard to the former statement respecting the divine institution of the Roman Empire, the commandment of God that all nations must obey them and their successors was regarded as evidence of the virtues of the Romans, their victories as God's judgments, the oracle and finally the fact that Christ was born under Roman rule, that by which God recognized its legitimacy. This is the account even of the great and sober Dante.[43] The right of the Jewish people to destroy the Canaanites, which Michaelis inappropriately enough judges by today's principles of international law, had as its basis such directly expressed divine will and concrete command. The leading of the Jewish people was in truth theocratic by way of exception; for the Jewish people is the type of God's eternal kingdom. But the medieval writers treated the whole of world history in this manner.

---

[42] Cf. this work, Vol. II, Book IV [*The Doctrine of State and the Principles of State Law*], ch. 4: "The Divine Institution of the State."

[43] Dante Book II, pp. 120–128. Andlo, p. 100.

PART III: THE REFORMATION, AND PREVIEW OF SUBSEQUENT DEVELOPMENT

Anti-Theocratic Character of the Reformation

The work of the Reformation in relation to the social condition is simply the overthrow of the theocratic character.[44] The Christian element, the personal will of God, remains, albeit not in a theocratic way. The Reformers likewise base the ruling authority and the spiritual office on divine institution; but they base this on God's order and commandment, not on an immediate act of God, by which He introduced a particular constitution or ordained particular persons. Therefore, all of those investigations as to whether God set an emperor or many kings over Christendom, whether the Romans held world rule by right, whether the pope or the people transferred it to Charles the Great, all get dropped. In their place comes where and how ruling authority exists, it being from God and deserving of obedience. There is then no divinely prescribed form of the constitution of church and state, and the uninterrupted succession of the apostolate (*successio personae*) is no condition of the rightful church and its promises. In this manner the earthly world assigned to men is independent, and does not coincide with the eternal kingdom of God; the supernatural aura of express authority and its unlimited power over faith and action fades; the individual person receives a sphere in which he stands immediately under God and his conscience.

Lack of a Scientific Development of Its Principles

But this healthy evaluation of the ethical and political situation was still without scientific support, and initially even an attempt at any. Melanchthon's work on moral philosophy cannot be considered to be such. He deals with human duties, moral and legal, in pure positive fashion, under the direction and arrangement of the Decalogue, as those that just exist and are questioned by no

---

[44] Cf. my lecture, *Der Protestantismus als politisches Princip* [Protestantism as Political Principle], 1853, pp. 12–22.

one, without even examining the inner ground and the meaning thereof. For instance, he writes: sexual intercourse is necessary for the preservation of the human race, but God does not want stray copulation (*vagi concubitus*), so marriage is necessary. But why does God not want *vagi concubitus*? What is the meaning of this prohibition and its morally persuasive force, through which, even apart from revelation, it must be clear to us and so vouch for the authenticity of the revelation? Likewise: the human community must have a ruler, therefore mastery or subordination is necessary, as is obedience to superiors. The human race needs protection, so penalties are needed, war is needed, from which proceeds bravery, the champion of justice. The abundance of sound striking views and doctrines which this book contains in specifics does not make it into a book that builds on and executes a scientific principle, namely one that realizes the spirit of the Reformation. It is an expression of the life valuation of the Reformation, but not of the scientific system, for which it sowed the seed. Similarly, the natural law of Oldendorp treats legal commandments simply on the basis of the Ten Commandments, as a given, and the same is true of Winkler, namely giving a general introduction about ethics (natural law), which contains the Christian concepts of divine law, human nature before and after the fall, etc., without scientifically bringing them into contact with specific conditions, the legal system, the formation of the social condition.

The Cartesian-Grotian Development and the Reformation

It was therefore a necessity that, just as with the Middle Ages, the new world epoch founded by the Reformation should give shape to its life valuation in a scientific system. That was the impetus for the development that begins with Grotius and Descartes. But this only represents the life valuation of the new world epoch in its negative side: the overthrow of the theocratic character, the liberation of the earthly life-order from the ecclesiastical hierarchy, the liberation of science from any external authority. On the other hand, it also relinquished the bond to God Himself, which the Reformation held onto despite being liberated from mediating powers.

With the destruction of false authority, with the strengthening of the individual mind and its demand to exercise its own investigation and its own freedom, the principle of subjectivity was first unleashed, the power of free personality creating from itself and resting in itself, and it tore itself away from all authority and all content over itself. The complete self-sufficiency of human knowledge (of reason) by which it finds itself in its true condition, capable from itself of recognizing all truth, the complete self-sufficiency of human morality [Sitte], whereby man in his own thinking, separated from God and the moral order given by God (albeit formed in free economy), possesses the ground and content of all morality, and the ability to fulfill it – this is the fundamental character of rationalistic philosophy, indeed of the general scientific orientation from the Reformation to the Revolution. This cannot be held to be the science of the Reformation and of the world epoch founded by the Reformation, in the way that medieval philosophy is the science of Catholicism, since it only appropriated one aspect of the Reformation, and not even the decisive one – the negative polemic. Such is already confirmed beyond all doubt by its contradiction of the fundamental teachings and the life-principles of the Protestant church, while medieval science was in full compliance with the Catholic Church.

Nevertheless, rationalist philosophy in terms of its final destination, of which it was unaware, is the initial prod toward realizing the true and positive principle of the Reformation in science. Because even with all the error in standpoint and result, it is yet at the same time the innermost intellectual contemplation of man in himself. Making thought itself into an object of thought, seeking the connection to the eternal power in the withdrawal from the world into itself, only considering that which is clearly and distinctly acknowledged ("clare et distincte" in Descartes' expression), the systematic Only [Einige], to be truly known – this really is the precondition for Christian truth to penetrate completely into the sphere of science, similar to the way self-examination functions in the ethical sphere.[45] Nevertheless, the error lies in adhering to the sufficiency of human thought as a prerequisite, and thereby refusing the object offered to thought – experience and revelation. If this error is removed, then contemplation necessarily leads to an inwardness and self-awareness, notably also to a self-awareness in all knowledge about its relation to the Christian revealed truth, and thereby an assurance regarding it, hence a true intellectual enlightenment such as dominated the scientific insight of the past. To fulfill this and thus to bring the life valuation of the world epoch founded by the Reformation to scientific development in all its fullness according to its positive aspect as well,

---

[45] *Der Protestantismus als politisches Princip,* pp. 59–64.

from its center outward, is therefore the problem of the present time. The latest scientific endeavors in the aftermath of the Revolution wrestle to find the solution to this, more or less consciously, in greater or lesser approximation, and often partially in yet further aberration.

The Latest Approximation of Medieval Catholic Elements to the Protestant Standpoint

These latest scientific endeavors should not merely scientifically give shape to the inherent drive, the principle of the Reformation according to its true, full, positive aspect, but at the same time revive an aspect which even the Reformation left to one side. That would be the ethical significance of world history as the work and manifestation of the World Power. The Middle Ages comprehended this significance theocratically in the sense that the history of the world, as far as the possession of power is concerned, in church and state, was determined by the direct indication and formation of God. For its part, the Reformation completely prescinded from world history. It was only concerned with the ethical rule, the commandment; this alone is divine to it; by contrast, the whole of reality and history provided it no ethical defining moment. So, it measured the church purely in terms of doctrine which stands outside and above all history. By contrast, the historical realization of the church, the catholicity or the historical continuity (the unity and the connection of all those who confess Christ, and the uninterruptedness of the doctrine and constitutional development of the church throughout the ages) is not at all decisive to it.

For Luther this element is still active, but only as the residue of his Catholic education. It is not his own and therefore not his energetic principle. His preservation of the status quo is often only a concession. For Calvin, it is entirely absent, indeed it is fundamentally rejected. The standard of doctrine is applied at each moment anew, not only to rectify the church, but to decide whether the church is present, as if there had not been a church.[46] Similarly, science (ethics and politics) here simply has to do with the rule that stands outside and above all time in itself, and the world-historical progress of moral consciousness and the formation of states simply takes its place to be judged according to this rule, not to be considered a fellow determinant or manner of application of the rule

---

[46] *Der Protestantismus als politisches Princip,* pp. 71–88.

itself. The general ethical commandment and the action of individuals are the only factors, with the latter standing totally isolated over against the former, without any mediation by world-historical conditions. This trait characterizes not only rationalist but also Protestant education; it characterizes the scientific era from Melanchthon to Kant. This is the field of pure Protestant science.

It is unmistakably an enrichment of this purely Protestant conceptualization, indeed a resumption of an element pertaining to the medieval period, when in the wake of the Revolution scientific conceptions attribute an ethical significance to history itself in one way or another. Thus, speculative philosophy finds the highest ethical standards in the development of world history, the gradual progress of its ideas, and so constructs the history of the world in a manner similar to Augustine and his successors, and, in distinction to Melanchthon or Kant, as a divine work, although as the work of an entirely different God than the person in whom both Augustine and Melanchthon believed. This is the manner of the Historical School of jurisprudence, which attaches to everything that exists, everything that is traditional, a binding regard, an ethical necessity of recognition, a commitment to piety. Likewise the recent political school [i.e., legitimacy], which grounds the regard of historical dynasties not merely, as the Reformation did, in "where there is ruling authority, it is from God" – which *de facto* is true for every government – but is also suffused with the holiness of the divine dispensation in history.[47]

Nevertheless, the ethical significance which the true and evangelical principle must allow to world history is of a very different kind than that which the Catholic-medieval conceptualization ascribes to it: namely, it is always of only *secondary* ethical significance. The supremely ultimate must always be that which is above history: the Word of God and the ethical rule. If one does not wish to fall back to the theocratic viewpoint, there are only divine order and divine arrangements for the social condition (the state and the external church), not divine acts, not pure and direct divine sanction of specific circumstances and persons. The historical event is never the source of the ethic as it is in the Middle Ages, wherein ethics consisted in: thou shalt recognize the *event*, the *act*

---

[47] This thought also corresponds with the actual practice in all times by which, preferentially, only dynastic lineages come into consideration for a new occupancy of the throne.

of God, whereby He constituted the Pope and through him the Emperor, while all ethical rule (truths of faith, regulation of life, legal order) only indirectly issues therefrom (that is, as the current statutes of the pope and emperor). Rather, the source of the ethic remains the commandment (the rule) alone, and every event is ethically valued only by subsumption under the commandment. But this latter is recognized in its enriched content. While the older Protestant intellectual culture [Bildung] recognized the ethical commandment merely as a commandment for the *sporadic* actions of (individual) people, in this advanced insight it is recognized at the same time as a commandment for the actions of the human community in its *historically cohering unitary condition*, as a commandment: thou shalt not interrupt this coherence without reason, thou shalt have reverence [Pietät] for what has come about by God's *providence* or *allowance* in this condition, to the extent that it does not contradict the order of God (the God-given ethical rule) – the unified faith and the traditional consciousness of the church (which is not without the Holy Spirit) shall have an authority over you and yours, as long as it is not contrary to the clear Word of God – thou shalt not merely obey the ruling authority, where such exists, but thou shalt render piety and devotion to the dynasty rooted in history, as ordained by God.

This therefore distinguishes the *principle of legitimacy* from the *theocratic principle*. For the former, the chief ground of regard is always only the general rule that obedience is owed the ruling authority, although it not only is not conceived abstractly, but also in the deeper meaning that over a lengthy period of possession a divine arrangement is honored, and this deeper ethical valuation extends to long-existing, prescriptive power. By contrast, according to the theocratic principle the ground of regard is not the rule but simply the act of God, by which He ordained authority, and of course this must be a purely divine act without the human admixture which is in all mere historical dispensations of God. The theocratic principle therefore is not satisfied with the ever so lengthy duration of a dynasty, but it goes back to the divine source, to the appearing of Christ, in order to examine whether its absolute origin is really such a divine act. For this reason, the Protestant church does not consider the unbroken succession of bishops from the apostles onward to be a condition of the true church and its promises, but holds the ministry (even if, in an emergency situation, it were to have emerged anew out of the congregation, still directly) to be derived purely from itself, and thus manifests itself as something ordained and dispensed by God, not as prescribed by the congregation. Just as the ethical rule is supremely ultimate in the lives of individuals, while secondarily the divine guidance and the promptings they mediately contain, detectable by the foreboding mind, are likewise ethically determinative ("do nothing out of your own will")[48], so also secondarily there is an ethical guideline in the history of mankind.

Finally, that which according to the newer conception is considered binding, recognized as ethically significant in world history, extends not only to the mere acquisition of external power but also to the entire development of ethical consciousness and life-shaping ideas.

Herein, then, lies a resumption of, or at least a stronger emphasis on, an element left unheeded in the Reformation's manner of looking at things, albeit purified by this and therefore also homogeneous with it. What is manifested in the most recent trends in Protestant science, whether more manifest or more concealed, is a reconciliation of the Protestant and Catholic principle, as far as such is possible.

---

[48] [Perhaps a reference to Philippians 2: 3, "Do nothing out of selfish ambition or vain conceit" (New International Version).]

PART IV: THE START OF THE NEW LEARNING

Character of the Writers at the Start of the New Epoch

At the turning point of both ages, that is, at the beginning of modern history, there is a class of writers which does not, like Descartes, Grotius, Locke, bring to bear, in accordance with the framework of the modern world, a simple energetic principle, but instead makes the object of treatment an unprejudiced, often noncommittal conception of public life, without any clear-cut statement of the problem. Their writings are the product of education based in classical antiquity, which with its broad knowledge rather than a one-sided preoccupation with Aristotle had become widespread, together with the intellectual movement and sober assessment which was opened up by the Reformation. In the freshness of these newly acquired intellectual elements, they seek after the relations between civic order, which not long before had begun to consolidate, and scientific knowledge. Among these pertain especially Bacon and Bodin, and to some extent also Thomas More.[49]

Thomas More

In his *Utopia,* Thomas More provides a replica of the Platonic Republic, a description of an ideal state of human common life as it lies outside of reality and possibility. Even the form of government is platonic: an elected Senate of excellent families, with a lifelong magistrate from the ranks of scholars (Plato's philosophers) at its apex. Similarly, as with Plato, the main and fundamental idea of his ideal is the subordination of material interests and pursuits, their limitation to indispensable necessity, and the community of goods, or more precisely, a communal economy: fields distributed equally, the harvest brought to market and the requirement of every householder distributed to him without payment, legally determined daily working hours, and in small amounts at that, so that the remaining hours are free for intellectual pursuits.

---

[49] Thomas More († 1535), *De optimo reipublicae statu deque nova insula Utopia,* 1517. Francis Bacon († 1626), *De augmentis scientiarum,* the chapter entitled "De fontibus juris." Jean Bodin († 1597), *De Republica.*

But in this picture More does not present the actual ideal of his nation, as Plato did; he provides, not a moral life assessment which is already active in the formation of states, but only the scientific expression. On the contrary, he completely abstracts from this, both from the conditions and the life assessment of his nation. His account is therefore nothing else than the enchanting game of a noble and educated mind, an attempt to prove itself in the newly acquired antique form, and from this it is understandable that it was and remains without effect. Incidentally, a complete sketch of the outlines of today's socialist economic system was given in More's book, only with the glorious difference that he did not make possession and consumption the final end, like the latter does.

Francis Bacon

Bacon is much more important. Compared to More, he once again represents the empirical standpoint, and does so with an independence gained from permeation in classical education, drawing from his own life experience and contemplation of national conditions, focusing on life, the national condition. With him there is no question of a peculiar scientific principle, of a system peculiar to himself. Rather, he enunciates profound insights which could have served to rectify subsequent systematic theory. Standing out among them are his conception of the state, by which public law ought not be restricted to being the guardian (*custos*) of private law, but also of religion, public mores, military power, public welfare; furthermore his theory of the origin (sources) of law, in particular the meaning and value of customary law and court practice. His teaching about the sources of law has only in recent times come to the fore again, through Savigny. As a philosopher, on the other hand, he planted the seed of a scientific development that immediately followed him, and in its later stages exerted the most important influence on the views of law and the state, although quite opposed to those that he himself held to; this will be discussed at the close of Book III [pp. 259ff. below].

Jean Bodin

Bodin's *Six Books on the Commonwealth* eminently manifests a new era of science [Bildung] arising in the sixteenth century. In terms of subject matter, it is similar to that of Thomas on the "government of rulers." In addition, in terms of structure one sees in it Aristotle's *Politics*. But the freedom of the modern era is already dominant here. Bodin joins Aristotle not only in concepts and doctrines but also in problems and the procedure of investigation. Likewise, the theatrical performances are eliminated. Hence, the legal-philosophical elements of the Middle Ages are all abandoned, and his book is therefore also completely or at least predominantly political theory (politics), not legal philosophy: herein it is the exact obverse of the subsequent work of Grotius. He seeks no principle, no basis and standard of all law; not even the legal basis of the state and the duty of the subject is a subject of his study. Although he presupposes the transfer from the people as the actual ground of state power, since everywhere the first and natural mode of conceiving the matter is the introduction of the existing constitution by conscious act, which can only be an act of the people, yet he admits that this in itself is not sufficient for the legal basis thereof. His aim everywhere is more oriented, on the one hand, toward laying out the extant, toward penetrating the richness of the existing political situation, and on the other hand toward recognizing the salutary, the wholesome, but not in order to establish some absolute legal necessity. He therefore begins by giving sharply delineated definitions of the state, of the family, of sovereignty ("majesty"), of the various forms of government, even the various types of monocracy (*dominatus – regia potestas – tyrannis*). He then seeks out the proper political maxims about conservation, change, the development of the state and its institutions. Finally, he compares the forms of government with each other in order to discover among them the more perfect, the more salutary. Especially prominent is his doctrine that the laws and forms of government necessarily must correspond to the conditions and manners of the people, together with the already extensive investigations he makes in that regard; for this reason he has rightly been characterized as Montesquieu's predecessor, while he himself had Aristotle as his predecessor.

But in terms of substantive content and intention, his book is mainly a scientific justification of monarchy. With the emancipation from Aristotle and the weakening of theocratic ideas, it was a requirement, indeed it first became a possibility, to comprehend the constitutional situation of the Germanic states, hence the monarchy and specifically the peculiar Germanic monarchy, in itself and independently, so that the nation, which emerged in terms of monarchy, also find its satisfaction in it, and especially that the true legal relationship between king and people (which theory and life might already have shaken) be recognized. Bodin meets this requirement. He teaches the advantage and higher perfection of the monarchical form of government, partly from earlier commonly-accepted reasons, partly from essentially new and often witty conceptions, but he only praises monarchy moderated by aristocratic and popular elements. He declares sovereignty ("majesty") to be a power [Gewalt] released from the laws, which, however, in his sense only means that the sovereign prince unites all regard [Ansehen] in himself and is subject to no judge on earth. Finally, in accordance with this he teaches the absolute illicitness of killing or dethroning the king when he really is king, i.e., sovereign.

It is with Bodin as it is with Bacon: there is no sharply delineated principle, or system based on that principle, but rather the considerations of a judicious man regarding political problems. There can be neither followers nor enemies of Bacon or Bodin; but anyone anytime can learn a great deal of truth from them, and base much that is truthful on their authority. The writings of both contain richness and solidity of ideas. But this entirely unprejudiced conception, which however does not penetrate to the ultimate grounds and is not systematically rounded off, had no lasting effect on the age. It pursued thoroughly conscious and self-contained knowledge, and the intellects which extracted a single aspect from the wealth of the subject, but situated it in all its sharpness and carried it through to the final consequence, were therefore, despite their one-sided fallacy, the ones which initially achieved scientific predominance.

The beginning of the world era which followed the Reformation is also characterized by the higher esteem in which the ethical element is everywhere held. That element is nurtured more carefully in science even than the material and mechanical, and ethical significance is recognized as supreme, especially with the state. Thus, Melanchthon declared the respectability of outward behavior to be a goal of the state (*honesti mores in externa vitae consuetudine*), Bacon likewise with regard to the common good (*bene vivere* in the sense of Aristotle), namely religion, discipline, etc. Bodin discusses in detail the notion that the outward comforts of life form a very subordinate purpose of the state vis-à-vis its moral purposes, and among these sets the "contemplative" purpose (the worship of God) as the supreme one. More, finally, starts from the complete suppression of material interests. It was the subsequent period that came to the profane conception that the protection of life and property is the actual, indeed sole task of human community.

BOOK III: ABSTRACT LEGAL PHILOSOPHY

PART I: ABSTRACT PHILOSOPHY IN GENERAL (RATIONALISM)

In the free treatment of the Greeks, every philosophical doctrine, indeed every conception, had its own independent life, and the ethics of Plato or Aristotle can be understood and appreciated without taking into consideration how, in their view, the existence of the world and the coherence of it is to be explained. This is not the case with modern philosophy. Logical consistency, through which alone it aims to attain all its knowledge, establishes the particular in its entire existence on initial assumptions. Each branch of philosophy stands and falls with the supreme philosophical viewpoint [Ansicht]. Therefore, for insight into the newer philosophy of law it is absolutely necessary to take the entire system of philosophy into consideration, and the former only as a consequence of the latter. This is true not only of the particular form of natural law as given by the founders of the particular systems, but quite as much of its general development. Because its entire existence is a result of the viewpoint of abstract philosophy in general.

Essence of Rationalism

The essence of abstract philosophy is: only accept what follows from reason, what is logically necessary. That something exists, is not sufficient; the opposite must be impossible. Every particular content with which reason is filled, is initially manifested as something random which could just as well be something else. What cannot be thought otherwise if it is to remain reason, is reason alone, what it is, its own laws, forms, and determinations: for example, the rule that something cannot be its opposite at the same time, the idea of the one and the many, the finite and the infinite, the relation of cause and effect, etc. Only that which already contains these has the character of logical necessity. That something follows from reason is the same thing as saying that anything else would cancel the determinations of thought. Hence, pure reason – thought prior to all content outside itself – is the principle of abstract philosophy. What it contains, is also to be recognized from itself, prior to all experience (*a priori*). And on the other hand, that which is known through experience can never have the character of logical necessity. For experience shows only that something is, never that the opposite would be unthinkable.[50]

Everything that is to be proven, must therefore be found purely *a priori*. This is true of the things of everyday perception no less than the invisible objects of faith. The proof of the existence of God, for example can only be conducted when it is shown that the non-existence of its concept, which one has to construct apart from any experience, is a contradiction (the ontological proof); the proof of the immortality of the soul, when the characteristics of which the concept of the soul consists, logically exclude mortality.

Common to all investigation and knowledge is reason in a *negative* sense, i.e., the elimination of everything that contradicts the laws of thought, as the standard. The peculiarity of the rationalist orientation is reason as a *positive* standard: only to recognize what these laws already contain in themselves, and to exclude anything that in terms of them might be this way, might be that. Insights should be discovered not merely *by* reason, but *from* reason. Reason is not to be the means and organ, but the source of knowledge; it is not through its activity to find a content lying outside of itself, but to find the entire content solely from its own nature and its laws. That is why this orientation is appropriately referred to as *rationalism*. It is like holding the eye to be the source of light, and wishing to see things not by looking at objects, but from the internal structure of the eye and its analysis.

Motivation for Rationalism

The motivation for this is not skepticism, because the philosopher who destroys the world by means of abstraction, has in advance the hope of rebuilding it out of himself. Nor only admiration of the intellect, because this for its own sake, as experience shows regarding the Greeks, leads to the quest for meaning in things, not to prescinding from them; rather, it joins to itself the *interest of freedom*.

The independence and inwardness of man (the principle of subjectivity) is what propels the entire history of the modern age and the European-Germanic populace – an insight that has been widespread among us for a long time. It has

---

[50] "Experience teaches us that something is constituted in this or that manner, but not that it could not be something else." Kant, *Critik der reinen Vernunft* [Critique of Pure Reason], p. 3.

become the basis of the current aesthetic view. Regarding the legal institutions and the formation of states of the Germanic tribes, it is also recognized that their origin consisted in free self-determination and personal ties. In like manner, scientific investigation resists the constraint which the objects outside it exercise upon it. One comprehends when one allows something to impact him, when one allows himself to be determined by it. Cognition [Erkennen] presupposes recognition [Anerkennen]. The Germanic spirit – liberated by the Reformation from the church's authority and energized in its innermost depth – does not wish to be determined by anything but what it itself determines. A world pre-existing outside it acts oppressively upon it; it is a foreign power, to which it is to submit against its will. It frees itself from that world by abstraction, and refuses to submit as long as it finds no compulsion to do so within itself. Only when the thought determinations themselves demand it, is room made for that existence; for then, the recognition is based on its own existence, not on this other's.

Such disdain to accept the real as real because it is not derivative of self would have to be reckoned the height of arrogance, if it were certain that it occurred arbitrarily. But this process is reflected in the entire development, without any awareness of choice and intention. It permeates all branches of knowledge and constitutes at least the scientific form even for the positive content. It is as if scientific treatment could not otherwise go about its business. Therefore, reason is also defended in general; but the attempt to justify its *particular* use, which is the important thing, is not even made, because one believes it not to be something particular, but the general and solely possible. And indeed, the possibility of abstraction leads of itself and almost inevitably to this conclusion, until the complete trial first makes clear the enterprise and its necessary end, in doing so safeguarding against it.

All philosophy, in fact, is only intended either to obtain a guarantee for specific results (God, immortality, etc.), or to recognize the unity in the mass of diverse things. The former can be called its practical, the latter its theoretical interest. Both are universally human and eternal. It must look for something unconditioned for both ends, which imparts the guarantee and unity to all others. If it is possible for human consciousness, through reflection, to break away from all existence outside of it, to feign even for a moment that it is alone, that everything else apart from it either does not exist at all or does so in a very different character than it really is: what is more natural than to seek that supreme guarantee in what one can no longer think away – one's own existence, and thought itself? The desire to gain certainty about God and immortality, to rescue these from the destruction of that flood of thought washing everything away, must lead to the attempt to see whether they were not already given in those first assumptions. The same free activity of thought that is cognizant of the ability to accept or not to accept any existence or the validity of any commandment, also removes the correspondence between man and the world. It has found what the Greeks stipulated in vain, a position outside of the world and thus a capacity to act against it. It is itself its own world. It stipulates recognition by necessity, it feels everything to be dependent solely on its choice. It is no longer incorporated into the world, and when it wishes to eliminate the contradiction and restore unity, no attempt lies closer to hand than to incorporate the world into itself, to find the world's coherence with it in its thought determinations, just as it finds coherence in itself. If all of this is achieved, then it appears to it, and to the thought pertaining to it, to be the harmony in all things, the only cause from which it imagines something existing to be such; and it possesses for its desired results the confirmation that it alone can be sufficient, its own existence. It has achieved what all philosophy desires, and has achieved this in the manner that its motive force and sense of independence wished for.

In the early period, the practical interest is still predominant. It proves the immortality of the soul – the reality of which is, that we can only be certain of it through faith in the revelations and promises of God – from the characteristics of the soul (its intangibility, its non-compositeness), thus in a way that God Himself could not annihilate or make mortal if He wanted to, any more than He could make a round triangle. Later, from the time of Fichte this interest recedes completely, leaving only the scientific [i.e., theoretical] interest: to derive the world from one's own reason.

Progression of Rationalism

This explains the entire process. Philosophy must find everything *from* reason, *in accordance with* reason. The motive of abstraction – to have the absolute in itself – likewise sets the restriction on its own thinking and existence. Besides, one might just think away even this, and how then could anything be found? That is what is meant when philosophy supposedly emanates from nothing.

Abstraction is immediately carried out until it arrives at some very simple idea, of which one cannot divest himself if he exists and thinks, which underlies all thinking, e.g., substance, the concept of being, the absolute, and the like. All determinate existence must proceed from these remains of abstraction – the simplest that reason contains – and it must do so according to reason, the merely logical. It must contain things such that their opposite is unthinkable. This applies just as much to the systems of necessary opposition, which have to form one thing in opposition to another (Fichte, Hegel), as to those which merely follow from the principle of contradiction. In both, science can accept no object, no concept as something that is there; it must itself build everything in its own way, by showing that with the preceding – beginning with the first assumption – this likewise is posited according to the laws of thought, and their not-being or being-something-else is a logical impossibility. It must then in the same way be possible for it and incumbent on it, conversely, to resolve objects apprehended by it in some manner into the simplicity from which it made them. This is the meaning and the high importance of *definitions*. The characteristics of the definition should be entirely adequate to the defined, should exhaust the matter; these features, even themselves in turn defined in the same way, should be able to be converted into already given general conceptions. In such a way one is to arrive at that which is simple, the general substance. It is, when one completes it, the transition backward, which the philosophical system aims to take forward.

Thus, all living coherence in the world is now repealed, freedom is impossible, the relationship of cause and effect is only appearance, in truth everything is as it is in logic and geometry: mere ground and consequent. Every cause, namely, can be distinguished in its effects not only in thought but also in reality. It is possible for the former to be extant and the latter not to occur, for example, when the sprouting of a seed is suppressed. Besides a positive cause, then, one can accept a negative one, the non-existence of possible prevention, if it should manifest itself. Yes, it is at least conceivable that the cause itself is free either to produce the effect or not, for example, a man and an action. Time – it might now be a true or a false idea in itself – at least refers correctly and clearly to the relationship of cause and effect, separating them both. By contrast, in the logical context the generating and the generated – ground and consequent – can be kept apart in thought but not in reality, as for example with the nature of the triangle and its consequence that its three angles together are equal to two right angles. We cannot put the notion of time between them, nor a prevention of the ground by the will or any other way. We know, as soon as the ground is there prior to all investigation, that the consequence is likewise inevitable, because it is not separate from it; it is the thing itself. Therefore, if all existence is inferred from the initial assumption according to reason, then that existence must already be given in it, apart from any process, and it is inconceivable that anything could have been done differently than it is, or rather that it should be different than it is. And rationalism must stand fast on this conceptualization. For if any free production were to exist in the world, i.e., something else likewise feasible and conceivable, then it could not know from mere thought determinations that precisely this is real. And what follows from reason, cannot be the result of a process, an act, or otherwise it would not have existed before these events, and it would really have been a logical contradiction. Just as little can things be exhaustively defined when they are effects and not mere consequences. The radius being logically *contained* in a circle, is absolutely nothing other than everything else that is already given for all circles. By contrast, the son as *engendered* by the father is by no means denoted even by that descent and by all that is posited in the concept of the father.

Reason as the principle of philosophy, therefore, does not tolerate any occurrence, any creation; it endures nothing new, nothing only adventitious. It is nothing more than what follows from it, and what follows from it could never be lacking, because it is it itself. *The entire development of abstract philosophy is actually continually driven forward by one single postulate: There is no change!* This postulate necessarily led – as will be shown below – from the early stage to Kant's, and thus connects the new systems with the ones preceding his.

Contrast with the Historical Viewpoint

The historical view, which, as was maintained above, the Greeks lacked, here is thus virtually denied. Now this emphasizes all the more that the historical view is not to be understood as if there were eternal change without unity of purpose and control, or as if the past had a higher value than the present, or as if one wouldn't know anything if it hadn't been for events from which one could learn. Quite the opposite! In fact, the historical view is the one by which something has happened and is happening, according to which there is a free act. Schelling called the Christian view of the world the historical as opposed to the logical view of modern philosophy. For the latter would have it that the world and all particular things are necessarily contained in the essence of God, while the former says it only arose (came about) through His voluntary creation. I have referred to the Judeo-Christian view of ethics as historical for the reason that it views law as law because God willed it so. Thus, man had the ethic before any incident of his own; but he has it only by the act of God; it does not exist by itself, with the concept of its existence or of being in general. And the past is not the higher, the present is; and the highest is the future, because God leads the world and law to it – just as the uniqueness of the Historical School of jurisprudence consists in nothing other than having this as its ultimate foundation, as will be shown below.[51]

Herein likewise lies the difference between negative and positive knowledge. What is found from reason (*a priori*) is, according to Schelling's deeply significant expression, not "being" [Seiende], but only "not-capable-of-not-being" [Nicht-nicht-sein-könnende]. Thus, for example, that a triangle has three angles that together add up to two right angles, or that, as Wolff deduces, "seeing is the property of an animal with eyes" (thus a seeing animal), is only a negative knowledge; on the other hand, that the earth is round and not triangular, that there are plants and animals, this is positive knowledge. Another would not be unthinkable. Positive, and the object of positive knowledge, is, if I may put it in an absolute and exhaustive manner, the person, what is specifically primordially determined for him (i.e., holiness, the love of God, etc.), his act, and the product of his act. Therefore, it is merely negative knowledge that there is a being, a power, a ground, by which the world exists, because the opposite would be contrary to logical concepts; on the other hand, it is positive knowledge that there is a God in the true sense, a personal, self-conscious creator; likewise, that this God is gracious and merciful. It is positive knowledge when we consider the world to be the act and creation of God, and only negative knowledge when we consider it to be the eternally necessary consequence of reason. Philosophy which derives all knowledge from reason, can have no other than negative knowledge.

According to that view, then, the entirely consummated All is merely an

---

[51] [Book VI, Part II; included in vol. 1 B of this translation.]

emanation of empty determinations of thought. God, as was referred to above, is what remains of abstraction. The latter, and thus God Himself, is likewise the world – logically, it is contained in Him. This is logical pantheism, which rationalism necessarily must confess or else give up its peculiar method, that is, itself. Different things were adopted in the different systems as what is most simple, which is where the abstraction has to halt – thus, as the god of the world of reason. For Spinoza and Hegel, it is general being (for the former as real, for the latter as thought); for Kant, the notion of the categorical, necessity itself; for Fichte, the I (the concept of self-consciousness). But all assumptions can be traced back to a dual basis, the real existence of the thinker (the I) and the pure determinations of thought. Both principles, as we have shown, are given necessarily with the abstract method; they alone are what remains. Therefore, they confront us immediately in the motto of the first founder of this orientation: *cogito, ergo sum*. But they are *in conflict with each other*. In terms of its essence, the real existence of that which thinks [das Denkenden] is living, acting, generating something outside itself as effect. Reason, however, is static, ready-made, including in itself everything it has produced as a result. The former is free, self-determining and freedom-demanding; the latter is merely determined, necessary, and necessity-imposing. Therefore, what is built on the one is destroyed by the other; thought-necessity abolishes the freedom of the I, and the free activity of the I does not allow for everything to be thought-necessity. They thereby attest to the falsehood of the motive, which encouraged both in a form such that they could not be carried out at the same time.

Subjective and Objective Rationalism

These principles, depending on whether the one or the other is used as a basis, divide the systems in two main directions. The one may be called subjective rationalism, the other objective rationalism. For the latter, impersonal reason is God, while for the former – if it were capable of accomplishment – thinking man himself is God. The representative of the first is Spinoza, the last is Fichte.

These principles come into conflict in the individual systems themselves and in the various branches of science, above all in the philosophy of law. The law of reason continually receives the impetus for its development only from the vain attempt to unite these foundations, and only from them is it possible to look into its innermost working. However, since the living cause of the entire orientation, against the power of which no logical consistency makes headway, is only independent personal existence, then of course subjective rationalism must predominate. It attains predominance right after Spinoza, and maintains it up until Fichte.

Only in the modern period has it been ousted, and all power again turned to the objective, namely by Hegel's system. For there arose a certain awareness that severance from the world does not lead to what is true, and it was believed that objective rationalism avoided this. But this is deception. Pure thought, which it makes into a principle, may not be the person of the thinker; but nevertheless, it has no existence elsewhere than in the abstracting individual. Hereby was the person connected to his own forms of thought, but not to the creation. And if one absolutely refuses to refer all particular existence to a cause that is outside us, recognizing it only insofar as the determinations of thought that are inseparable from our consciousness contain it, then nothing else could have prompted this than the subjective motive whereby man in his isolation wishes to be the center of creation.

Objective rationalism, where it is sincere, is also well aware that it denies a personal God and the historical creation. This is not always so with subjective rationalism, which is wont to invoke the scholastic distinction between the principle of being and the principle of knowledge.[52] Reason is not supposed to be what causes things, but only what causes our knowledge of them. Such an appeal might be less deceptive with general systems of philosophy, in which things can be traced all the way back, than with individual doctrines, for example in theology and natural law. Because reason is to be the *principium*, the originating thing, what is intended here is not a merely negative standard added as a second one to the positive standard, in order to test its conceivability. The distinction would yet have weight if reason were taken merely as the beginning and starting point of the *investigation*, as a fact which is itself to be explained — but not as the ground which alone grants the explanation. For then it would immediately have to go beyond itself. One would have to call for help from laws outside of it to attain to the principle of things. If, for example, I explain the

---

[52] [Apparently a reference to Kant's appeal to the distinction between *ratio essendi* and *ratio cognoscendi* in the Preface to the *Critique der praktischen Vernunft* (Critique of Practical Reason).]

existence of a Creator by the fact of my existence and the forms of my reason, then this happened according to a rule learned from experience. For according to which logical laws is a Creator given in the concept of my existence? How does it follow from the forms of pure reason that it is not me that is the Eternal One?[53] Supposing we had now arrived at the true principle, then the procedure would take on its enduring shape in terms of the nature of this principle, which does not already contain reason. If, for example, this principle were a personal almighty Creator of the sort that rationalistic theologians have found it to be, then it is clear that He could not prescribe to Himself things to do or have done beyond those from which He could not refrain; for example, there could be no miracles, simply because *reason* can produce nothing other than what it must produce.[54] With such a method (which is no longer mere rational inference, but empirical-historical) there would then be no reason as to why *pure thought* is made the starting point, and not rather our whole manifoldly filled nature, thought and desire, volition and conscience, and the endless supply accumulated in it through experience and history. This totality as undeniable fact is the agency from which one would have to proceed in order to discover, likewise with the help of our whole faculty of knowledge, the cause of the forms of thought, observation, intellectual vision, even intuition. For only if we seek the logical unity of the world in ourselves do we have to conceive of ourselves as simple.

The difference of the scientific course as here described, appears to me to have been meant by Plato in the sixth book of his *Republic*, and he would have delineated it more clearly if he had been acquainted with rational philosophy in its modern iteration. There he esteems the mathematical and similar sciences to be lower and insufficient, because they abstract general forms from visible things, and from these abstractions as assumptions move *forward* to results, which then, in order to have some meaning, need the sensible things through which (not from which) they were obtained. True science, on the other hand, must first explicate *backwards*. It must start from the objects, certainly, but

---

[53] Similar reasoning by Kant also refutes this kind of demonstration (*Critik der Urtheilskraft* [Critique of Judgment], pp. 331ff.).

[54] See for this generally, Kant's *Religion innerhalb der Gränzen der bloßen Vernunft* [Religion within the Bounds of Bare Reason], Book Four, Part One.

considers them to be conditioned [bedingte] and therefore seeks not that which is in them (the general form), but an independent cause outside them, as the absolute [das Unbedingte]. If it goes to work like this, then, when it has ascended to this absolute, it will no longer need the sensible things from which it proceeded, but will move among the pure forms. Among these forms (εἶδος) Plato certainly understands not that which is without specific content, the abstract, but rather the opposite of the sensible (αἰσθητόν), the intellectual, in constant freedom, not inhibited by any immovable substance, acting – the creative archetypes and counsels of God.

But all of this is precisely opposed to rational philosophy, including the subjective kind. Here, pure thought is the beginning. With this, we directly relinquish the creaturely character. According to the pure consciousness of existence and the pure forms of thought, we would have to consider it eternal if it only were possible to abstract from the particular sensations which we have at every moment and the changing conceptions with which we must fill those forms. Further, with this thinking as starting point, explication can only occur in the forward direction, according to its own laws. What then results cannot be a cause outside of it, but only a consequence in it. If with the existence of reason everything that truly should be is already logically necessarily posited – and this is the requirement – then there is no need for a Creator outside of it, and according to the same laws of logical necessity, there cannot even be one. If one were to postulate Him, thereby making the concept of Him real – erroneously, because what it requires of existence must also be there even without a Creator, as necessary as logic itself – then the Creator Himself could only be a creature of reason, which is the higher Creator, as can be seen from the Kantian proofs of God.

It therefore comes as no surprise that the logical systems lead to atheism. Rationalism does not first end there, it has already begun there. It immediately *denies* by its own method, *prior to any investigation*, the question the *affirmation* of which it is in the practical interest of all philosophy, even rationalism, to *attain certainty about*.

Admittedly the abstract method largely lingers midway, unconscious of its basic requirement and its inevitable outcome, contenting itself with eliminating details the logical needlessness of which is evident.

Logical Pantheism – Spinoza and His View of Law

Spinoza is the example to which all later efforts of this sort refer as the most solid model, even when they are battling amongst themselves. That does not come because of his exceptional intelligence alone, but also from the special nature of his scientific work. All the later philosophers implement specifically rationalistic systems, but *Spinoza did nothing less than set up the canon of rationalism itself.* Thus, with him it is the magnificence of the enterprise, without the pettiness and inconvenience which in the execution (for example, by Fichte and Hegel) it inevitably gets caught up in. And he, like everyone devoted to him, can find no doubts and no difficulty against his view, because he does not try to put it to the test. He assumes that the only thing in the world is rational coherence. And he does not show how specific objects really follow from reason, but only what kind of coherence with it and with each other they must have according to that assumption. What he says about this cannot be refuted, because, as people are wont to repeat after him, it is true. One simply has to deny the assumption itself, the rational coherence of the world.

The essential content of his teaching therefore consists merely in the character traits of rationalism, which we give here as the generalities of every logical system:

The absolute (*causa sui*) can only be something the existence of which follows from its concept (i.e., the non-existence of which would be logically contradictory), and this is Being itself (substance): this is God. There can only be one, which is simple (because the original idea of thought is necessarily empty, undifferentiated, therefore simple and indivisible). Every cause must lead inevitably to its effect, which is to say, there is no cause and effect, but everything stands in the correlation of ground and consequent. All specific things are only necessary consequences (modalities [Affektionen]) of pure Being (God). He is in them like the essence of the stone (*lapideitas*) is in individual stones. He has no mind and will; He had no freedom to create the world or not to create it; rather, He contains the world, according to necessary laws. There is no freedom at all, as little for God as for men. We consider our actions to be free because we do not know their causes. For what exists, and therefore every individual action, is only a consequence of general necessity, is already given with the substance itself, therefore inevitable, etc.

Ethics in the true sense cannot be expected of Spinoza, for the essence of objective rationalism excludes the freedom of the actor. The universal law [Weltgesetz] is everything; no action takes place that did not follow logically from it (from God). Anything which happens there, therefore cannot help but be lawful, good, and right. Injustice would only be that which did not follow from this necessity, but precisely for this reason is also not possible – "what no one wants and no one is capable of." Human beings can act against religion (the revealed), but not against the eternal law of God. There is therefore no injustice, no sin. What we call such refers only to the consequence that an action has for us, for the well-being of people, not to its intrinsic character.

The objection that there is evil in the world is thereby obviated, in that it is denied and the notion of it is declared to be a sham. Spinoza's entire view of law is only the implementation of this idea. People need to enter into the state, bear its dominion, in order to gain security; because nature drives them to choose the lesser of two evils. If they did not enter into the state, then nature has effected this as well and they do no injustice thereby. By unifying, the government gains power, and therefore right, over all. It may order what it wishes, because it can do so; citizens must obey because they are unable to resist. The government must ensure the public good, because this consideration is a lesser evil than imminent rebellion and thereby doom. But if it does not wish to, it does so at its peril, it does no injustice because nature has given it the power not to. Citizens may not transfer their rights fully and unconditionally to the government; that is, it is physically impossible to give up their (natural) power completely and forever. If they could, the government would no longer be obliged to govern well, namely, it would no longer have the mechanical drive to that end.[55]

Seemingly, and in terms of a literal reading, Spinoza's view of law has the same basis as Aristotle's – nature – the power of generating everything by necessity. But a closer examination shows most clearly the difference between the empirical and the abstract method. Aristotle recognizes a nature with characteristic laws and purposes which his thought does not possess, but which he learns from observation. Spinoza's nature at bottom is nothing other than the abstraction of a logical necessity. Aristotle always derives new data for his knowledge from the world around him; he finds an existence of an entirely

---

[55] See the entirety of Spinoza's *Ethics* and *Theological-Political Treatise*.

different sort in conscious than in unconscious nature, and accommodates his knowledge to this, here establishing freedom and a true ethic. Spinoza, closed to any experience, to everything newly adventitious, holds firmly to his initial assumption, and conversely forms the objects according to the shape of his knowledge, and denies freedom and ethics. For Aristotle the equitable is what free being does, in correspondence with nature. For Spinoza it is what nature itself does, and that's it.

Standpoint of Natural Law

So the peculiarity of objective rationalism is that, carried out logically, it allows for no ethics. All actions that can occur are given with the initial adoption of general substance by ineluctable necessity. Even the question regarding justice must cease, because it would foresee an independence and a condition of being severed from this general necessity. But the logical interest which is satisfied thereby is only derivative. What is original desires causality, not on the part of the laws of thought, but of the living person, which calls for a doctrine of obligation that recognizes his power and freedom, which makes his personality the center while allowing the realization of logical deduction to depend in the first place upon him.

Such is the natural law as it has progressed from Grotius up to most recent times. Natural law thus owes its existence and formation to subjective rational philosophy. Because it emanates not only from reason but also from the existence of the thinker, this philosophy is at once aware of the freedom to exercise in action what is demanded or not by thought; it therefore derives from reason only the prescriptions, while leaving actions to be effected by the free person. So the prerequisite of ethics is not lacking. For this it eschews the postulate that everything is just reason, since free actions, which it admits, may just as well be *counter* to reason.

This is what distinguishes natural law from the legal view of Spinoza; it is the difference between subjective and objective rationalism in general. The basis and the characteristics of natural law are already given with the generic characterization of abstract philosophy, and only need to be substantiated in the particular subject matter. For in no other scientific orientation can the treatment proceed so evenly as in this one, the essence of which is precisely to regard what is newly created not as something newly generated from the appertaining life principle, but as given with the universal, in terms of its concept. Natural law takes on a different shape when it manifests itself as an integral part of a universal (subjective-rationalist) system, with Kant and Fichte, or when it is formed from a doctrine as independent as it is isolated, such as from Grotius up until recent times, whether because its cultivator did not practice philosophy as a whole, or because his philosophy consisted of individual fields without connection. In the latter it is more dominated by the characteristic of the object, in the former more by the specific, often random results of theoretical philosophy regarding this object. It will thus be altogether appropriate to illustrate the development of natural law first according to its general motives in the thread of the subject matter, and then according to its peculiar shape in the individual systems in the thread of the preeminent practitioners.

PART II: GENESIS OF NATURAL LAW IN GENERAL

Chapter 1: Ethics (Natural Law in the Earlier Sense)

The question: How can I tell what is just and what is unjust? presupposes the higher question: how is it that there is just and unjust, what causes these differences, what is the source of all ought? The answer to the latter question is therefore the decisive one for any sort of ethics. The philosophy that only recognizes what follows from reason cannot very well look elsewhere for this source of the ethic than in reason. In this consists natural law.[56]

---

[56] For the development of abstract philosophy in general, and therefore for this entire approach, it is of the utmost importance that reason be held in the truly intended sense of pure thought, rather than to presume any specific content (e.g., a design [Absicht] or attribute of God supplied up-front), which of course solves many problems, but also abandons the basic requirement, which is to accept nothing without logical necessity. Now the threat of such tacit assumption is greatest in ethics. For a long-standing custom that is hardly ever doubted, by which existing mores [Moral] are derived from reason, has lent to this term the signification of morality itself, a word which everyone understands immediately; this might lead one to wonder whether our derivation of obligation from reason is well-founded, since reason is understood to be equivalent to morality. This is further supported by the current confusion of language in philosophy and the usage adopted by many since Jacobi, whereby reason is understood to be the immediate perception of everything divine, holy, good, just, thus precisely the opposite of discursive reasoning [vermittelnden Denken].

The principle upon which natural law and the entirety of rational philosophy is based, is pure thought. It does not wish to proceed from mores and justice, but rather to derive them from itself. Further, it is static, merely existing thought: the epitome of the pure determinations and laws is what it *is,* not what it by its activity produces.

What is proper to the rationalistic treatment can be explained from this, and apart from it, could not arise. Reason in those other meanings would lead to a legal philosophy of an entirely different character. Even the teachers of early natural law stated that by reason they understand thinking, e.g. Pufendorf, *De Jure Naturæ et Gentium,* Book 1, ch. 1, §. 2 [English translation: *Of the Law of Nature and Nations*]; Thomasius, *Institutiones Iurisprudentiae Divinae* [English translation: *Institutes of Divine Jurisprudence*], Book I, ch. 1, §. 38, who refers to a statement of Descartes: *homo dum intelligit, cogitat,*

The Conception of the Origin of the Ethic

The Platonic idea of the good, by which what corresponds with it is good and what conflicts with it is evil, is a source of the ethic outside of reason. It has an original independent existence. And Plato could not even raise the question, why exactly is it that the good is good, and that it should exist? The newer ethic, on the other hand, is based on this question. What does "ought" mean; is it something good or bad? I can deny all of that, even abolish these conceptions, and still exist and think without contradiction. I will only consider the "ought," the "good and evil," to be something if, apart from them, my thinking itself would cease to exist. The good must therefore be logically deduced and must be defined, that is, it must be composed from pure thought-determinations, able to be decomposed into them again. With Kant, for example, it is only the form of all thought itself (necessity and universality); with Hegel likewise, a product which the empty *thought-determination* of being brings about with the *law of thought* (dialectic), *apart from any other component.*

History of the Conception of the Origin of the Ethic

Prior to philosophizing, the Christian world recognized a cause of the ethic independent of reason in the will of God and in the content thereof, divine holiness, which is of specific determinacy, positive, not susceptible to and without need of any further (logical) deduction. To remove this cause was therefore the precondition, the first step that natural law had to take to clear space for itself. The beginnings of this were already given in the philosophy of the Middle Ages: in the *lex aeterna*, which the scholastics set in holy nature over God, which was

---

dum vult cogitat, dum sentit cogitate [Man thinks while understanding, while willing, while feeling]. And though subsequently even important men, such as Leibniz, quite often attribute moral laws which are independent of thought, to thought, as contained in the *ratio;* though they occasionally understand active examination and not logical elaboration as *ratio;* this is merely a lack of consistently clear awareness in their work. Since Kant, who emphasized precisely this clear awareness, there is no longer any such wavering among rigorous philosophers; but non-philosophical writers are now taking all the meanings of reason and combining them into *one* meaning, to turn that into a principle, namely reasoning from reasons [Raisonnement aus Gründen], as did the late lamented Wolffian school.

in Him prior to any resolutions, from which they believed they needed to derive the ethic (*convenientia cum sanctitate divina antecedenter ad voluntatem divinam*). This abolished freedom of decision and determination in God, and it was now requisite to explain reason as that which by necessity is determinative of Him and the world. This took place by asserting that the differences of right and wrong would stand according to reason, even if there were no God. Because in that case God could not possibly be the cause of them, neither His *sanctitas* nor His *voluntas* – otherwise without Him the consequences would lapse as well – this cause could only be reason. Leibniz took this assertion, which was adopted by the founder of natural law, Grotius,[57] (although he by no means was its author), under his wing against adversaries, and emphatically asserted: as the laws of geometry would have to be found necessary even if one denied God, so also the laws of justice. And the differing requirements which, according to the Bible (which Leibniz acknowledged), God issued at various times, form no hindrance to this, because these exemptions are no less necessary consequences of reason than the rule;[58] God Himself is praised because He is righteous, and acts *ut omni satisfaciat sapienti* [to satisfy every wise person].[59]

Wolff[60] posits the law the source of which is the will of God, as positive, over against the *lex naturalis,* which has a *ratio sufficiens* in the nature of man, a classification that can still be found in most textbooks of standing law. As can be seen, it is not the intention here that, as was indicated, good and evil exist by themselves (*perseitas honestatis et turpitudinis*); but that good and evil are such by the laws of thought. This view was indeed contradicted by prominent natural law teachers. Following Pufendorf, there is no good and evil without the *impositio* of a suzerain, and this is God; man did not even have the *socialis* and *rationalis natura* in a manner *ex immutabili quadam necessitate* but rather *ex beneplacito Divino.*[61] Thomasius protested against the distinctions of the

---

[57] Prolegomena, *De Jure Belli et Pacis,* §. 11.

[58] *Observationes de Principio Juris,* c. 13.

[59] *Monita quaedam ad Samuelis Pufendorfi principia,* in Dutens, *Opera Omnia,* vol. IV, part III, p. 275ff.

[60] *Institutiones Iuris Naturae et Gentium,* Part I, ch. 2, §. 39.

[61] *De Jure Naturae et Gentium,* Book I, ch. 2, §. 6; *De Officio Hominis & Civis Juxta*

scholastics[62] – comparing their *lex aeterna* to the matter of pagan philosophers – and also against this assertion of Grotius,[63] and declared that while his principle of reason should be the standard (*principium* **cognoscendi**), it should by no means be the cause of the ethic (*principium* **obligationis**).[64]

But all of this was only words, without application and consequence. The treatment proceeds in such a manner as if everywhere the opposite view were accepted. And this could not be otherwise, if reason is to be the standard of the just, regarding which no doubt prevails amongst the collective caretakers of this doctrine. Because now, what is just is what reason itself contains, not what a cause external to reason requires, a cause the effect of which reason views as if such were independent of it. Reason, then, is not merely the eye, but itself light and color. What reason is, could not suffice to find the differences between right and wrong if there were anything else outside it which caused the differences. The assertion, then, that God is the cause of the ethic is therefore annulled by the other assertion, that reason is the (positive) standard thereof. Certainly an association could lie in God having given us reason, and that therefore He wills what follows from it.[65] But in that case, did God only create the pure determinations of thought and the concept of our nature, stripped of any specific life, and not our specific ethical determination? Should what unfolds in history, which He in fact likewise directs, not similarly be acknowledged? And how can we arbitrarily attribute to Him the wish to have the drive for morality produce its requirements in the same way that logic produces its results, given that the former is given to produce deeds, the latter simply to take up and grasp objects of thought [Gegenstände]?

Legem Naturalem Libri Duo [English translation: *Of the Whole Duty of Many and Citizen*], Book 1, ch. 2, §. 2.

[62] *Institutiones Iurisprudentiae Divinae,* book I, ch. 1, §. 31; "Dissertatio Prooemialis" [Introductory Dissertation] in *ibid.*, §. 39.

[63] *Programma* [apparently the "Collegium Privatum über seines Institutiones Iurisprudentiae Divinae," in "Die Grund-Lehren des Natur- und Völker-rechts, nach dem sinnlichen Begriff aller Menschen vorgestellet...," pp. 57ff].

[64] *Fundamenta juris naturae et gentium ex sensu communi deducta* [English translation: *Foundations of the Law of Nature and Nations*], Book I, ch. 6.

[65] E.g., Wolff, *Institutiones Iuris Naturae et Gentium,* Part I, ch. 2. §. 43.

Hence, it is not merely individual statements by which Pufendorf, Thomasius, and those professing to follow them, come into conflict with themselves. Just so does Pufendorf require that every suzerain, from whom all obligations proceed, not only have the power but also *justus causas et rationes*.[66] The *impositio* as the final cause of obligation thus itself has a higher cause of obligation over it, rational laws, a contradiction already criticized by Leibniz. So Thomasius praises the benefits of natural law in order to have a law common with pagans and atheists.[67] Therefore, for him, *ratio* also has force *etsi daretur Deum non esse* [even if it is given that God does not exist].

But this is not all; their systems in their entirety are driven by the rationalist principle. In practice they everywhere bind the will of God, which they make into the cause of the ethic, by reason. He shall not be subject to the *lex aeterna* and His own *sanctitas;* but it is prescribed to Him that what follows from the drive to sociability etc., and that alone, is what He shall will, while He shall not will other things outside this. Therefore, with them as well as with their opponents, He plays no other role than a *Deus ex machina*. To wit, He has to undertake everything that reason can no longer achieve. He must invest moral duty with its real power over people,[68] secure entitlement,[69] and be the cause of such obligations for which one can provide no *ratio*, for example, the prohibition of incest. With such an approach, controversy is entirely in vain; though initially the subject of the most careful debate, during the course of that debate it also became increasingly lackluster, since God increasingly disappeared,[70] until finally Kant expressly declared reason to be the *cause* of the ethic. Since Kant, the relation of God to duty is no longer discussed, and it may well be surprising to see this controversy once again stirred up here as something of importance.

Thus, from the start of abstract philosophy, the opposite mode of conception is everywhere connected with it. But already here, the effectuating element in scientific treatment is reason alone. It only need be expressed unequivocally

---

[66] *De Officio Hominis et Civis* [English translation: *The Whole Duty of Man according to the Law of Nature*], Book I, ch. 2, §. 5.

[67] "Dissertatio Prooemialis," at the end.

[68] Wolff, *op. cit.,* Part I, ch. 2. §. 41.

[69] Thomasius, *Institutiones Iurisprudentiae Divinae,* Book I, ch. 1, §. 84.

[70] Compare Gundling, Darjes, Nettelbladt, Höpfner, with earlier generations.

to banish entirely even the appearance of that conflicting element.

Basic Concepts

Reason, from which the ethic is to follow, now requires a basic concept from which it is inferred, which, as goes without saying, must still remain after all abstraction is accomplished. According to the subjective-rationalistic stand-point of natural law, this concept is the existence of the thinker, human nature. In reality, this nature is always something specific, determined by individuality, environment, fate, time, matter, in short, by history. But in such determinacy, it possesses no logical necessity. The only characteristics which are inseparable from the concept of man are sensibility and thought. A man without moral feeling, even if he has never yet existed, is at least still conceivable; but a man without physical existence or without the capacity for thinking would be a logical contradiction.

The *sensorial-rational* (i.e., thinking) nature of man is therefore the basic concept of abstract ethics. It is actually premised by all natural law doctors. But initially one did not know how to make any direct use of it, and was forced to found the system on some drive of the human being, for example, the drive to sociability, which one hoped would suffice for the inference. The premised concept of thinking nature was only used to justify the rational *inference* from the drive as law. What is of note here is that every system of natural law is built exclusively on such a drive, and no attempt is made to derive such a system from *all* of the drives of human nature. This has to do with the abstract treatment. In our nature, the manifold instincts and feelings are actually connected; but they have no logical unity, no concept that is common to all and yet individual to each. But rationalism urges just such a simple principle. It contradicts living fullness as principle, but no less what is merely aggregated. Syncretistic treatment does not show up as long as there is vitality; such comes along only at the time of exhaustion, when the original confidence to achieve simplicity has abated. To take an isolated drive as ground, therefore, lay of necessity in the character of the natural law; what was arbitrary was the choice of one or the other.

Therefore all possible exchanges were made between sociability, fear, happiness, perfection, etc.; the whole gamut of human drives was run through, and the natural law schools succeeded each other following this thread. The development knew no rest until at length Kant secured that basic concept and summed it up in its complete abstraction: thinking nature as mere consistency; the sensorial as the restriction of that pure consistency contained in any of its expressions. From this point, the concept of a being that thinks, but is limited by sensoriness (finite) remains as principle. Only this has a logical necessitation, it is the last remnant that is left standing after abstracting from the existence of man.[71] And from the concept of thinking nature, it is also only by pure reason – as required – that it is possible to deduce. Any other drive than that of logical consistency itself, for example happiness, acts externally and is energized externally. In order to say what it requires, both the consequence of action in the world and the repercussions of the external object on one's own condition must be observed.

This provides the concept from which nothing more can be abstracted (the necessary beginning) and from which now the entirety of ethics must ensue, merely from logical reasoning; as Wolff previously expressed it: *Principium ex quo continuo ratiocinationis filo deducuntur omnia* [The principle from which, by the continuous thread of reasoning, everything is deduced].

History of the Basic Concept

In the series of ethical systems, Hobbes is customarily highlighted as opposing rather than promoting the development of natural law. But this is certainly unjust. He is in no way any different from the others, since he simply elevates one drive from human nature, just as they do; only he elevates the drive of fear rather than some other drive, and from this he deduces his results, to which he certainly has the same right. It follows from the conception of a fearing being that protection is sought for life and limbs – *pax quaerenda* [peace-seeking]. It does not follow from it that agreements are kept outside of the state; for when

---

[71] Hoffbauer (*Untersuchungen über die wichtigsten Gegenstände des Naturrechts* [Studies regarding the main objects of natural law]), prompted by Kant, thought that he had to go farther. The *abstractum* of man is still too concrete for him, and so he arrives at the concept of a rational being, which is not like this, and therefore is not exactly human. The original and acquired rights that are derived from this concept of the rational being thus form the pure natural law, those derived from the concept of man, the applied natural law.

such agreements are kept, they provide security which at the same time harms someone else. Therefore, for Hobbes the state of nature is without rights, and one takes offense at this. But it follows from the drive of fear that a civil condition be established in which the supreme rule must be *pacta servanda* [agreements are kept].

For this reason Gros unjustly accuses Hobbes of confusing what people do with what they ought to do. This is because to Hobbes, this utter arbitrariness [of what they do] is really nothing more than the minor premise; prior to this he has the major premise, what they *ought* to do: "protect themselves" – as elsewhere: "please themselves" – from which the state follows as conclusion. Equally unfounded is Thomasius' objection that the *pacta* presuppose a law. This law is just dictated by human nature as fear. Even Hobbes is not empirical. If he was, he would have made the multiplicity of drives in human nature, which experience demonstrates, into the principle. Because he is not empirical but abstract, and only for that reason chooses the one of fear only, and has everything proceed from it as reason would have it, *necessitate quadam non minore, quam qua fertur lapis deorsum* [a kind of necessity, not less than what is said of a stone falling]. So in every respect he belongs to the development of natural law. He stands or falls on its foundations and is far from opposing it; his approach is only a variation on the theme, consistent with the others in principles, requirements, and procedures, and is only distinguished from them by an entirely incidental assumption.

Abstraction from Relations

Turning now to individual ethical requirements as conscience makes them known to everyone: the diversity thereof is linked to the diversity of circumstances in which we function. In industry, we feel obligated to be diligent, in trade to be honest, in social interaction to be benevolent; one particular course of action is required for the family, another one for the state. So it would be natural to seek the reason for the difference in these circumstances. To this end, it would not suffice for these to be regarded merely as different material, but as a different source. Each must be conceded a peculiar moral objective that has its origin in itself; but then the unity of these various objectives would have to be sought outside man.

And so rational philosophy immediately annihilates these relationships, in order to recognize them again only if they contain its fundamental concept of ethics. This abstraction stands in relation to the condition of the *state of nature*. Such has been constructed in different ways, as a historical fact, as a presumption, a fiction, finally, arriving at self-understanding, as a scientifically necessary abstraction. In all these ways, the drive to its adoption is the same: since I can imagine myself without the state, such is therefore not *a priori* required by reason; I must now assume that the state was not in existence, in order to see whether my concept as a thinking being leads me to it. In the same way, one can oppose the state of nature to the condition of the family or of social interaction (mutual contact), and this has been done, even if not expressly. If, for example, with regard to the question of breaking up landed estates, the necessity and the objective of agriculture is not the deciding factor, since the freedom of the individual should decide everything, this presupposes that it is not the actual relations of agriculture but the prescinding thereof, the state of nature, that is taken as starting point.

Consequences of this Abstraction

Since the actual existence of these conditions is abandoned, their actual requirements are as well, and they can only apply, and apply to that degree, if this deduction yields them. Thus, the configurations of the ethical world no longer impose laws on persons; instead, they receive these first from the concept of persons' existence, and therefore *of necessity are entirely different* than what the nature of these configurations requires.

To wit, when man conceives himself to be released from any connection and still recognizes a rule over himself, this rule can only be enacted for him as an isolated case – he is its exclusive subject. Only what he is capable of, only what still makes sense when one looks at his action and fulfillment in isolation, is his goal. And it is satisfied when he fulfills it, when he attaches no blame for it to himself. A general condition the achievement of which also depends on the participation of others, cannot be demanded of him, and thus cannot be the object of the rule. Thus, for example it can only command: "Thou shalt be prepared for the state!" not: "The state shall exist!" Otherwise he would not be summoned as an individual but as part of a totality. So while the Greek ethic is directed to ordering the world, and is to be established to satisfy this without considering how people's actions are constituted, here the quality of these actions is what is requisite. The result, and what is constructed by the same in the world, is only adventitious, and is not the originally willed.

Nearly all of the earlier systems of natural law begin with the concepts of action, its kinds, its attribution, etc. Hence with the Greeks, the duty of the citizen is discovered from the ethic of the state; but with the modern versions, the duty of the state is imagined from the duty of man apart from the state. This has supreme influence on the content of the ethic. Because with the former, requirements must arise for man which could never be made for him if one thinks of him individually. With the latter, however, the state itself is robbed of its peculiar duties because the individual cannot or may not meet them. The meaning of punishment, for example, cannot be retribution; because which persons are entitled to administer justice? That it therefore likewise does not accrue to the state, is then self-evident.[72] The existence of social ranks [Ständen] must be abandoned as an ethical requirement ahead of any investigation, because it is not a matter of my action. If every rank, exclusively pursuing its orientation, excels in doing so, but only while accompanied by extreme one-sidedness – brave but brutish warriors, pious but shiftless priests, highly educated but effeminate scholars – then this view would rightly deprecate the imperfection of the individuals, but it would not notice the admirability of what they provide in the way of wealth and power to the entirety. This is because *the content of this entire ethic consists merely in commands over the isolated actions of individuals.*

Content of the Ethic

What actions these might be, should indeed, according to the requirement, arise from the basic concepts. But since, as will be demonstrated in the issue, such abstraction never leads to positive results, the interest of the school as a whole gets immediately involved. Accordingly, the goal of bidden actions is simply man. Either rationally to pursue one's own satisfaction – as Hobbes, Thomasius – or, since virtue does entail a certain sacrifice [Hingeben], to pursue the satisfaction of others, their welfare, their freedom, etc. Apart from the beings who resemble him, his abstracting reason and its interest offer him no object. Unity, the development of the strength of the state, the symmetry and

---

[72] E.g., Fichte, *Grundlage des Naturrechts nach Prinzipien der Wissenschaftslehre* [translation: *Foundations of Natural Right*], Part II, p. 129.

beauty of life, faith, devotion, honor recede into the background or disappear entirely. They do not provide well-being to the individual. Kant consequently removed the duties towards God from ethics, which the ancients and many of the moderns held to. Hence, the duties towards Him (who, in terms of His concept, is the absolute cause of all being and duty) obtain their sanction through a second absolute, the nature of man, and take their place alongside other duties, even though the duties to God – assuming they exist – are the only thing which make these other into duties. This is tantamount to a Kantian wishing to range duties to the moral imperative alongside the duties to neighbor, parents, children, and spouse.

Now after abstracting or prescinding, reason finds a goal outside human existence, which is itself, the form of thinking. To satisfy this in action is its own fulfillment. Such is conceived partly as a second task in addition to the satisfaction of others, partly as the epitome and ground of all other tasks. But its concept is none other than the uniformity of action according to principles, regularity, immutability, unaffectedness by changing emotions.

This negative virtue of never contradicting itself is found in Spinoza's view of the rule of the soul over the emotions, in the *pax interna* of Thomasius, which consists in discouraging the passions, and at its most conscious, finally, with Kant in the supreme rule of ethics: act according to a law which is a universal law, one through which a contradiction with itself can never arise.

Chapter 2: Division into Moral and Natural Law

Factual Division of Duties
Now reality shows two kinds of ethical [sittlicher] prescriptions, their obvious difference being that, with the one, compliance is compelled by the state, while with the other, compliance is left to the individual; and in accord with this, the latter focuses on disposition, the former on the act. Science has to demonstrate the basis for this difference.

Scientific Division of Duties by the Greeks...
The Greeks found this difference in the subject of the ethic, whether it is directed to people individually or to the state as a whole. It aims for the same everywhere and in the same way. But the requirements it puts on the state, when the state fulfills them, are thereby in themselves automatically compulsory for the individual. The state, which has the obligation, is therefore not compelled, and the individual who is compelled, does not automatically and directly have the obligation, and his disposition is irrelevant.

To the Greeks it is not at all strange that man is limited in his actions so that the world can reach its perfect form. There is thus no necessity here for a distinction in the ethic itself. Plato distinguishes between the just man and the just state. Aristotle distinguishes between ethics and politics; apart from the state (πολιτικὸν δίκαιον) there is only *one* justice (ἁπλῶς δίκαιον). In general, the Greeks do not seem to consider the question as to how the ethic relates to the individual, whether in compulsory fashion or not, to be of great significance.

... and by the Moderns; Thomasius, Kant, Feuerbach
In modern philosophy, however, precisely this must be the cardinal question: how does the law affect me, does it merely exact, or does it compel me? Now then, the newer philosophy does not even recognize duties originally placed on the state; how much less, then, a restriction on the individual stemming from the state? A sufficient ground to coerce the individual must be given with man himself, even apart from the state (in the state of nature). By one basic rule, therefore, and for one and the same subject, the necessity of the variety of commands, enforceable and unenforceable, external and internal, must be

demonstrated. This can only be done if an original division of the same is identified, two different objectives of the ethic, each of which by its concept demands compulsion for the one, excludes it for the other – juridical law and morality.

The subjective principle of the new philosophy was constrained to find this difference. Although the task remains to purify this discovery from the dross of abstract treatment, still it is a great step forward. For the Greek conception can explain neither the dependence of compulsion on the will of individuals (law in the subjective sense), nor the dissimilarity of law to other public objectives.

To Leibniz is owed the honor of having predicted the shape of the newer ethics – its division into morality and law. The execution, however, was carried out by Thomasius. The sociabilistic[73] system, even in its development by Pufendorf, knows only these two ethical sciences without subdivision: the positive, i.e., theology, and the philosophical, i.e., natural law. Pufendorf also has them correspond to the distinction between the *forum internum* and *externum*, so that all inward, or as we now say, moral, obligations are referred to theology, while the outward are left to philosophy, i.e., natural law. But this does not keep him, in the title *de promiscuis officiis humanitatis* [of the common duties of humanity] from treating alongside each other the rules of international law, *de accessu ad litus alienum* [of access to foreign shores], *de foro praebendo* [of granting a market], and the duties of charity and gratitude.

By contrast, Leibniz, in his letters discussing Pufendorfian natural law, claims the internal forum also for philosophy. He concedes that the inward duties are not appropriate to natural law proper; but neither may they be left to theology; they have to be discovered from the *ratio*. Therefore he sets up, separate from natural law and (positive) theology, a rational doctrine of inward duties, i.e., a *moral philosophy*.

It was left to Thomasius, this man who, even though devoid of ideas (as is the entire orientation), nevertheless through the freshness and bluntness of his mind, contrasting as much with the earlier scholastically crimped treatment, which he combatted from the outset, as with the dullness of Wolff and his successors, put into effect what Leibniz surmised. His first writings were indeed

---

[73] [German *sozialistische,* i.e., the system, initiated by Grotius, that derived law and society from man as a creature of a sociable nature, seeking social life.]

occupied with implementing the sociabilistic system in the received manner, nor is the title *de promiscuis officiis humanitatis* absent there. But the arbitrariness with which the *forum externum* and *internum* are intermingled with the sociabilistic thinkers, caused him to seek a principle of ethics enabling him to give a peculiar basis to each of the two classes of obligations, so that their different characters could be derived from reason, with evidence, as he says, that must be clear even to the most narrow-minded (*stulto*).

For this reason he jettisons the sociabilistic system, the principle of which, the drive for sociability, could not accommodate such a separation, and substitutes for it the drive for happiness. From this follows that double law: to seek outward and inward peace. This distinction corresponds to law and morality – the negative duty not to violate the other, and the positive one, to do to him what he himself wishes for – *forum externum* and *forum internum* – enforceability and unenforceability of duty. Thomasius is therefore the first to provide a foundation for the classification of perfect and imperfect duties, which was already found in Grotius; he first truly distinguishes the obligations according to the criterion of enforceability, in the *regulas justi* and the *regulas honesti, decori, officia humanitatis.*[74] The first book of his later work, *Fundamenta Juris Naturae*, is occupied with the discussion of his new principle; the subsequent ones, which maintain the arrangement of his first work, the *Institutiones Jurisprudentiae Divinae*, are merely intended to specify the later deviations from it. These deviations consist nearly entirely in separating out all the obligations which exist for the sake of inward rather than outward peace – which he earlier, following the sociabilists, had treated together with those and largely characterized them as enforceable – and characterizing them as unenforceable, for example, the paternal power.

The Wolffian school did not progress any farther in this.

The system of Thomasius achieved the mutual correspondence between the material character of inward and outward peace, positive and negative duty, and the formal one of compulsion and non-compulsion, albeit not in such a way that the formal manifests itself as a necessary consequence of the material, which is what is demanded. Namely, no ground is given as to why the

---

[74] *Fundamenta Juris Naturae*, Book II, ch. 6, §. 4 [p. 217]. This was attributed to his students, unjustly so.

commandments which have inward peace as their object rule out enforceability, while those with the object of outward peace demand it. Whether they should be fulfilled or not could be left to free will either for both types or for neither.

In order to be able to provide this ground, and thus to be able to deduce the different effects of morality and law as necessary from their different natures, inward and outward *freedom* had to be substituted for inward and outward peace. This was Kant's accomplishment. In terms of its content, inward freedom excludes constraint. The laws which merely have this as their purpose – which do not directly resolve upon specific acts – contradict themselves when they compel. The laws that have outward freedom as their objective, however, must compel, because outward freedom cannot result from accidental fulfillment and non-infringement, as can, for example, well-being, because freedom ceases where the result depends upon others, even if this result actually comes about. For example, if someone gives me my thing, but he was not compelled to give it to me, then even though I did receive the thing, my freedom over the thing did not and does not exist.

In this manner, morality contains the laws for the purpose of inward freedom, while natural law contains those for the purpose of outward freedom. Although the difference existing in life between enforceable and non-enforceable obligations only prompts the quest for a principle by which this difference can be justified logically, and only guides that quest, so conversely, what exists now gets assessed by this principle. The separation in life must now be just such a one as can be deduced from life. Therefore, from this point on it is held to be decided, as a requirement of reason, that *only those laws which have outward freedom as their purpose, shall be enforceable.*

The Problem of Deducing Law in the Subjective Sense

This development could have concluded here if not for the fact that the characteristic concept of the legal sphere, to which outward freedom likewise automatically leads, remained unaffected – *law in the subjective sense.* Just as the compulsion which juridical law of necessity requires must accord with the peculiarity of its object – freedom – so also does this compulsion depend on the discretion of that freedom, the freedom for which the law exists. Because even if I securely obtain the object of my freedom, if my obtaining it or not does not depend on me, then I am not free. The compulsion by which I obtain what is mine, must absolutely be the result of my will, if my freedom is to be attained. The ethic wills this freedom. And the decisive thing here is: not only does it have this freedom as its objective, in favor of which it requires others to act, but it imparts it directly. He for whom it is established has the awareness that freedom does not first have to be produced for him, but that he already has it and may make use of it. It is not like, say, the good, something which, although required by the ethic, yet only arises in fact and exists in fact, but it is an effect of the ethic and is itself ethical.

Since the Romans, this immediate sanction of freedom can be found decisively in human life and consciousness, especially in the Germanic. It is a fact; science could not remove it and not deny it, it had to assimilate it. But it also generated a new distinction between morality and law. What is moral merely effects a requirement and only has a consequence for those subject to this requirement. The person for whom something results from the fulfillment of its command, e.g., whose good is to be effected, has no connection to *the command itself*. His relation, which Grotius calls *aptitudo*, is therefore without any ethical significance, and the concept of *aptitudo* was also soon lost to ethics. But juridical law not only imposes a requirement, it also imparts freedom; it has a double relation not only when it is fulfilled but by the very fact that it exists, the one to whom it is given, the other for whom it is given, to the obligated and to the entitled. Even coercion itself, because the duties of law are different from those of morality, materializes only as a result of that freedom, and as evidence of this, it is not directly applied by law, but only by the person entitled, if he so desires. In this manner, requirement, which law imposes just as morality does, recedes as secondary, while freedom, which law constitutes, emerges as primary – [subjective] right [das Recht]. For this reason, Feuerbach ended up expressing the difference between morality and natural law like this: *morality is the science of duties, natural law the science of rights.*[75]

The Two Problems Facing Natural Law

But this separation embroiled ethics in two contradictions, the solution of which is its problem. The first is that between the moral and juridical law, on the one hand, and what those laws entail by way of requirement, and on the

---

[75] *Kritik des natürlichen Rechts* [Critique of natural law].

other. The second is between the laws and competence.

Firstly: since reason posits outward freedom as its goal, it will inevitably come to the point that the same actions that it secures as law, it forbids as morality. According to juridical law, no one may stop someone who wishes to kill himself or to waste his substance, from doing so, even though the moral law demands that such acts not happen. For this reason, the Wolffian school restricts competence to morally licit actions. But morality permeates all action, and since idleness is against morality, we would lose the competence to be idle; by the same principle, given the existence of needy people, we would lose the competence to use property. Kant seeks to resolve the contradiction by having reason impart outward freedom as a means for its own ends, as a way for its commands to be freely met inwardly. A person would not contradict himself in such a case. Reason might lead one into temptation, to make the victory all the more glorious; it might not at first will what it actually ends up willing, out of consideration for the final end. But this relinquishing and restriction of self for future purposes, this free choice of tactic, is not the essence of a rational law. Outward freedom is by no means rationally necessary for inward freedom. Experience shows how much they interact, but in terms of their concept, they are independent of each other. When people are prevented from suicide, dissipation, idleness, by outward force, still their inward disposition can also be that they not waste, not commit suicide, not be idle. If this were not the case, reason would have to ensure not only against restriction by other people but also against restriction by nature. For example, it should make all people rich so that they can be frugal voluntarily, and also make them all poor so that not abundance but honesty deters them from stealing.

Indeed, the contradiction goes even further. As morality, reason demands that force be withheld; as law, the contrary, that force be applied. But because reason as morality extends itself to all actions, it comes about that reason needs to prescribe the same act in two ways, on the one hand having to do something (force), commit something, that on the other hand it cannot permit. The law obliges me to pay my creditors, so according to reason I must be compelled to do so. But now morality commands the same thing of me; it is then contrary to reason that I be compelled. Therefore, Kant made this distinction: morality also imparts to legal obligations their sanctions, although the content of those sanctions is given not by it, but by the law.[76] But that does not resolve the contradiction, for as morality also makes legal obligations its own, it is compelled to require the uncoerced decision for these as well.

That is why, in the later period of natural law, the ambition is everywhere expressed to provide an independent principle to rights [dem Rechte] completely divorced from morality. This, it was believed, would remedy the contradiction. But it is not sufficient to separate law and compulsion from morality; rather, they must be separated from ethics altogether. This was accomplished by Fichte, and he was aware of finally having satisfied a long-recognized requirement.

Secondly: rights [Recht] and juridical law are contradictory in terms of their concept. The question here is not why a juridical law exists, a law that forces me to protect another's freedom, even when opposed to moral purposes; rather, given its existence, how a competence can be derived from it. Because right, the freedom to do or not to do, cannot possibly follow from a law that only contains what is necessary. Trying to combine these two concepts is the locomotive engine in the history of the fundamental concepts of natural law.

Development until Fichte and Feuerbach

The earliest practitioners did not yet feel the need for such a combination. With them there is a sudden break from the deduction of law [des Gesetzes] and obligation, in order to treat of rights [Recht] as a *facultas moralis*, as a *potentia activa*, the cause of which is then only perfunctorily attributed to *natura, lex, consensus,* or *Deus*.

A serious endeavor to find a systematic relationship here soon emerged. Because it was conducted in terms of the abstract character, the viewpoint which held competence to be a new concept was resisted as long as possible. The next attempt therefore was to consider it as being another side of obligation, positing it immediately with obligation. "What I ought to do, that I also may do;" therefore in terms of its concept, every command already contains entitlement [Berechtigung]. Thus Wolff, Nettelbladt, et al. But that is not entitlement: for entitlement may be refrained from; furthermore, there are rights to things that

---

[76] *Metaphysische Anfangsgründe der Rechtslehre*, pp. xv–xvi [p. 21 in *The Metaphysics of Morals*].

one ought not to do.

Entitlement was now sought in the obligation of others rather than one's own: "if I am obligated to you, then you are enabled; my limitation is in itself an enlargement for you." Thus Heydenreich, Hoffbauer, et al. But it does not follow from the fact that I should allow myself to be compelled, that others may compel me. If I act unreasonably by not allowing myself to be compelled, it does not follow that others act reasonably by compelling me. The freedom of the entitled would thus factually exist if the obliged party actually fulfilled the command; but it would not have the ethical content which is intended by the concept of law, and its actual usage would even be irrational, because one may not at all limit the freedom of another.

Likewise the other characteristic of legal obligation, e.g., that its fulfillment is to be preferred before moral obligation, can be explained only if its essence is that an antecedent right requires it. But then one cannot turn around and derive a right [das Recht] from it. The deduction of a right from a duty, be it one's own, be it another's, had then to be abandoned. Now there remained no choice but to derive obligation directly from law. The concept of law, as it was posited, contains that of entitlement as well. But here one ran into the contradiction of the *lex permissiva*. A law [Gesetz] can only command and not permit, and so the specific content of the juridical law would cancel the general nature of the law [Gesetzes], which is absurd. Now of course, a law imparting freedom is indeed not at all contradictory if we are speaking of actual, functioning laws. Because it can never be said of any living cause, prior to experience, what it is capable of and what it is not; and experience shows that freedom arises according to laws. Thus, the natural law of procreation makes the son independent of the father, the law of the state sanctions the freedom of the citizen, and the command of the lord frees the slaves. But the law of reason cannot grant freedom; because the actions for which it should provide, it must contain, as consequence, in order to prescribe them. The generally perceived contradiction in the *lex permissiva* therefore by no means concerned this truth: no freedom can arise from a law, but rather this one: what should arise logically cannot arise as something possible, but only as something necessary.

Still, there was no turning back, and entitlement had to be found entirely in the concept of juridical law. Kant then resorted to the expedient that the law does not contain competence immediately but mediately: the law which commands or forbids some things but not all, thereby establishes an empty sphere, out of which action can be taken arbitrarily – this is competence. But this is only negative, not positive allowance; a non-prohibition is not yet a right. Freedom here, notwithstanding the obligation of compulsion of others, would follow only as something *de facto*, and the peculiarity of legal obligation would be left unexplained, just as it was with the attempt to derive a right from the duty of another. Thus the law must contain competence immediately as positive permission – lately even Feuerbach insisted on this – which on the other hand is not possible, since a positive permissive rational law is a contradiction.

Hence the final step of natural law had to be taken: the right of man [das Recht des Menschen] had to embody the condition of something original, from which even the juridical law arises. The progression, then, runs like this: first, it appeared to be the result of obligation – for it is in the nature of the ethic to will obligation originally; then as ground of obligation, but still a result of the law; and finally as ground of the law itself. But thereby it ceased to follow from reason, for it is itself the initial assumption; and it also no longer need acquiesce to the empire of law; natural law drops from ethics. This step was taken in this respect, as in the aforementioned, by Fichte, and is only an integrating member in the formation which all of philosophy gained through him. For this reason, both it and its consequences are to be considered there.

But we must now answer the question: why does natural law strive in vain to derive right from obligation or obligation from right; why can it not have both, at one stroke, follow from the juridical law? Then the character of perfect obligation would be explained from rights posited at the same time with obligation, and vice versa, positive entitlement explained from the simultaneously posited obligation of others. The only thing standing in the way of that conclusion is that such production is no longer logical. In a living body, certainly, something is at the same time cause and effect of another. But rational deduction can only find the one in the other; or both, not mutually conditioned, in higher concepts. The attempt to have right and obligation emerge at the same time, which by no means was lacking towards the end of this school of thought's career, is therefore merely syncretistic; they emerge alongside each other rather than becoming a whole by means of a living drive; and therefore, as Feuerbach already demonstrated,[77] this attempt cannot attain what was intended. Abstract ethics, as stated above, does not exact conditions, but only actions on the part of individuals. The law cannot speak into the world: let there be the state! because only isolated persons hear it. Nor can it say: thou shalt be secured in your freedom! because this is not an affair of its power. It can only say to the one: I do not forbid it! and to the other: you are to acquiesce in this! But what is said for the one has no existence for the other. Each must declare what refers to him, as a right or an obligation, to be his "own reason," which speaks to him but not to the other.[78] The non-prohibition of the one and the restriction of the other come as little into connection as do two people dreaming of each other. It is not a real power over them and not a real condition around them, which associates them. The law would only appear as a natural result of the law of reason if the latter read: thou shalt secure thy freedom, claim ownership! With this it really would impose a necessity. But the law does not read like that, and if it did, only obligations would exist, not rights.

Natural law, due to the character of its principle, necessarily encountered all of this difficulty. Reason cannot give rise to heterogenous things which freely restrict each other. Reason cannot generate a product independent of itself. Man, thinking in isolation, is encouraged only to isolated actions; no condition to which he pertains with others can make known to him regulation or sanction.

Therefore one cannot consider the difficulties and contradictions laid bare here to be superfluous subtlety. What is subtlety is above all the effort to get results through such reasoning, which adheres strictly to the characteristics of the *concept* alone, and does not acquiesce in, or take up, the living reality constituted from the *matter*. And in what consists abstract philosophy other than this endeavor? Its essence is subtlety, and to investigate what can be attained hereby is the only way it can be understood and appreciated. It would have won the day if the requirements that it generally lays down and busies itself to accomplish were not linked to its works, to which it was strictly referred. It would not have it any other way. Because everything that this subtlety necessitates, as we have shown, is actually recognized by the outstanding intellects of this school of

---

[77] *Op. cit.,* pp. 209ff.

[78] So declares Feuerbach most decisively, *ibid.,* pp. 147–148.

thought, and scientific progress has been arranged in terms of it. That which was claimed above, is here demonstrated: the historical progression itself forms the tribunal.

Chapter 3: Legal Doctrine (Natural Law in the Later Sense)

Logic can be called the heart of the newer philosophy, which emits its pulses and receives them back in itself; natural law is its countenance, in which its soul is reflected. For the freedom of man, the secret driving force in all its efforts, is here manifest as express principle.

Equality [Concept of Man versus Ideal of Man]

If freedom is inferred from the *concept* of man, then it must arise for everyone in equal measure. And if this freedom is the exclusive objective of all coercive laws, then there is nothing that could abolish that equality. Now then, an ethic that derives from the objective of relations leads to inequality of the law. If a rank [Stand] of honor, a representative of the divine majesty is to exist, then the latter must be permitted sanctity and inviolability, the former advantage of birth. The purpose of the family assigns a different legal position to the man than to the woman. The *ideal* of man, the highest quality of being for which he is intended, would *mandate* inequality of the law. The closer the approximation to it, the greater freedom and entitlement it would generate. The *concept* of man, however, is present in all men and in all circumstances. Therefore, complete equality before the law is the requirement of the law of reason; it is made by all the doctors of natural law, from the earliest to the latest. Consistently implemented, it prohibits advantages of birth, rights of majesty (at least those that are irrevocable), the taking of individuality into account, whether in terms of wardship [Bevormundung] or in recognition of the ideal [of man]. It leads to women being granted an equal share in the affairs of state along with men; even children who have attained the age of rational thought, in which, therefore, is the concept of man, should have the right not to be put under wardship, and to be granted the same position as the rest. The Platonic principle: "to each the position appointed to him by nature!" and the principle: "to each the same!" are complete opposites.

The Deduction of Natural Law from the Concept of Freedom

Freedom as a principle of natural law is initially without content, that is, without a particular object and without restriction. The natural thing would be for every right first to be determined by its object, and its restriction to follow from that. But here, the determination must proceed in the opposite direction. For the object cannot be found from that empty freedom, but the restriction can: in such freedom on the part of others. From this restriction, then, the specific objects of rights are to be derived, if they are to be derived merely by reason. The various objects of experience are posited as minor premises under the concept of the equal freedom of all as major premise, and the conclusion must yield the specific rights and institutions. It is precisely the business of natural law to carry this out.

The Concept of Primordial Rights and Its History

Among the objects subsumed [as minor premises], two classes immediately can be distinguished according to their generic difference. To wit, there are objects regarding which man is already in possession by virtue of his existence, for example, one's own life, own thoughts, the use of limbs, etc.; and there are those with which he comes into contact only in different ways, combines with them and again separates from them, or which do not need to be conceived in connection with every human being. This is the distinction between *innate* and *acquired* rights (*jura connata* and *acquisita*). The diversity of relations already leads to this in the process of deduction. One only needs to analyze the existence of man to get the *jura connata*, and he gets specific ones. I have a right to these, i.e., my limbs, etc. For the *jura acquisita*, on the other hand, objects external to people must be subsumed, events must be subsumed, in which case we only get them as abstract rights, such as rights over things in general; the factual first decides to which things we have a right.

The relevance of the distinction manifests itself directly in the consequences. According to the postulated equality, innate rights must accrue in the same way to the one as to the other, while with regard to acquired rights the question is first, to what degree was that original equality effaced by the occurrence which led to them, and to what degree is it effaced in specific cases. This yields the consequence for alienability and burden of proof. For this reason the earliest writers already had the distinction between innate and acquired rights. Pufendorf's distinction between *obligatio connata* and *adventitia* is entirely of a piece with this; because to the former he reckons the "obligatio omnium hominum adversus quoslibet homines qua tales, per quam invicem jus naturae usurpare socialemque vitam agere debent."[79] But with Thomasius the definition is still imprecise. For him, *jura connata* are those which one has apart from the consent of the obligated party, which means that *patria potestas* also pertains to them. Wolff comes closer: *jus connatum homini ita cohaeret, ut ipsi auferri non possit* [the innate right of man cleaves to him, so that it cannot be removed]. Hoffbauer summarizes the difference in all its sharpness.[80] He separates innate rights not merely from those that presuppose any occurrence of contract, but all that presuppose any particular occurrence at all.

This is the generally leading concept, even though it is not everywhere clearly recognized. But Kant seemed to have abrogated it. The earlier proponents, namely, treated the natural equality of human beings and the *jura connata* quite separately from each other. Kant, systematically penetrating, sought their connection; he found it in the fact that they both explain one and the same concept. He denied the majority of innate rights and derived them all from what is none other than primordial, content-free freedom itself, according to Kant's definition: the right not to be a mere means for another. From this point, the *concept of primordial right* [Urrechts] took the place of the *jura connata*.

But Kant had to concede that innate rights when taken individually, for example, the right to a good name, not being directly expressed, first have to be deduced logically, and that this deduction is of a different sort than the one involved with property, contracts, etc., a difference which shows itself to be operant in the burden of proof. Hence, although he banished the words *jura connata*, he did not banish the fact. Rather the empty concept of freedom, the primordial right, is now the midpoint of natural law, from which first arises that which is immediately contained in it, and then that which requires other occurrences.[81] The analysis of the existence of man yields the rights to one's own life,

---

[79] Pufendorf, *Elementa jurisprudentiae universalis libri duo,* Book I, defin. 12. §. 1. [English translation: *Two Books of the Elements of Universal Jurisprudence* (Indianapolis: Liberty Fund,), p. 109: "the obligation of all men towards all men whatsoever as such, by virtue of which they ought to employ the law of nature in their relations with one another, and to live a social life."]

[80] Hoffbauer, *op. cit.,* pp. 122ff.

[81] Kant, *Metaphysische Anfangsgründe der Rechtslehre,* p. xlv [p. 30 in *The Metaphysics of Morals*].

limbs, reputation, the possibility of acquisition. When the objects outside of him are subsumed, then there result the rights to things and to the actions of others, either temporarily or in permanent relations. This is the system of natural law.

The Negative Character of Natural Law

The abstract character in natural law lines up in just the same way as in philosophy generally. In both, everything is only the logically necessary consequence of a basic concept. In philosophy, this basic concept, from which no further abstraction can take place – substance – is empty being, while in ethics it is the concept of the thinking being. This in turn becomes the basic concept of the philosophical doctrine of law, so that all individual rights and institutions only manifest themselves as its modalities. Therefore, natural law bears a negative character like abstract philosophy does generally. Just as the substance of Spinoza or Hegel is that which cannot be thought away, pure being without content, mere not-not-being, so also here, what is taken as the basis of freedom is not positive power (like the freedom of God to create the world, the freedom of the Platonic wise men to govern the state), but something without content, only that for which, if absent, the concept of freedom no longer exists – the *not-being-a-means*, *not-non-person*, *not-being-a-slave*. In the same way, the development of this concept is a negative, i.e., a merely logical one. Namely, no right, no institution, may emerge that first arises and then is joined to that empty concept of freedom as something new, but only those of which it can be shown that when they are expressed, their non-existence is likewise impossible.

Relation of Natural Law to Roman Law

The affinity of natural law with Roman law is generally recognized. This already indicates that Roman institutions could be received into the natural law textbooks, and this in fact took place. To elucidate natural law, therefore, nothing would be more conducive than clearly to delineate its agreement and divergence with Roman law, and to demonstrate the basis of each.

Roman law, like natural law, recognizes a right of the individual independent of any divine requirement over him. But where a person, in whatever relation, ever breaks from the connections in which he was created, there arises a paucity of cultural drive and force, and thus the abstract character. With the

ancient Germans – although they towered above the Romans in independence
and the love thereof – yet every right was also permeated by obligation; honor
– perhaps only another expression for freedom – inspired their lives; it was not
merely an inviolable good but also a sacred power that required as much of every
act as it authorized that act. That is why the Germanic legal viewpoint is always
situated within the totality of life; every entitlement is created, develops, varies,
with the manifold relationships that, all around it, passively and actively affect
it; and it is constantly assessed together with them. By mutual permeation with
them, there arose ever new kinds of applications that had not been originally
delineated by their mere existence; Roman law, on the other hand, in that it
conceives of every entitlement in isolation, precisely thereby prescinds from all
living relations, and could only receive that which is given invariably with its
concept. Herein consists the Romans' abstract procedure of reasoning from existing rights and the laws which indicate their content. Emptied of life, the logical character everywhere emerges automatically; for there is nothing [new] to
be expected, but only what must always remain. When the force that forms
anew recedes, then everything remains as it is and is fixed spellbound in an immovable concept.

To this degree, Roman law and natural law agree. But Roman law only conceives the already existing entitlement in isolation. Its abstract procedure of reasoning thus begins first from given rights and laws. These themselves, however
– the starting point of the rationale – have come to it from out of the totality
of the consciousness and the relations of the nation; religion, patriotism, family,
forms of diet; these living causes have determined it, which by their nature effect
something positive, having to produce something which they were not already.
For this reason, it embodies a variety of rights and laws, each of which has its
own existence, which are not included in any concept – one may presume
whichever one he likes. It is positive law. By contrast, natural law isolates people
right from the start. What emerges here has already arisen in the abstract. The
origin of rights and legal provisions is the empty concept of freedom, and nothing new must be added to this basic concept. Not only the application, but the
production itself is stamped by the absence of life.

Alongside personal entitlement and in agreement with it, there could also
exist in Rome an independent law of the state, a recognition of the public condition not dependent upon men. For the legal condition had a living source

there. Natural law seeks logical unity; it can only have one concept as basis. In that it emanates from the rights of the individual, this rules out its deduction from the state, and it tolerates no obligation of compulsion which does not proceed from the freedom of individuals. Ultimately, as explained above,[82] all logical connection is timeless. What reason demands is contained in it before any occurrence, and what is based on an occurrence does not follow from reason.

By contrast, rights which have arisen through history and presuppose it are not logically necessary. Roman law recognizes the real manner of the functioning of action and incident; it does not abstract from time and history. On the contrary: what it grants to every man according to specific statutes at a specific time, is precisely his inviolable right (*jus quaesitum*) and this is held to be sacred to him. This explains why the nation, with the same virtues and defects, nevertheless manifests such opposite action in its two classes [Ständen]: in the patricians, the recklessly passionate pursuit of their prerogative, in the plebeians, unprecedented moderation while enduring outrageous hardship. It is the sanctity, in the eyes of the nation, of every acquired right, i.e., rights arisen in history. In the entire struggle, the upper class manifests itself as that which protects its own, for which reason the use of any means is not viewed as a bad thing; the lower, by contrast, as the one that offends without justification. And it is certainly not prejudice or ignorance on Livy's part when he conceives the struggle in this character, leans as a Roman to the patrician side, and even in the speeches of leading plebeians, characterizes the undertakings of this class as riots and illegality. The characteristic Roman sentiment holds everything which is acquired to be inviolable, regardless of the results to which it leads, how its use is related to humanity, and finally, without any regard to what would exist if we think away the occurrences by which it was acquired, it being conceivable that they had not happened.

Now the logical derivation of rights leads to quite the opposite: the disregard and annihilation of all acquired rights. In every moment reason requires anew – for it requires it incessantly – that incidents be ignored, that the truth be discovered from it alone, and therefore that anything formed outside of it be destroyed.

This is the train of reasoning that abolished all prerogative of rank and guild,

---

[82] Book III, Part I.

in order to restore the eternal condition of reason, that is, a condition outside of time and action. Certainly the disregard of the condition then existing contained in itself an emphatic requirement; but it was not taken into account that this desire to allow only the logically necessary to exist would lead to continuous acts of destruction for the goal to be achieved, precisely because life, it being life, is not without history and change. So then, the principle of freedom developed purely logically does not in any way secure the rights of living people; on the contrary, it abolishes them, so that only consistency can exist.

The description of the peculiarity of Roman law, by which each entitlement is more isolated than even the natural-law deduction, is reserved for another place.[83]

---

[83] See Stahl, *Private Law*, appendix: "Regarding the Value of Roman Private Law."

Chapter 4: The Individual Institutions of Natural Law

The Two Conflicting Principles of Rational Philosophy and their
Implementation in all Doctrines of Natural Law

The real existence of the thinker, and the law of thought, were referred to above as the two necessary principles of rational philosophy, and the conflict in their modes of production was also highlighted.[84] The general development of natural law contains just these principles, and therefore also their conflict. Because of this, rights [Recht] and juridical law could not be brought into connection – natural law makes human freedom into its foundation, and yet does not recognize acquired rights.

The genesis of the individual institutions is now also nothing more than a repetition of the same difficulty, the same mutual fuss, when one tracks any one of them. The exclusive principle of law must be freedom. If one comprehends this as real freedom, then right is what it *does*; if one comprehends it as the concept of freedom, then right is what it *is* (in both cases, excluding curtailment by others). In terms of the manner of operation of real freedom, there results from it a change in the initial condition which can progress to its complete opposite, in which it cancels itself and tolerates no restriction. But in terms of the concept of freedom, no change is possible. The condition is given by necessity, and freedom does not have freedom if somewhere it is restricted from effectuating anything in opposition to the logical conclusion. For the mode of action of freedom and of the logical conclusion are precisely opposed, in that the latter ever only posits what it already is, while the former can indeed bring about something else. This is the reason that in natural law one finds two opposite opinions regarding each and every institution, one of which is unconsciously based on the former principle, the other on the latter, and which are never able to arrive at a final settlement.

Controversy over Innate Rights

With respect to innate rights – rights to life, body, honor, opportunity to acquire property – logical deduction demands that their being flow directly

---

[84] See above, Book III, Part I [e.g., p. 88].

from the concept of man. Therefore they are always necessary, and it is contrary to reason if for one moment they do not exist. As such, giving them up cannot depend on discretion. But if life or reputation really are my rights, objects [Sache] of my freedom, then I should be able to keep them or not keep them, and even to renounce them if I so desire. Hence, Fichte[85] admits that one legally could sell his freedom of thought, if factually this were possible. According to the latter line of thought, the murder of a man who himself demands it, is no violation of the law, *non fit injuria volenti* [injury is not done to a willing person]. According to the former, it is such; because although it is not against that which this free person wished, it is to act against what follows from the concept of his freedom. Therefore, one and the same writer, and no second-rate one at that, can profess first the one, then the other opinion.[86]

Over Property

Consistency stemming from equal freedom would correspond to the arithmetically equal allocation of objects, community of goods, alternating use. But this contradicts living freedom, which cannot allow objects to be allocated without its will; it itself must be the cause of possession; but if it desired and took them, it wishes to lord over them exclusively, because by its very nature it must be able to effect something, and it cannot do so in a community of goods. To it corresponds property and the original acquisition thereof by seizure, the derivative acquisition thereof by transfer. But now it happens that the legal condition is determined by events which might or might not have occurred. One person is deprived of objects by the act of another, which he could not prevent, and an inequality arises in actuality, in the particular case, even with initial and, in terms of the idea, equal opportunity for control of the external world. In Roman law this is completely consistent, because Roman law recognizes the deeds of the free man as the determining factor of the legal condition; but natural law recognizes only the logical consequences from the concept of his freedom, and

---

[85] Fichte in the anonymous publication, *Beitrag zur Berichtigung der Urtheile des Publikums über die französische Revolution* [Contribution to Correcting the Verdict of the Public regarding the French Revolution], Part I, p. 228.

[86] Feuerbach, *Revision*, 2nd ed., Part II, p. XXIX, and *Lehrbuch* [Manual], 1st ed., §. 40, note.

a condition is not logically necessary which did not have to be effectuated.

Over the Content of Contracts

The history of the philosophical doctrine of property therefore manifests the eternal vacillation between the horns of this dilemma. According to Grotius, there follows from reason a community in all things, as now exists in public places, such as the theater. No one can acquire a lasting privilege vis-à-vis another for one particular object; he only has a right not to be disturbed in the factual possession thereof, not by virtue of a right to the thing but by virtue of his personhood, and only as long and as far as this factual relation extends.[87] Pufendorf, following the moderns in this, misunderstands Grotius when he attributes to him the idea of a positive-law community of goods. Pufendorf's own opinion only differs from Grotius' in that he denies this claim to non-disturbance of the factual condition: if someone collects fruit, another may snatch it from him again.[88] Although Thomasius rejects the latter as a *jus Hobbesianum*, which Pufendorf had actually already refuted, he returned to the view of Grotius.[89] Later, however, he seems to consider a positive-law community of goods to be the rational one.[90] This is decisively the case with Nettelbladt,[91] although all practitioners of natural law before Kant agreed that the community of all goods (*communio primaeva*), of whatever sort, flows immediately from reason, and the possibility that several property arises through occupation could only have its legal basis in an express or implied contractual establishment. Even according to Thomasius, reason advises occupation; but not so *praecise* and *distincte*, that a *pactum* would not be necessary for this.

Kant is the first to go the opposite direction and allow things to be linked permanently to one's legal sphere [Rechtssphäre] through his voluntary action. In this he is followed by the later Fichte and by Fries, although they again, like the earlier proponents, justify the institution of property solely from the

---

[87] Grotius, *De Jure Belli ac Pacis,* Book II, ch. 2, §. 2.

[88] Pufendorf, *De Jure Naturæ et Gentium,* Book IV, ch. IV, §. 3.

[89] Thomasius, *Institutiones Iurisprudentiae Divinae,* Book II, ch. 10.

[90] Thomasius, *Fundamenta Juris Naturae et Gentium,* Book II, ch. 10 [pp. 232ff.].

[91] Nettelbladt, *Systema Elementare Universae Jurisprudentiae Naturalis* [Elementary System of the Universal Law of Nature], §. 255ff.

agreement of the people; but they arrive there from a completely different position. Whether and why contracts are sufficient to transfer property, or to make the institution itself rational, does not pertain to the doctrine of property. The concern here is only whether the free act of an individual who has been granted the capacity to appropriate, can abolish equality, which lies immediately in the concept of freedom.

Over the Binding Nature of Contracts

The controversy which can be called perhaps the most important one of natural law, namely the *binding nature of contracts* (although only becoming the general subject of treatment in the later period) revolves around this same pivot. Any objections to this are based on the fact that one does not adopt a historical, act-generated relation between the moments of consent and of performance, but rather, in accordance with the abstract character, measures each against the concept of freedom. But this cannot explain how I must do something now simply because I once wanted to. Suppose I once made a lawful promise, but on false pretenses; now, i.e., without reference to time [zeitlos], my freedom entails that I am *not* obligated to keep that promise. Enforcing the contractual obligation is therefore contrary to reason. The binding nature of contracts is to individuals what legal inequality is to the whole. The deeds of the nation yesterday, even the deliberate ones, could not bring about the existence of a situation today that did not already have to exist apart from any deeds. And as with the people regarding its history, so can and must I abstract from my history, namely from what I did and wanted yesterday.

In opposition to this, the defenders of contractual obligation reason from consideration of the living person. He must act, connect the different times of his actions, and thereby make something happen for the legal condition. This, however, creates something contrary to his present freedom and hence likewise against the concept of his freedom. This dispute about the binding nature of contracts is made clearer in its essence when it is extended to the possibility of its contents.

Over the Distinction between Alienable and Inalienable Rights

Contract is the predominant institution not only for the emergence of legal claims, but for natural law as a whole. In it, everything is effectuated by the will of man: the right, the obligation, *that* they are, *what* they are. A system that is driven by the interest of human freedom can use no other lever than contract. With it, one seeks to actuate the most heterogeneous, the most peculiar, in the same manner. From it, one tends to derive even the validity of testaments, and thereby indirectly, intestate succession as presumptive testament.

He who is permeated by this spirit even for a short period – and who has not been! – must remember how this solution everywhere initially presents itself. But if contract itself is an act of freedom, then its opposite comes to pass simultaneously with its completion: he who has acted freely, is now bound. So with contract, it is only for a moment that freedom exercises its full existence. Like a flash, it dies with its birth. And with contract, natural law has called upon a dangerous assistant. One uses it to justify what one wishes, but does not consider that he also justifies that which he does not wish, and that, if it should have the power to build, it must also have the power to destroy. The rights of subpoena [Strafandrohung], of property, of paternal authority, the rule "sale breaks rent," if they cannot be derived directly from the principle, become established by contract. By contrast, compulsory morality, prerogative of nobility, tax exemption, trade restrictions, which their defenders must have the right to ground on tacit agreement, are unconditionally rejected. And where will the limits be set on what can be agreed upon? Will one, like the old Germanic tribes and the earlier natural law, allow contractual slavery? Will one limit the duration of a function, like the French Code prohibits the permanent hire of services, or the scope, and to what extent?

Therefore, it was in the latter period of natural law, when everything in rapid development hurried to its end, that one became preoccupied with the separation of alienable from inalienable rights. No tolerance could be found for acquired rights which, in view of the fact that they only could arise because of a fact, could only lapse because of a fact. The difficulty first became apparent with innate rights. It was already demonstrated above that those two principles require on the one hand their alienability, on the other their inalienability, and therefore neither of these opposing conceptions has lacked defenders. Nevertheless, both led to results that could not be accepted.

Alienability could not be accepted, as it made even full slavery possible. Nor yet inalienability, because innate and acquired rights are in such indissoluble relation that, with the rigidity of the former, the latter would also lose their flexibility. The possibility, for example, for someone to acquire things by his actions, to move about at his own pleasure, as contained in primordial right, must at least be relatively abandoned in order to engage any run of the mill contract. To find the boundary here, one would have to separate, in abstraction, the innate right, without any specific content, from this content, declare the latter of any sort to be alienable, the former alone to be inalienable. So to be consistent, we arrive at this: the original right itself, that is, the not-being-a-slave, cannot be abandoned, but every specific use of it can be, as long as only it itself remains. Hoffbauer, one of the clearest and sharpest proponents of this orientation, distinguishes: "I can abandon individual rights which I have as component parts of my innate right; but I cannot deliberately give up one of my original rights such that nothing more of them remains to me."[92] Fichte, who in his anonymous work on the French Revolution[93] conducted a sprawling investigation into the alienability of rights, and whose interest is precisely their inalienability, nevertheless comes to no other result than what has just been delineated: pure personality is inalienable, while everything specific, in which it expresses itself, is alienable. Thus he admits that someone can entirely divest himself of his right to engage contracts, and even can enter into slavery; only in the latter case, the right of the slave to be nourished by the master remains as a right, so that the concept of a person, the primordial right to life, is thereby preserved.

Natural law itself thus accomplished the reduction of inalienability to this mathematical point, so to speak, and thereby believed it had brought those contradictory principles into harmony. But it did not achieve this, because it is entirely impossible to achieve. Either there is a historical connection between the act and its consequences – in which case, slavery is not against freedom, when it is only willed; because it happens to him who is now a slave only by his will, and therefore he is not treated as a means. Or there is no such connection, and it cannot by any means justify being bound by a contract; because he who is compelled does not now wish to be so, and thereby is treated as a means.

The solution of this dialectic is this: the contradiction arises only from the

---

[92] *Op. cit.,* p. 254.

[93] *Beitrag zur Berichtigung der Urteile des Publikums über die französische Revolution* [Contribution to the Correction of Judgments by the Public regarding the French Revolution].

fact that human freedom is founded on a concept. If it is deployed by the free will of God and as part of His specific moral order, then all difficulties are smoothed away: it reaches as far as it wishes to, it has its limits in how far it may alienate itself in the determination that He gave it; but within this boundary it has its truly free, change-effecting movement, because God, unlike reason, brings forth more than what is only logically necessary.

Over the State

Among contracts, the *social contract* plays the leading role. Through it, even lasting relationships of mutual dependence (marriage, parental relationship, the state) which are removed from freedom, can be derived from freedom. *Nullum imperium sine pacto.* These relations, which by their very nature dominate mankind by their inherent idea, are thereby brought under the social contract. For any society [Gesellschaft] only has a passive object and does not entail any submission other than that which reciprocally exists and is mutually adopted. In this way, the existence and the arrangement of the family, the state, continually depend only upon the arbitrary will of the parties to the contract. Its shape is only governed by the restrictions of private contracts – where such is recognized. Hence the state is, e.g., denied the right of capital punishment because private individuals cannot dispose of their lives – as if they had a greater right arbitrarily to dispose of their health, their freedom.

Thomasius distinguishes himself in this, that when he was still a sociabilist, he derived the law of society and the power thereof from the goals of these relations themselves, rejected the *consensus tacitus* and *praesumtus* of the other natural law doctors, and grounded paternal authority directly on divine institution. Consistent with this, he declared in his later works that the relationship between parents and children involves no compulsory obligation.[94]

In terms of this school's interest, the essence of the state must likewise consist solely in the satisfaction of the individual: It is an institution for either the good, or the moral perfection, or the freedom of individuals. But the task also was to derive this logically from the basic concepts: "Without the state, power or difference of opinion would topple the results which follow from the equal

---

[94] Thomasius, *Institutiones iurisprudentiae divinae,* Book I, ch. 1 §. 86; Book III, ch. 4. *Fundamenta juris naturae et gentium,* Book III, ch. 4.

freedom of all. But freedom calls for the protection of its results; this protection is the state; therefore, the state is included in the concept of the equal freedom of all." This is the final result of natural law from first to last. It was only in the later period that the attempt was also made to insinuate morality or happiness as an end for the state, in contradiction to the innermost motive of orientation and in contradiction with consistency. Because to be justified as a legal institution, it may only follow from freedom. Hence the will of the individual to be protected is the exclusive goal of the state.

But this still does not satisfy the leading interest. Because the state puts limits on this goal as well, and even protection should not be imposed. The will of the individual, therefore, must not merely be the exclusive goal, it must also be the only cause of the state. The state is founded on *contract*, express or implied, real or supposed. This reduces the institution [Anstalt] the power of which is obvious to the people, and which cannot be avoided like, e.g., the church can, but factually cannot be done without, to the individual will, at least in theory. And here the character of the whole orientation speaks most directly: outright rebellion against every given regime; subjugation only to a chosen one. From start to finish, all significant natural law doctors are therefore agreed on the creation of the state through contract. Even with Spinoza this is at least the form with which he cannot break, regardless of how much the thing itself contradicts his system's character of necessity. The bottom line for him is not consent but the real alienation of power; yet he characterized this everywhere as a contract.

That this ongoing contradiction must also prevail in the deduction of the state, is obvious. It follows from the *concept* of freedom that freedom *must* be protected – hence compulsion by the state and a certain unalterable form thereof. *Living* freedom, on the other hand, requires free choice in its establishment (state contract) and discretionary arrangement. Now this contradiction was not so evident to the older writers, but ever since Kant it has set everything in motion; hence the manifold opinions as to whether the state contract is voluntary or necessary, whether it is morally or legally necessary, whether it grounds duty to the state generally, or only to a specific one. This controversy as well can as little be brought to an end as can the one set forth above; and it is merely coincidence, or rather the interest of the antagonists, which has proven to be the decisive factor every time. Therefore, in different relations the most contradictory principles prevailed. Namely, with regard to establishment, the view generally was adopted which follows from act-oriented freedom: the state arises and exists legally by contract, so that if people did not want it, it would not arise or exist. By contrast, in the doctrine of the arrangement and formation of the state, almost all profess the result of the opposite principle: only those arrangements are permitted in the state which include the concept of freedom, and public legal institutions that do not follow from this concept are unjust, even if the people willed it that way.

Initial and Subsequent Position of Natural Law regarding Positive Rights

This, then, is the course of development of natural law taken uniformly as a whole, albeit with individual differences and disputes. For a time it both mingled with religious and devout notions[95] and tolerated positive legal institutions within itself, e.g., the feudal law, until finally it stripped itself of all foreign elements to present itself purely in its peculiar character. Initially, it was nothing like at odds with existing institutions, the intent of the deduction being to demonstrate the rational necessity of these as they really are, in order to sanction them. But it increasingly pushed against them until it finally forcefully tackled and upended the entire existing state.

A principle, and probably the most important one, which was followed above in its development, shows this clearly. This would be the principle separating out compulsory obligations. This was initially sought in order to justify the status quo; in the end, it was used to demolish it. Even the actual content, the primordial right of man – that he may not be a slave – which is what the entire development seeks, was obtained only at the end of that development. Oldendorp even venerated slavery and deduced it from the commandment, Honor thy father and mother, while also appealing to the authority of Aristotle.[96] Thomasius called for a less restrictive relationship in accordance with natural rights, e.g., *non invitus alteri vendi poterit servus perpetuus* [one cannot be

---

[95] To this pertain as well the investigations regarding morals and law prior to the Fall, regarding the Kingdom of Christ and the Devil, etc. Hobbes and Thomasius in particular busied themselves with this.

[96] Oldendorp, *Iuris Naturalis Civilis et Gentium Isagoge* [Introduction to the Law of Nature, Civil Law, and the Law of Nations], IIII Praeceptum [Fourth Commandment].

sold into perpetual slavery to another], but nevertheless calmly listed alongside it what positive law has enacted differently.[97] Wolff deems it justified by contract and insolvency; by birth, only until such time as the master recoups the costs of education;[98] Hopfner merely by contract. Only the subsequent period (Montesquieu, Rousseau, Kant) rejected this absolutely.

If one now looks back to the first requirement – to derive everything simply by logically subsuming passive objects under the ethical rule – in order to see whether it has been met, then we have to conclude that it by no means has been satisfied. Admittedly, property and obligation [Forderung] could be regarded as the object of such subsumption: things brought under the concept of freedom are property, etc. But with regard to the legal necessity of the state, the deduction is by no means only logical, but also derived from effects. Here not only is the object of freedom taken from experience, the rule that the state should exist is as well, and is founded on those premises, on the observation that people apart from higher authority do not respect rights, but that such an entity secures them. Already the concept of the end of the state, which underlies the deduction, entails this. For now the question is no longer: what lies in the concept of freedom? But rather, by what is that which lies in the concept of freedom achieved according to the laws of empirical nature? But what is found by this approach lacks the character of logical necessity. One can be persuaded that things subsumed under freedom yield property in the way that two times two equals four; it is not contradicted in terms of form. But that human drives make the state necessary already lacks this necessary form. For reason assures me neither that the state will really be capable of protecting me in my rights, nor vice versa, that they will be violated without it, even though to this point all experience, which in reality always has exceptions, speaks for both. For this reason the great divergence between Hobbes and the others had its foundation not in ethical but in experiential propositions.

The same is true for the various institutions of the state. For this reason, the objection has been lodged against the theory by which punishment, like the state, is considered to be a means (namely a means of protection): it needs to be seen whether punishment *always* achieves this; apart from this, it would be

---

[97] Thomasius, *Institutiones Iurisprudentiae Divinae,* Book III, ch. 5.

[98] Wolff, *Institutiones Iuris Naturae et Gentium,* §. 959.

lacking a rational test. This objection is entirely justified in terms of the requirements of abstract procedure, but it is valid with the same justification against the deduction of the state for the purpose of securing law as it is against punishment. Namely, in both the *continuo ratiocinationis filo deducere* [continuous deduction of the thread of reasoning] is given up, in order to turn the workings of experience, which are not without exception, and are not logically necessary, into the thread of reasoning.

Unfaithfulness of Natural Law to Its Required Method

But natural law is compelled to this infidelity to its method, because while it derives ethical rules from reason, it borrows the material thereof from experience. Now the outside world stands everywhere not only in logical, but in real connections, and the ethical construction itself must be affected by this. For this reason natural rights, as abstract philosophy generally, always had the urge not to borrow relations from experience, but to find them *a priori* as well as in their ethical arrangement. This took place with Fichte and Hegel. With them therefore, and preeminently with the latter, the uninterrupted thread of logical reasoning is implemented. For them, the state and its institutions do not result because they are needed for a goal, but because they are included in the basic concept of natural law by a rule of pure thought, without anything needing to be added from outside, as will be shown in greater detail below.

We have hereby characterized natural law in its general outlines. The final evaluation of it will be suspended until its various iterations with individual compilers have been pursued. Our purpose here has been to emphasize the internal contradictions which impelled its development.

PART III: DEVELOPMENT OF NATURAL LAW IN INDIVIDUAL SYSTEMS

Chapter 1: Hugo Grotius

Hugo Grotius is the originator of the system of philosophy of law which goes by the name of "natural law" and which for more than a century was the only one applied and cultivated; indeed, it was the only one held to be possible, because the various systems which were customarily distinguished during this period (sociabilistic system, system of fear, external peace, etc.), were merely particular implementations of one and the same system.

Principle of Law

His work *On the Law of War and Peace*,[99] in which this is laid down, had the law of nations as its intended and actual task. The old foundations – feudal law, knightly battle customs, ecclesiastical orders and temperaments – gave way for this, and new ones needed to be laid; indeed the evidence had to be provided that in relationships among sovereign states and especially in war, not merely advantage and violence applied, but justice. But standards to legislate and enforce among sovereign states over which no supreme authority exists, presuppose the idea of a law which is valid not by positive sanctions, but by its own intrinsic regard. It was therefore a necessary preparation for Grotius' task to show the law to be given by nature (*jus naturale*) and valid apart from any positive legislation, and indeed such a one that is invented and introduced by man not for the sake of utility and selfishness, and which therefore can be bypassed for the sake of utility, but which rests on an ethical reason, which binds man absolutely. To refute that doctrine of utility and prudence such as represented in particular in antiquity by Carneades, and to establish an ethical principle of law, is the endeavor of the Prolegomena of Grotius' work, with which the new era of legal philosophy mainly begins.

He constructs this law, in itself ethically binding, upon the gregarious nature of, or the drive of sociability in, man (*socialis natura, appetitus socialis*). Man has a drive for community with others, indeed a drive for a "peaceful and rationally ordered community." Grotius did not conceive this urge to community as mere reciprocity of physical needs, but much more broadly, as good will towards

---

[99] Grotius, *De Jure Belli et Pacis*. [On Grotius, see also Alvarado, *Calvin and the Whigs; The Debate that Changed the West.*]

others, especially in opposition to mere utility. It is to him the love of a condition in which common satisfaction is achieved for self and others. The gregarious nature in this sense now becomes the principle of law. What follows from it is the law of nature (*jus naturae*), is just, is commanded, while the opposite is unjust and illegal; and it is immutable (*mutari non potest*), and is the supreme law for all times and for all peoples. Thus did Grotius establish a principle for a system of natural law, a *purely ethical* one disregarding utility (*jus non solius utilitas causa comparatum*), and a purely *rational* one disregarding positive regulation. (It is not rationalistic because of its independence from positive law, but because of the source from which it is drawn, namely, human reason abstracted from God and the God-given world order, in which it, as shown above [p. 95], goes so far as to claim a validity for the same even on the assumption that there is no God.)

Delimitation of the Legal Sphere

The sphere that stands under this principle and is to be regulated by it is, according to Grotius' specific declaration, simply law in the actual or strict sense (*ejus juris quod proprie tali nomine appellatur*). He therefore firstly rules out law in the "broader" sense, which we call morality [Moral], namely the control of desires (fear and lust), as those regulated not by the drive of sociability, but by a different drive of human nature, namely, value judgments regarding the true lasting value or lack thereof of things, and secondly, as part of this broader law, the wise arrangement (*prudens dispensatio*) of the particular conditions of every man or every state, thus politics.[100] Therefore there remains to the sphere of law

---

[100] This is the undoubted sense of §§. 8 and 10 of the Prologue. Many places indicate that Grotius understood law in the broader sense to be morality, preeminently Prolegomena §§. 41 and 44, where it reads: "cum injustitia non aliam naturam habeat, quam alieni usurpationem, nec referat, ex avaritia illa, an ex libidine, an ex ira, an ex imprudente misericordia proveniat" [Whereas the very Nature of Injustice consists in nothing, else, but in the Violation of another's Rights; nor does it signify, whether it proceeds from Avarice, or Lust, or Anger, or imprudent Pity, or Ambition, which are usually the Sources of the greatest Injuries – Barbeyrac/Tuck, I, p. 121]. Likewise Book II, ch. 22, §. 16: "Illud quoque sciendum est, si quis quid debet non ex justitia propria, sed ex

[Rechtsgebiet] (the sphere that stands under the principle of the drive to sociability) nothing but *respect for mine and thine*, namely property recognition, fulfillment of contracts, damages, and upon transgression, the punishment that pertains to this (*alieni abstinentia – promissorum implendorum obligatio – damni culpa dati reparatio et poenae inter homines meritum*). The deduction of these legal propositions is simple and obvious, they being undeniable conditions of peaceful coexistence, and is exhaustive in terms of that principle; because for the mere purpose of peaceful coexistence, nothing more is required.

Contract as the Embodiment of Natural Law

As a result, only the sphere of private law as such is derived from the principle of natural law. From this Grotius arrives at the state only indirectly, namely, through the medium of *contract*. It is a command of natural law that contracts must be kept, because (for the peaceful community) there must be some sort of mutual obligation among men and none other than contract is conceivable (*fingi potest*). But then it must be assumed on the part of those who form a state (who have joined with a *coetus*), that they have promised by express or implied

---

virtute alia, puta liberalitate, gratia, misericordia, dilectione, id sicut in foro exigi non potest, ita nec armis deposci" [This we are also to understand, that if a Man owes another any Thing, not in Strictness of Justice but by some other Virtue, suppose Liberality, Gratitude, Compassion, or Charity, he cannot be sued for it in any Court of Judicature, neither can War be made upon him on that Account – Barbeyrac/Tuck, II, p. 1 1 1 2]. In this sense, therefore, Grotius also judges the duty of parents to nourish their children to be such a one that pertains not to law in the strict but in the broad sense (hence, morality): Book II, ch. 7, §. 4. This entire construction of the ethical sphere of Grotius' can only be explained on the basis of then-extant scholastic teaching [Bildung]. That which there was divided subjectively into various virtues, Grotius established objectively as separation into life-spheres [Lebensgebieten]. The sphere of *justitia commutativa* is what he construes as law in the strict sense; as law in the broad sense he allocates control of appetites, which according to Thomas was the object of other virtues but not justice, and the wise distribution of goods and positions according to the inner worth and calling of persons, which according to Thomas was the object of *justitia distributiva*. But when he transfers the separation to objective life-spheres, it automatically becomes a compartmentalization of the legal sphere over against morality and politics.

contract, to obey either the majority or those to whom authority has been transferred. For this reason, even according to Grotius' expression, obligation from agreement (*obligatio ex consensu*) is the "mother of all civil law." Upon it, in fact, is based the power that gives rise to civil law.[101] Indeed, even in the sphere of mine and thine he also derives the validity of several property from contractual introduction.[102] So it is only contract that directly binds according to the law of nature, everything else is derived from it, and one might say that the entire essence of Grotius' doctrine of natural law, without him being aware of it, is nothing else than merely *the binding nature of contracts*.

General Ethical Significance of the State

As Grotius proceeds from a general ethical basis for law, he also, in the same way and in accordance with this basis, attributes general ethical significance to the state. The state is the perfect union of free men, through which that law [Gesetz] of nature, a peaceful and orderly community, is to be realized.[103] In accordance with this general ethical significance, the state, as differentiated from the person of the prince, as a human community, is the subject of public legal relations and public authority. There remains, therefore, the state itself, and its rights and obligations continue through all change of rulers, dynasties, and even forms of government – the immortality of the states (*civitas immortalis*),[104] and the actions of the regent are binding on any successor, even those who are not his heirs, so that they are acts of state (*actus regii* as opposed to *privati*).[105] Similarly, the purpose of the state according to that general ethical significance is the common enjoyment (mutual recognition) of rights and the common utility. The public good is thus the supreme standard for decision (*salus publica suprema lex esto*), to which all individual rights must yield. From this in particular he derived the right of eminent domain (*dominium*

---

[101] Prolegomena, §§. 15, 16. Cf. also Book II, ch. 5, §. 17 and 23.

[102] Book II, ch. 2, §. 2. no. 5.

[103] "Est autem civitas coetus perfectus liberorum hominum, juris fruendi et communis utilitatis causa societas." Book I, ch. 1, §. 14.

[104] Book II, ch. 9, §. 8, nos. 1–3 and §. 3.

[105] Book II, ch. 14, §. 1, nos. 1 and 2; §. 11, no. 2; §. 12, no. 2.

supereminens).[106]

Identification of Nation and State

With this entire conception, the state is for Grotius entirely the same as the nation or people [Volk], the people [Menschen] united, and the public signifies only what is of common utility to all, not what is a higher necessity over them all. Certainly he considers the people to be the state only insofar as it is imbued with a spirit, namely, just that full civil life community (*vitae civilis consociatio plena*) the first product of which is the supreme authority.[107] But the state never manifests itself to him as a unity or institute [Anstalt] to be distinguished from the people; this is also expressed in the fact that he everywhere uses the concepts *civitas* [city], *communitas* [community], *coetus* [gathering], *populus* [people] as synonymous terms. In consequence, he grounds that identity of the state and perpetuity of its rights and obligations not on the unitary institute but rather on the fact that the rights and liabilities are *that same people's*,[108] and mediates the binding nature of the acts of state on the successor not through the state but through the people, because of its being obligated by the actions of earlier rulers acting as its representatives, and tacitly transferring this obligation to the later rulers, who derive their power from it. In consequence of this, and this is the main point, for him the people are the subject of supreme authority (*summa potestas*). In free countries, it remains so completely, while in monarchical states it is not the exercise but the right (*imperium in se retinet, quanquam non exercendum a corpore sed a capite*). Therefore, here the people remains the general subject of authority, while the prince, to whom it transfers that authority, becomes the special subject (*subjectum commune* and *proprium*), similar to the whole body being the subject of sight even though only the eye is first and foremost. Therefore the authority also reverts back (*redit*) to the people when the

---

[106] Book II, ch. 14, §. 7.

[107] Book II, ch. 9, §. 3.

[108] "Non desinit debere pecuniam populus rege sibi imposito, quam liber debebat, est enim *idem populus*" [A Debt contracted by a free People, ceases not to be a Debt, because they are at present under a King; for the People are the same – Barbeyrac/Tuck, p. 673], Book II, ch. 9, §.3.

dynasty dies out, as having proceeded from it.[109]

Grotius nevertheless does not arrive at any practical inferences against monarchy from this implemented theoretical popular sovereignty; on the contrary, he emphatically combats the then revolutionary doctrine of a supremacy and especially penal authority of peoples over their kings. This is because, according to his doctrine, the king, although only gaining authority by transfer from the people, nevertheless thereby receives it truly and irrevocably; the people forever remain subjected to his own will and act. Grotius teaches a sovereignty of the people and a sovereignty of the king, but the former is only potential, and therefore can never do harm to the latter.[110] Nevertheless, this conception, by which Grotius disposes of the natural consequences of his basic assumption, again is only possible through an inconsistency, a lack of awareness regarding his position, of the kind he is afflicted with generally.

Private-Legal Character of the State Contract

That is to say: in contradiction to the general ethical and thus necessary significance that Grotius ascribes to the state, he conceives the contract founding the state in strictly private manner, as of arbitrary content, and since, as the state in general derives from contract, so necessarily do the specific form of government; all forms of government are declared legitimate by the backing of such a contract or similar title, such as, in particular, conquest, which according to Grotius' position can be considered a (compulsory) contract. In this sense, he recognizes in particular the legality of a class of states which he already distinguished using private-legal characterizations such as patrimonial states or usufruct states, in which, namely, the ruler has full ownership of state authority, either because he has subjugated the people through war or contractually it has passed so completely into his hand that nothing is excluded.[111]

---

[109] "Nam imperium, quod in rege est ut in capite, in populo manet ut in toto, cujus pars est caput: atque ... adeo regis familia extincta jus imperandi ad populum redit" [For that sovereign Power which is in the King as Head, rests still in the People as in the Whole, whereof the Head is a Part: So that ... if the Royal Family be extinct, the Sovereignty reverts to the People – Barbeyrac/Tuck, p. 672], Book II, ch. 9, §. 8; Book I, ch. 3, §. 7.

[110] Book I, ch. 3, §. 8.

[111] Book I, ch. 3, §. 11.

Certainly this term patrimonial state initially signifies only the irrevocable and unconditional jurisdiction of power (including the power of alienation [Veräußerungsbefugniß]),[112] not absolutism. But in other places Grotius also allows the content, purpose, and scope of state power to depend on any contract whatsoever. In the way that a man of his own free will can give himself over to slavery, so also can the people bestow the sovereign power over itself in whatever way it wishes, because it is not utility but only will that is decisive according to the legal point of view, and therefore states are also justified in which the state power is intended solely for the benefit of the prince and not the people, thus entirely equal to the power over slaves, in accordance with the then prevailing Aristotelian characterization.[113]

There is obviously an inconsistency with regard to the concept of the general necessary essence of the state. If the legal basis for all relations only lies in the satisfaction of human desire for a peaceful and rationally ordered community, then a contract cannot be legally valid that allows the public authority to be used not for this purpose, but for the benefit of the ruler. This inconsistency had to be removed, and this led, from the other premises of Grotius, to the doctrine of Rousseau.

Now the same thing that holds for the state and the people within the state must also apply to the nations mutually. For these as well, there exist standards by agreement (among which, undoubtedly, not only express but also tacit agreement is to be understood) which have as goal not the benefit of an individual state but the benefit of that great unity of states (*magnae illius universitatis*). Accordingly, war in particular is also based on fixed laws. There are only certain cases in which it can lawfully be conducted, mere advantage is no authorization, there are rules and restrictions according to which it must be conducted, and there are even temperaments of humanity by which not everything allowed by principles of law should actually be implemented.

Evaluation

With this program of ideas [Ideenkonception], Grotius opened a new path for various scientific fields. Already for ethics generally, he laid the foundation

---

[112] *Ibid.* and Book II, ch. 6, §. 3.

[113] Book I, ch. 3, §. 8, nos. 1, 2, 14.

for scientific treatment by laying claim to an independent field separate from religion, and an independent body of knowledge separate from revelation; because if he also fell into error in this, by entirely separating God Himself from this purpose, he yet extracted the problem of recognizing the moral commandments not in terms of arbitrary divine commission, but their inner reason and essence.[114] Still more decisively, he is the founder of "natural law" as an entirely new science which did not exist before him. Not only did he establish a new principle for the philosophy of law, the socializing nature in his sense, but he provided a new boundary for its subject matter. He was the first to separate out the actual sphere of law, which until then was mingled with others. He established a natural law (*jus naturae*) as distinguished from morality and politics, while also distinguished from positive law. Legal principles shall exist which are not based on positive law and yet are not merely desirable principles worthy of pursuing, but which already are actually valid, legally binding principles that have nothing to do with the question of the appropriateness of the state constitution and state institutions, but are valid across all state constitutions and state institutions plain and simple, as unconditional legal standards. Such a science of general law, which is not morality, not politics, not the epitome of mere law-ideas, and not positive law, is precisely the specific nature of the discipline of "natural law" that Grotius founded and the entire construction of which, at least in its outlines, he already prefigured with a steady hand; and here again the mighty progress he achieved in distinguishing the legal idea from the political idea needs to be recognized, regardless of the untenability of his notion of such a law.[115] For regarding the doctrine and law of the state, Grotius mainly asserted the viewpoint of the public commonwealth as opposed to mere private entitlement to rule, as has already been pointed out in other places of this work.[116]

Above everyone else, however, Grotius accomplished a service for the law of nations, which was his intended task. Since it was no longer the church that maintained a joint order among the mighty of the earth, and no longer the emperor who was recognized as the supreme arbiter of their disputes, in international relations it was only the absolute will of the individual sovereigns which

---

[114] See Stahl, *Philosophical Presuppositions* (Vol. II, Book I), §§. 24 and 28.

[115] See Stahl, *Principles of Law* (Vol. II, Book II), §. 17.

[116] See Stahl, *The Doctrine of State and Principles of State Law* (Vol. II, Book IV), §. 37.

was valid, and there already had appeared the theory of mere utility which handed the European condition over to the thirst for unlimited aggrandizement on the part of courts. It was therefore a great thing to bring about the validity not only of utility but of law in the relations of nations, such that even in war laws are not silenced, and that even what the law allows, humanity does not permit. Grotius stands above all the subsequent practitioners of natural law up until Kant, not only by being the initial originator, but also in the execution, richness of thought, and the perception and living conception of conditions, as a result of which (which is also noteworthy) with him falsehood does not emerge as determinedly as with others; in part (in particular the severance from Christianity) it even remained hidden from him.

But as undeniable as these lasting merits of the Grotian doctrine are, he also, with this same doctrine, was also the first and already full-blown founder of that one-sided and therefore false orientation which in its consistency ends with the destruction of morality and justice. He sketched out the enterprise of implementing a legal construction by abstracting out not only the Author of the moral order but also the content of the actually given (objective) moral order, abstracting simply from the nature of man. He gave the initial expression to the manner of presentation in which the state has no authority over men in itself, but only gets it through their contract, and has no purpose in itself, but derives such from the purposes of (individual) men. This point of view is the decisive factor. The fact that Grotius personally and incidentally endorses the Christian revelation could not prevent the consequences of this from manifesting themselves.

This also clarifies his relationship to Aristotle. The tradition in which the social nature of man contains the basis of law and the state began with Aristotle and proceeded to Grotius; to this degree, the sociabilist system has been regarded as nothing new, and not as the Grotius' work. But the same expression has a completely different meaning in Grotius than in Aristotle. The same expression with Aristotle means nature as the power in the universe which appoints people to social life, while with Grotius it means nature as the character or desire of men. According to Aristotle, nature in the state seeks *its* completion for that which it establishes in smaller circles, and this is the reason that man is by nature gregarious. According to Grotius, by contrast, man has a social need, which is why the state is an end of nature. Therefore Aristotle comes to an (objective) doctrine as to how the state must be arranged according to *its* very nature, while Grotius comes to a (subjective) doctrine, how it must be designed to suit the nature of (*individual*) *men*.

Hence with Grotius a principle came to life which in its further development necessarily led to the doctrine of Kant and Rousseau, and eventually to the French Revolution. The doctrine of Grotius, that the duty of subjects has its basis in their tacit contract, is in itself quite insignificant and innocuous. But it only needed to be developed in all its content and its consequences to become what a century later would overturn the order of Europe. Likewise, one snow-flake which dissolves on the mountain peaks is inconspicuous; but [when combined with others] it rolls along and falls as a crashing avalanche into the depths.

Chapter 2: The Natural Law Doctors from Grotius to Kant

Hobbes

Thomas Hobbes[117] countered the doctrine of Grotius with another, taking the same point of view but from an opposite presupposition. Human nature is not the desire for community (shared satisfaction), but selfishness. Man seeks community not for the sake of comrades but merely for his own sake. The origin of great and lasting societies is therefore not mutual benevolence but mutual fear. The detailed implementation is as follows.

The state in which people by nature, i.e., prior to their mutual commitment by contract – the "state of nature" – is one in which all have the same rights to all things, but also the same inclination to hurt each other, particularly because of the desire for things. The state of nature therefore is a perpetual war and perpetual reciprocal threat and fear. But now the law of nature (*lex naturae*) or – a term Grotius used as meaning the same thing – right reason (*recta ratio*) is self-preservation (the protection of life and limb); what happens in accordance with this is justified and responsible, having taken place *juste* [justly] and *jure* [lawfully].

The fundamental precept of nature, therefore, is to seek peace. From this flows two corollaries: the first, that you cannot retain the unlimited right of the state of nature, but must partially transfer it in order to possess what you retain in peace; and the second, that you must keep contracts, because only in this way can peace be attained. From this source equally arise the duties of compassion, gratitude, etc. (in short, all moral obligations), since their reciprocal practice serves self-preservation. So Hobbes reduces everything having to do with law and ethics to selfishness.

Yet all of these commandments which follow from the law of nature are not binding as long as the state of nature endures, precisely in terms of their own principles; because as long as one is not sure of fulfillment by others, one's own fulfillment does not serve self-preservation. That is not only why the civil laws are silent in the state of nature, but the laws of nature as well; in it, there is no

---

[117] Hobbes, *Elementa Philosophica de Cive* [Philosophical Elements, the Citizen] 1642 (*Leviathan* 1651).

other legal standard (*mensura juris*) than actual benefit. But for this reason it is the law of nature to abandon the state of nature (*status naturalis*) and to establish the civil condition (*status civilis*), that is to say, to bind each other in overwhelming numbers to reciprocal assistance against disturbances of the peace. This combination is the state, and only from it proceeds the mine and thine, the obligation to respect other people's property, because only through it does the assurance exist that others will do the same.

Yet this security coming from this connection should not be a mere agreement (*consentire*) but a union (*unio*); that is, participants must cease to be separate independent entities, but instead need to become one will, so that individuals retain no will and no right of themselves, but rather transfer all their rights and all their power (*jus virium et facultatum suarum*) to a person or a consilium, waiving resistance and reversal of the transfer. That is the supreme power (*summa potestatis, summum imperium*) or, as we would say, sovereignty. In this manner the state is itself a person (*persona civilis*), distinguished from all individuals that make it up, so that all these taken together are not to be regarded as a state, excepting he who represents them (*repraesentant*). A dual contract is therefore necessary for the establishment of the state: the one through which anyone contracts with anyone, and the other through which they all contract with the future holder of the supreme power, to submit, and indeed to submit unconditionally.

This complete transfer of all right and all force to the supreme state power necessarily makes it absolute (*imperium absolutum*). In terms of its concept, there can exist neither a higher power over it nor a restriction on it, for the latter assumes a higher power. It cannot be bound by laws. There can be no right of subjects against it that it must take into account, no property, indeed no conscience, no judgment over good and evil, but in this as well, subjection to the judgment of the supreme state power (the sovereign) is unconditional, and therefore, whoever acts in obedience to state power does not sin. The opinion that the subject might have an independent judgment regarding good and evil, and that a sinful act that he commits by command of the sovereign is a sin for him, is a false and a revolutionary doctrine (*seditiosa opinio*).

Finally church teaching, i.e., the interpretation of the Holy Scriptures, must take place by state authority (albeit by means of the bishops of apostolic succession) because the individual, if he had the competence to such interpretation, would attribute to himself the highest standard of conduct, which would cause all civil obedience and indeed all of society to cease. Therefore, for Hobbes the church also coincides completely with the (Christian) state, which is to say, by the church he understands Christians united under an external authority. Here below, the inner invisible church is merely a church in *potentia* [potentially], not *actu* [actually]. Given the reasons already brought forward, such power may be no other than precisely the supreme state power. Only such a unified will, against which wills that are competing with and combatting each other cannot stand, is able to ensure the security of peace, which is the supreme law of nature. Selfishness, which is the core of human nature, can only be tamed by such unlimited irresistible power.

Accordingly, Hobbes stands unmistakably on the same presuppositions that are peculiar to his time, and which were first expressed by Grotius. Like Grotius, Hobbes does not recognize a given order standing over men with inherent ethical laws, but wishes to derive such only from the nature of the individual. He too, therefore, established the civil condition on an arbitrary contract of subjects, so that even the validity of majority vote, this "beginning of the civil condition," can only be decided by unanimity, and he knows no other concept of injustice (*injuria*) than that of contract infringement, so that no injustice can be committed against those with whom one has not contracted.[118] What is unique to him, though, is that he de-ethicized [entsittlicht] law and the state, indeed morality itself. The natural law (*lex naturae*), on which alone he erects law and ethics, is not ethical at all but the mere physical drive of self-preservation; his right reason (*recta ratio*) is a mere law of prudence. No less peculiar to him is his political result: the absolutism of the state, which before him had never been taught, nor after him, at least not to that degree, such that he even excludes the moral accountability of subjects, namely in the way that citizens are subjected, not as in Plato to a higher harmony, but to an arbitrary will. Hobbes arrives at this result by being consistent: The vacuity of social relations which is here assumed, the divestment thereof of ethical ideas in order to base them purely on human will, must lead to the absolute power of the united human will. Rousseau later attained similar results, in other ways. Grotius would have had to arrive at them, if he had exhaustively drawn the consequences from

---

[118] Book I, ch. 1, §. 3.

his principle *salus publica suprema lex esto.*

But Hobbes was also led to his absolutist doctrine from a practical motive. The religious and political divisions, the [English] civil war, the readiness of religious conscience to revolt that surrounded him in his own country, filled him with longing above all for peace and unity, and the idea that such cannot exist where any power of resistance, especially for the reason of conscience and religion, could burden it. In both respects, both in his materialistic conception of life and in the practical power of his political result, Hobbes is an excellent representative and cultivator of the orientation that found its development in the West, in opposition to the more ethical and inwardly contemplative manner of vision suggested by Grotius and cultivated particularly in Germany, even though the outcome of that orientation was quite different, indeed the opposite of the one Hobbes strove after. But Hobbes' deep insight into the foundations of the state had true scientific merit, namely, the notion of the unity of the state in contrast to a mere society; and connected to this, he first expressed the idea of sovereignty in all its profundity; in this he stands above Grotius. For Grotius distinguishes the state merely from the prince, while Hobbes also distinguishes it from the people.[119] In particular, Hobbes substantially developed the system of legal philosophy begun by Grotius; he brought many and significant doctrines to clear discussion which, although already available, were only veiled in the system of Grotius. In particular, these would be the doctrine of a state of nature, the deduction that the supreme principle of law cannot be fulfilled in the state of nature and therefore postulates the state, the description of the course of events (or the legal relation) by which the state is established by contract. These doctrines, if not true in themselves, are necessary for the position, and therefore built the construction of "natural law" up until the last moment.[120]

---

[119] With Bodin, the concept of sovereignty is certainly more concrete, is determined more vividly than with Hobbes, but merely as something given; it is not deduced from the essence of the state.

[120] Hobbes and Spinoza have often been set in parallel. This has been prompted by both the mightiness of the two intellects, and by the impression that with both, actual ethics disappears and is replaced by a natural power; and indeed, with both of them the nearest

Pufendorf

Pufendorf[121] is considered to be the one who implemented the principles laid down by Grotius, and in so doing to have perfected the sociabilist system. If one understands by this that he applied those principles consciously and logically to the subject matter, then that would be inaccurate. Such inner systematic development cannot be found in him, not even to the degree of Grotius

---

expression thereof is the natural law of self-preservation. Yet they differ from the ground up. Certainly, Hobbes founds law and custom on the natural instinct of self-preservation; but what he derives from this natural drive is for him nevertheless a demand such that man should freely fulfill or violate; his law, therefore, is truly ethical (at least regarding the form, i.e., the manner of accomplishment) even though in terms of content it is only physical. By contrast, Spinoza founds law and custom on the power of nature, i.e., the metaphysical necessity of the universe. His law of nature is not to be met by man, but by nature itself and inevitably, and man does not have the freedom to violate it. There is no demand, no ought in the actual sense. The form of ethics is also absent, the working of the law is not ethical but merely natural. The pantheistic position allows ethical content to the law, as for example self-sacrifice (Hegel's doctrine would later demonstrate this), even though there is not much of this to see in Spinoza himself; but it does not allow an ethical mode of action to the law. On the other hand, Spinoza did not share the absolutist result, and indeed he was concerned that he would be categorized together with Hobbes, who was hostilely regarded on this score. A sentence in his *Tractatus* refers to this: "People may not transfer all power to the authorities, because they cannot," and in his letters (*epistola* 50) he himself points up the difference between his doctrine and that of Hobbes: "quod ego naturale jus semper sartum tectum conservo, quodque Supremo Magistratui..., non plus in subditos juris, quam juxta mensuram potestatis, qua subditum superat, competere statuo, quod in statu naturali semper locum habet" [I will always firmly maintain natural right, and that the supreme magistrate ... does not have more of a right over his subjects than according to the degree by which his power exceeds that of a subject, which is always the case in the state of nature]. The position of Spinoza has no other refutation against this absolutism than that such is not possible according to natural law, and where the power of nature is everywhere acknowledged, the difference between the state of nature and the post-contract condition cannot be established.

[121] Pufendorf, *De Jure Naturæ et Gentium, De Officio Hominis & Civis.*

himself. But Pufendorf did implement the material of the ethical and jurisprudential discipline in a completeness and external order that hitherto did not exist, and thus gave to the Grotian doctrine an outward systematic form. Moreover, he brought the philosophy of law into connection with the overall philosophy of his time, as it in the meantime had been founded by Descartes, albeit only superficially, in that his system of natural law presupposes the philosophical results thereof. It must also be recognized as an achievement, that he investigated the anthropological foundations of law – intellect, will, action – precisely in consequence of the general philosophical point of view and thus provided the instigation to cultivate significant legal doctrines, in particular, imputation [Zurechnung]. All this taken together assures him a place in the history of natural law. But that he furthered natural law in terms of content as well, must be denied. He rather renders the notions of Grotius superficial than develops them; he summarizes the drive to sociability not as Grotius does, as mutual benevolence, but merely as mutual need; he decisively renounces the bond with God and the Christian revelation, which Grotius (albeit inconsistently) still maintained, and declared (despite the opposition of theologians) natural human reason to be the sufficient source of moral knowledge; he binds God to the natural law not as Grotius does, by virtue of moral necessity, but because God mechanically cannot maintain people otherwise than via the drive to sociability; he thoroughly confuses the spheres of law and morality, which Grotius separated. In fact, he transforms the pure discipline of law founded by Grotius into a discipline of moral philosophy, a doctrine of duties. Nor did he contribute any new aspects for the systematic expansion of the natural law system. In the final completed form of natural law with Kant, therefore, one is reminded of Grotius, Hobbes, and Thomasius, as those who provided the elements, but not Pufendorf. Rather, his main significance is only the external dissemination of doctrine via his catchy exposition.[122]

---

[122] Pufendorf is best evaluated in Warnkönig, *Rechtsphilosophie* [Legal philosophy], pp. 50ff.

Thomasius (Gundling)

By contrast, Thomasius[123] established inner and indeed essential progress in the discipline of natural law through his separation of morality and law, as was treated in a previous chapter [pp. 106ff.], by which the provisions for inner peace are moral and cannot be compelled, while those for external peace are legal and can be compelled. But this is not a completely new element, because even Grotius himself, as is evident from the above presentation, separated the legal sphere [Rechtsgebiet] from the moral under the names law in the stricter and the broader sense, and ranged them under different principles, the former under the drive to sociability, the latter under the proper valuation of things. Indeed, the innermost character of the doctrine founded by him is precisely that it strives to highlight pure legal principles. But the distinction is not presented by Grotius in clear concepts and is not energetically executed. Hence it was that Grotius' successors blurred, indeed completely lost this distinction: Hobbes derived the duties of compassion, gratitude and the duty to fulfill contracts equally from self-preservation; and in the same manner Pufendorf summarized the right use of language (not to lie) and the right use of things (property) in the same chapter, and the like. With Thomasius, the separation of the two spheres is secured for good, in that he emphasized a different motive or goal (inner and outer peace), a different ethical character (*justum* and *honestum – decorum*)[124] and a different effect (enforceability and unenforceability), hence delimited it in terms of all relations, and set for himself the specific task of implementing the distinction through the entirety of ethics.

Moreover, Thomasius was governed here by a practical motive, which pertained to the innermost driving force of the entire development, by which his distinction procured a very different result than it did with Grotius. For him, namely, the important thing was to keep external force far from the inner moral, especially the religious sphere . It is mainly the interest of freedom of religion that drove him to make the distinction between the two spheres , and

---

[123] Thomasius, *Institutions Jurisprudentiae Divinae; Fundamenta Juris Naturae et Gentium.*

[124] With Thomasius, *decorum* comprehends duties towards others, *honestum* duties to oneself, and therefore they are based on the Pufendorfian system; but both together are opposed to *justum* as a completely separate sphere of coercible duties.

therefore he first formulated it, prior to the publication of his *Fundamente des natürlichen Rechts* [Foundations of Natural Law], for a practical reason, namely to defend the Pietists against religious oppression by the orthodox, which he did in the publication *Das Recht der evangelischen Fürsten in theologischen Streitigkeiten* [The Right of Protestant Princes in Theological Disputes]. This led him to the result that, for the purpose of salvation and thus of piety and faith, no provision of a legal nature, hence coercible, can exist and be maintained,[125] and therefore he emphasized not only, as Grotius did, the different origin and purpose of moral and legal precepts, but also and especially the different effect, the coercibility and uncoercibility thereof. In this regard he brought in one mighty stride not only the scientific system of natural law but also the lively intention that underlies it, closer to the goal, so that Kant only had to apply the finishing touches. This is reflected also in Thomasius' practical achievements, his struggle against torture and the witch trials.

Since then, the formal criterion of the legal sphere [Rechtsgebietes], coercibility, which would not again be forfeited, was especially emphasized and developed by Thomasius' successors, Gundling, Gerhard, Fleischer, *et al.* The distinction between the two spheres, a vital question for Thomasius, became an academic subject and remained so up until Kant. The scientific result of that distinction manifested itself in full evidentness with Gundling, Thomasius' most significant successor. His natural law (*jus naturae et gentium*) is a pure doctrine of law to the exclusion of morality, which he treats in another work under the name of ethics. Gundling is to be regarded as a pure follower of Thomasius, even if he did not admit to it. Certainly, he often goes back to Hobbes and establishes his proper position against widespread misinterpretation. He also seeks to rectify various and sundry controversies according to his own manner, selecting the proper viewpoints from among all previous authors. But his basic concepts

---

[125] In my book *Die Kirchenverfassung nach Lehre und Recht der Protestanten* [The Church Constitution according to the Doctrine and Law of the Protestants], I referred to the erroneous nature of this Thomasian doctrine in relation to the church, by which he confuses coercion regarding individual salvation and individual faith with coercion for the maintenance of ecclesiastical order, hence public doctrine, preaching in the name of the church. See the more detailed treatment of the territorial system founded upon this, in the same place.

and teachings are from Thomasius: happiness as the principle of ethics, its division in terms of outward and inward peace, the restriction of the legal sphere, and the perfect or enforceable obligation, to the former: this is how he constructs natural law. If he sought to found that principle of happiness more deeply, by attributing to the laws given to mortals the object of the conservation and perfection of their nature, while this conservation and perfection consists precisely in happiness – well then, this is hardly worth mentioning.

Wolff (Darjes, Höpfner)

A different method for dealing with natural law came on the scene with Wolff.[126] Wolff deals with natural law entirely as a moral philosopher. The principle he newly issued for morality, the perfection of man, is for him the law or right of nature *tout court*, and he implements it throughout the entire sociable condition. He does not entertain a separation of law and morality like that of Thomasius. While he retains the distinction between perfect or coercible and imperfect or non-coercible obligation, this distinction is incidental, marginal, and does not determine the shape of his system; he did not have a standard, like Thomasius, for determining which duty is coercible and which is not.

For this reason he again divides the entire ethical sphere merely in terms of the moral system, as sketched by Pufendorf: duties towards himself, towards others, toward God; and competence is only the result of (private) obligation, and actually is nothing other than permission: what I am obligated to, I also need to be free to do. Wolff's moral principle is certainly more correct than the earlier one of happiness.[127] But for natural law he accomplished nothing as far as content is concerned, for nowhere did he either enrich or more narrowly specify it. At the most, one can thank him for the development of various concepts: the *status moralis*, which consists in being the subject of law and obligation, the distinction between absolute and hypothetical rights and such like, as a promotion of clarity in the ethical sphere. If anything, he lost the measure and delimitation of the ethical sphere gained by Thomasius and furthered by

---

[126] Wolff, *Jus Naturae Methoda Scientifica Pertractatum* and his *Institutiones Juris Naturae et Gentium*.

[127] Nevertheless, on this point cf. *Philosophical Presuppositions* [Volume II, Book I of this work], §. 29.

Gundling. He took a wrong turn that quickly had to be retraced. On the other hand, he gained significance for the formal or general scientific character of natural law by applying the demonstrative method.

In general, Wolff's philosophy is of a character whereby demonstration is its innermost essence. Other philosophers are led by some material foundational view, which to them is the supreme truth, or at least the supreme problem. For example, Spinoza by the oneness of God, therefore His impersonality and the absorption of the creatures in Him; Leibniz, by contrast, by the formation and existence of independent individual creatures (*principium individuationis*). On the other hand, for Wolff there is no such supreme material truth; rather, for him the syllogism as such is the supreme, only truth. He takes from Leibniz the two principles of demonstration, the principle of non-contradiction (*principium contradictionis*) and the principle of sufficient reason (*principium rationis sufficientis*), and implements them through the entire sphere of knowledge. That which he and every other person knows, he presents in the form that it does not contradict itself (because "the essence of a thing is its possibility," that is, precisely conceivability, non-contradiction) in that everywhere he takes the features from the definition which he himself put in it (according to experience), which then for him is valid as having been demonstrated. For example, "seeing is founded in the essence of an animal that has eyes," thus it is a characteristic thereof, which obviously is to say nothing other than that seeing is the characteristic of a sighted animal.[128]

The most characteristic aspect of this method and of Wolff's intellectual organization is that he thinks that we have no immediate certainty even of our own being, but gain it (even if, for most, this occurs without realizing it) only by means of a deduction: "If we wish clearly to realize how we are convinced by these reasons, that we are, then we will find that the following conclusion is contained in this thought: Whoever is aware of the being of himself and of other things, is. We are aware of our being and that of other things. Therefore

---

[128] When Wolff allows himself to act beyond this purely analytical manner, it goes badly for him. Thus, for example, he proves: because God had to create that which is most perfect, the planets must have inhabitants. He could just as well have proven from the perfection of the divine creation that people do not have to have only legs, but also wings.

we are."[129] Hence not even Wolff believes that he is, if he is not convinced by reasons for it. Wolff also applies this syllogistic method to the ethical sphere, and if in itself this is nothing more than an absurdity, nevertheless the requirement which underlies the rationalist philosophy, to find results purely from reason, is thereby first actuated, and the inevitable alternative is therewith posed for a subsequent, more rigorous scientific conception, of either abandoning this requirement, or making an attempt really to use bare concepts of reason. Wolff's demonstrative treatment of the entirety of philosophy and hence the philosophy of law has no other value than that of being an impetus for Kant to take the rationalist principle seriously.

Subsequent legal-philosophical treatment closely adhered to Wolff. Yet there was still the need, even without full awareness of it, to return to the more correct position of Thomasius that had been lost. Wolff's most significant and most successful student, Darjes, indeed retained the entire structure of the Wolffian ethical system, but he used the second part, obligations towards others, to derive the Thomasian segment, the field of compulsory duties, or, as he calls it, to gain "jurisprudence" as opposed to "ethics." But with Höpfner the diminution of the Wolffian system and the return of the Thomasian one is on full display. Höpfner unites the perfectibility- and happiness-principle and treats them synonymously; he departs from the Pufendorfian-Wolffian division of natural law into three classes of obligations, and instead delimits his discipline according to Thomasius' and Gundling's method as the doctrine of "natural compulsory duties." Nor does he treat primarily of obligations in order to derive rights from them, but rather everywhere originally treats of rights. At the same time, the way in which the general texture of ideas leads to Kant is already reflected in him, in that the will is already roundly asserted to be the ultimate principle of rights, thus especially in the deduction of property as well as contract. Wolff's doctrine in relation to legal philosophy is only a provocative episode between Thomasius and Kant.

---

[129] Wolff, *Vernünfftige Gedancken von Gott, der Welt und der Seele des Menschen, auch allen Dingen überhaupt* [Rational Notions of God, the World, and the Soul of Man, likewise All Things in General], §. 6.

Opponents of Natural Law (Selden, Coccejus, "Dubia Jura Naturae")

Resistance to the natural law system was by no means lacking during this period of its development and rule. Such resistance stemmed from the accurate realization that the natural law system completely dissolves the bond between the human world and God. Selden and Coccejus take this position,[130] as does Crusius later on, in relation to moral philosophy. But these opponents were not able to indicate either the innermost seat of error and separation from God, nor were they able to provide any doctrine maintaining the bond with God which scientifically sufficed.

Selden objected to the grounding of natural law on mere human reason by referring to the absence of a binding power in human reason, and the conflict of reason among a number of people and doctors, which all point to a higher author of, and a higher sanction for, natural law. But his own reasoning contains nothing further than this: the natural law that comes from God has an obligative and a permissive component; the obligative is that we must remain faithful to the contracts and state constitutions that we, again by contract, have entered into (*pactis ac regiminum formulis civiliter initis standum*); the permissive is that the sphere left free [frei gelassene Sphäre] can be precisely determined by the people through their agreement in a binding manner,[131] however, the binding force does not arise from the contract as such (*ex simplici hominum ratione et consensu*) but from God's permission that they by mutual agreement prohibit or enjoin what is free in itself (*ex consensu mutuo inhibere*). Finally, however,

---

[130] Selden, *De Jure Naturali et Gentium*, in particular Book I, chs. 7 and 8. Henricus Coccejus, *Disputatio Juridica Inauguralis de Principio Juris Naturalis Unico, Vero, et Adaequato* [Inaugural Juridical Disputation regarding the Only True and Adequate Starting Point of Natural Law], and in particular in the *Positiones pauculae & generalissimae loco quasi postulatorum explicationi juris gentium & praelectionibus Grotianis praemissae*.

[131] "Simulatque ex ejusmodi permissione quid ab hominibus sociatis coercitum, vetitum seu constitutum est, ad illud in quod sic consenserant ipsi (sive pacto sive deditione sive aliter) .... observandum obligatos esse" [Similarly from such permission by which human society coerces, prohibits, or appoints, regarding that to which they consented (whether agreement or capitulation or whatever) ... they are obliged to observe it]. Book I, ch. 8, p. 106).

God's laws are promulgated by the revelation in Scripture, which are mandatory everywhere and of necessity.

Hence Selden fought a side of the natural law system that was the least relevant, because the natural law doctors themselves often and gladly admitted that obligation has its final (remote) ground in God, and his own result coincides with natural law's in the essential thing, that at the origin contracts are the source of all law. The only thing in which he has the advantage is that, clinging to the divine origin of all moral precepts, he can vindicate the supreme position for the immediately revealed commandments, which the exclusively rational moralists left completely sidelined.

Coccejus essentially agrees with Selden in his polemic: he does not see a binding power in human reason and (admittedly less decisively expressed) a content for commandments necessarily arising from the principle of social and peaceful life. His own doctrine, however, which he sets in opposition, is more thoughtful and decisive than that of Selden. The divine will, which he makes into the principle, is to be recognized from His deeds and works and the perfection of the divine essence (without any mention of revelation). From this will proceeds the entirety of the commandments of natural law – freedom of action, the prohibition of harm to another, the necessity of the common life among men (*societas communis*) and the rights which arise therefrom, the legal effects of declarations of intent, disposition over one's own, the right of inheritance of children, domestic authority, the necessity of the state, the regard for and power of the magistracy – rather than by means of contract or deduction from one simple principle, which supposedly includes everything.

To this degree Coccejus truly opposed the error in that system, the ratiocination and foundation of the legal system on the human will and contract; and the accusation lodged against him at the time, that he did not teach anything different than Pufendorf, because the latter also recognized reason to be a work of God, was unfounded. But there is lacking, firstly, any mediation between the divine will (His deeds, His perfection) and the results that Coccejus teaches to be the content thereof; we do not see how the inheritance of children, regard for government, and so on, follow from divine perfection; secondly, the ethical and legal order in itself is not at all comprehended by him, indeed he contributed little to their deeper understanding; it is all set down as positive [as opposed to natural], and indeed the basic concepts thereof (the concept of law, competence, and the like) are much less sufficiently and correctly comprehended than with Grotius and his more significant successors.

And so, such opposition to natural law achieved nothing.

Other objections to the same thing, especially as recited by the author of the then highly celebrated writing *Dubia juris naturae,* were based on mere skepticism and therefore even less likely to affect its reign.

Chapter 3: Kant's System

Kant's Doctrine

As is well known, the train of Kant's system is this: we form all our knowledge by means of certain forms and concepts which we do not draw from experience, but which we must already have within us before we are capable of experiencing, as for example the relationship between cause and effect. We would never consider the real causes and effects in these conditions to be anything but isolated phenomena if this relationship were not already implanted before all perception. The embodiment of these forms of thought and law is reason.

The question is now whether reason, without which we cannot experience, is also able to furnish us with perceptions apart from experience (*a priori*). Here we are not speaking of such perceptions which contains nothing but what reason itself is, a mere extension of what lies in the essence of those forms (analytic knowledge), for example, that the cause precedes the effect, which indeed the concept of cause declares. Rather, this has to do with the perception of objects outside of those forms (synthetic knowledge), for example, God, immortality. The question is, "are *a priori* synthetic judgments possible?"

This is the question that rational philosophy of necessity must raise when it has arrived at consciousness of itself; in fact, it is that in which its consciousness consists. The result of Kant's investigation is this: we have no pure rational knowledge (no *a priori* synthetic judgment). For reason only vouchsafes the form of knowledge, while the material comes to us through experience, i.e., by means of the impressions of external objects upon our senses. Only both factors together provide knowledge. For example, the statement of pure reason: "everything that occurs has a cause," is not yet knowledge; a specific occurrence and a specific something that is its cause are obligatory for it to become knowledge. All our knowledge, then, is experience-knowledge, and beyond possible experience, hence of extrasensory [übersinnlichen] things that do not affect our senses (God, freedom), we can have no knowledge at all.

But more than this: Even our actual knowledge, thus experience-knowledge, is untrue, for we only attain it through the medium of our two sensory perceptions, *space* and *time*, and these are merely our (subjective) inherent forms without truthful (objective) existence. It is not the existence of things that is subject to doubt, but the opposite: without them, we would have no sensory impressions and thus no conceptualizations at all. Only its true quality (*"the thing in itself"*) is not perceived, because things (objectively) do not exist in space and time, even though we can only observe them as they are in space and time. Our perceptions therefore obtain only phenomena, not the things in themselves. And the objects of our knowledge (not, of course, the objects in themselves) comply with our manner of perception, and not the other way around.

The sum is this: we have absolutely no perception of transcendental things, and our perception of sensory things is mistaken, it yields us only the phenomenon, not the thing in itself.

This, then, would be a renunciation of all knowledge. But now comes help: all of this is only true of theoretical reason, that is, thought directed to perceiving objects that exist outside of itself. By contrast, practical reason, that is, thought directed to the generation of objects (actions) that are not already in existence, thus where it manifests itself as Ought, discovers these objects as goal without external impressions on the senses and therefore apart from the medium of space and time, purely from its own laws. To wit, there is a commandment of the good within us, which we do not derive from experience and which commands us to do the good without taking experience into consideration, i.e., without taking a consequence, a utility, a convenience to us, into account, but only for the sake of the good – a "categorical imperative." This then is pure rational knowledge. From this unconditional commandment of the good follow, purely *a priori*, freedom, immortality, God: freedom, because without it a commandment would be preposterous; *immortality* or a world beyond this world, because reward and punishment do not follow upon fulfillment or violation of that which reason consistently must require; *God*, because without Him reward and punishment could not be realized. Practical reason, accordingly, is the area in which truly pure rational knowledge (*a priori* synthetic judgment) exists; through it alone, therefore, we gain knowledge of transcendental things, and only its perceptions are true and reliable, while theoretical perceptions, because they borrow from experience, are fictitious.

Its Scientific Motivation

Obviously this fictitious nature of all experience which Kant takes as the basis, is not mere doubt but a positive confident assertion, and at once presents itself as the actual character of his system. How Kant was forced into this conception must be demonstrated in order to clarify the essence of the critical philosophy.

The basis upon which it rests is the assumption that space and time, chiefly time, is merely a notion pertaining to our own sensorial nature, corresponding to nothing in the object. Certainly, from the fictitiousness of the notion of time, Kant inferred that time has no subsisting and inherent existence in things, and therefore is not a derived concept. But such reasoning about an individual element of knowledge cannot possibly be the deepest mainspring of a system upon which a philosophical epoch is grounded. With the same reasoning, Kant could have denied the truthfulness and objectivity of all logical forms (ground and consequent – unconditional). Rather, a much deeper mainspring underlies it which itself determines this line of thought.

Every glimpse of the world shows change, act. But rational coherence is timeless – "universal and necessary." Should Kant wish to recognize this changing world, he would have to recognize a cause and a coherence of the same, which is not reason, and therefore cannot be discovered by reason. That would be impossible for it, because it would contradict the basic conception of rational philosophy. If he should wish to deny the existence of changing things, then he would also find this to be impossible, in that he very well saw and declared that without the existence of these things it would be absolutely impossible to comprehend why we imagine this or that and not always the same thing,[132] and that the thought forms are not yet knowledge unto themselves [für sich], but require an object and content to arrive at knowledge.[133]

There remained only one escape for him: maintain both: there is rational coherence, *and* things really exist, and only deny the rock of offense, the mutable character of the latter. He builds his system upon this foundation. Space and time are only fictitious because they are the forms of mutability. In Kant's view, if we weren't bound to these forms, "the same determinations which we now perceive as change, would yield a perception in which the conceptualization of time and *thereby that of change* would not even arise,"[134] and in that case we

---

[132] *Critik der reinen Vernunft*, pp. 274, 275.

[133] *Ibid.*, p. 146.

[134] *Ibid.*, p. 54.

would recognize the true nature of things. But now, space and time are the medium for all knowledge of extant objects; this can, then, only yield phenomena.
In this way he solves the difficulty in which he denies mutability, causality, act,
along with time, indeed denies reality itself as nothing other than "time-filler,"
so that only mere logical relations remain; everything shrinks to mere determinations of thought as in a mathematical point.[135] This is the basic viewpoint that
rationalistic philosophy by no means derives from investigation, but rather unconsciously smuggles into the investigation. Kant believes he can flee from such
a result's absence of result, to the area of practice. That is to say, thought as ethical demand requires objects that are timeless, eternal, immutable. For it was the
undoubted presumed conception of his time, that the ethic be a system of bare
logically connected rules, and this conceptualization cannot be refuted as mere
logical coherence in physical things could, by any and every glance at the world.
But the ethic could only therefore be assumed to be such a system if it were
based upon bare rational coherence. Here or nowhere could pure *a priori* be
recognized, and the results thereby attain the certainty of logical laws. God, immortality, and freedom had to be demonstrated on these grounds in order to be
elevated beyond any doubt.

Kant's Relation to Spinoza

Thus, this entire system develops from the basic assumption of rationalism:
there is no change. Spinoza asserts the rational coherence of the actual world.
Kant, by contrast – both the later Kant, and the Kant prompted to investigate

---

[135] For Kant, even our *a priori* function is contaminated by the mixture of a false perception of time. That is to say, even the *a priori* judgment, in that it applies the categories
to an object (if not to a specific one, then to any conceivable object) which comes to our
observation from the sensory world, contain a time relation, e.g., "that which occurs has
a cause" is constructed upon the unity of time, denying thereby that anything can begin
anew, or can drop out of the unity of time. For this reason our judgments *a priori* are by
no means valid for the objective relation, but only for our experience. They are the foundational principles according to which alone we can have an experience, but they are
not the laws of the objective world. Accordingly, Kant even establishes contradictions
("antinomies") in reason itself, in connection with its supreme conclusions or ideas,
which have their origin in the fact that they everywhere are based on the view of time.

by the Wolffian school's endeavor – gained the insight that the world of experience does not allow the problem to be solved, because we here find undeniable
change, freedom, act. He therefore abandons this world as fictitious, and flees
from it with his rule of reason into another, which he first fabricates by his
thought, in which he is capable of completing the task because he first arranges
it in terms of the task.

He seeks something unconditional, a *causa sui* in Spinoza's sense, i.e., such a
one that is not, like God, the first that *is*, but is the first in terms of what we
think of. For him, this is the notion of unconditionality itself, with the character
of universality and necessity that necessarily adheres to it. From this, likewise
according to logical laws, all actions must flow; in this consists the ethic. It may
produce nothing else, or else the absolute would no longer be what its concept
testifies, the foundation of the conditioned.

For this reason it postulates freedom of the will. That is to say, it denies that
it is determined by covetousness (thus by objects outside of thought), but it
likewise rejects every motive outside of rational thought itself – love, enthusiasm, as well as self-interest – as being contrary to morality. Hence, reason requires actions categorically, unconditionally, only as consequences of itself.
Good and evil are not characteristics that precede our thought, and condition
it; rather, they first arise through the form of universality and necessity that un-
derlie our thought.[136] But the ought itself is yet a real power and contains in
itself the notion of change, since an action is to be generated which does not yet
exist. It therefore had to be referred to the world of phenomena. Thought manifests itself to us as ought, the imperative, as commandment and prohibition,
only because we belong to the fictitious world of change. Apart from this, there
would be no question of ought; rather, reason itself would faultlessly accomplish the actions that flow from it;[137] considered more precisely: there would be
no ought and no act; rather, reason would exist simultaneously with its consequences. Not only the condition of action but also the condition of the intelligible world would be deduced from that absolute. As a statement of universality
(non-contradiction) it contains the agreement of the act corresponding to it
and its consequences for happiness, thus a condition of allocation according to

---

[136] *Critik der reinen Vernunft*, p. 102.

[137] *Ibid.*, p. 36.

desert ("the highest good") and a world disposer that makes this happen – God. The latter, as product of that absolute, is therefore bound to the law thereof, and cannot exercise pardon and grace. The actual God is therefore also in this intelligible world the abstract thought of logical universality and necessity, a God without understanding and will, as with Spinoza.

Contradiction in Kant's Demand on Reason

This makes clear that Kant completely grasped and followed the canon of Spinoza. The construction of his intelligible ordering is arranged entirely in accordance with it, even though for the things of observation he surrenders it. For this reason, a double world runs through the Kantian system: that of the phenomenon, i.e., the real coherence of act and event, and that of the essence, i.e., logical coherence. Spinoza, for his part, solely recognized the latter, and believed he had resolved the former only because he insufficiently took it into account. For Spinoza, the world as we observe it is merely the unconditional in terms of its concept, with its necessary consequences. Kant identifies these observations as something wholly other, and therefore also as fictitious; but for him as well, the ethical actions, the intelligible ordering, i.e., the true existence of things, is only the substance which underlies all thought (universality and necessity) and its modalities. Spinoza denies freedom (the choice to do this or that) in the real world. Kant accepts it and names it freedom of choice [Willkür]; but at the same time he denies it in the true world, where everything is necessity: reason contains the actions appropriate to it, the last judgment [das Weltgericht], etc., without choice [Wahl]. This unavoidable determination by reason Kant calls freedom of the will [des Willens] in contrast to freedom of choice [Willkür]. With Spinoza nothing can occur in the real world which is not necessary and thus just. The distinction between good and evil drops out; but with Kant such can occur, and it is only in the kingdom that we ourselves have to construct, or that lies beyond our experience, that this infallibility lies. He therefore does not need to justify the evil shown by experience; in the realm of phenomena he can praise and reject, and is empowered to establish tasks which are not already fulfilled, and for which – as we see ourselves – we are given the choice, and so can contrive a real ethics.

It turns out, then, that both of these apparently scarcely related systems, which above all construct the shrillest contradictions in ethics, nevertheless in turn are based on one and the same basic requirement.

Usurpation on behalf of Practical Reason

Kant is generally accused of a string of inconsistencies, but these have their deep-seated origin in the task that he gives to all philosophy, which he must of necessity give to it, holding fast as he did to rational philosophy while nevertheless not being blinded by it. For this task is in itself contradictory. He requires synthetic perceptions from pure reason, i.e., perceptions in which predicates are not derived from a concept, are not already given with that concept, but to which others are added, which are not contained in it. "Which are not contained in it" – what is that, other than: those which, according to reason, are not inseparable from the existence of reason, thus are not bound to reason through a cause outside of reason. If Kant thereby only wanted rational coherence and knowledge from reason, he would have required no synthetic judgment, he would simply have had to deny the possibility of such. Or, there is synthesis. There are effects, predicates, which are not contained in their causes, but could be produced or omitted by them. In that case, however, there is, truthfully, act and change, even if the form of time and space would be the prejudice of the senses. In that case, it is not possible to consider the relation of things as truthfully immutable, because it is change; nor to recognize it through the power of necessity (reason), because it is something free; nor as *a priori*, because it is directed not in terms of the laws of thought but in terms of causes which precipitate change.

We might attempt to consider this dilemma even to be a product of our prejudice, the truth being that the unchangeable is in fact a connection of new, and thus an object of synthetic, knowledge; but that would be inconceivable to us. That would have pushed us beyond all ground of human thought and imagination, where no further examination could follow; but such an appeal would by no means be in Kant's spirit. For he only rejects the forms of sensory observation, not the logical law of contradiction. But now it is demonstrated that without reference to time and space, simply in terms of thought, synthetic knowledge and change are inseparable concepts, while synthetic knowledge and mere rational coherence (thus discovery from reason) contradict each other.

Basis of the Deception

Therefore, it is quite natural that this greatest of all investigators, who by virtue of the strict account he everywhere renders, undoubtedly lays claim to the rank of the most thoroughgoing and venerable of all rational philosophers, was led by his investigations to this place: reason vouchsafes no synthetic knowledge in the theoretical sphere. But when in the practical sphere he nevertheless commits the contradiction, he is deceived by the following mistake: our sense of ought, the drive, the longing within us, really precedes all sensory impressions, and to that degree is *a priori,* and certainly also has a synthetic force; it impels us to certain actions, requires conditions, and points with certainty to a relation with God, the future, and blessedness. *But this drive is not reason,* it is a real power, and in terms of its innermost essence continues to have an effect as act and change, by no means in a logical manner, by no means according to the nature of reason. It is also, even though free of visible influences and elevated above them, still not an initiating cause but rather effected by a higher cause preceding it and distinguished from it. Precisely the character in it by which it is what it is, and by which it alone can have the synthetic power to generate something from itself, namely what is real, what is capable of action – it is precisely this character that Kant denies to it and declares to be a delusion. What he allows to remain to it as truthful, the emptied thought of the *a priori,* is what the synthetic power does not have. He thus makes use of the actual drive (which he denied) in order to attribute its force to thought, which in terms of its nature it cannot have.

Three Resulting Inconsistencies in his Practical Philosophy

From this stem the inconsistencies in Kant's practical reason, among which these three can be distinguished: that a real moral law follows from pure reason; that on the basis of this moral law, not only actions but general conditions can be commanded; and finally, that not merely practical but also theoretical knowledge can be derived from it.

The world of action, in which, because knowledge is directed toward what exists, thought is transcended, is precisely what Kant needs for the knowledge of what is to be produced. Like every idea, every commandment must also have an object, and this – the act, the human relation – pertains to the world which he regards as mere appearance, and which thoroughly bears that character. He cannot escape the fact that the essence of practical reason itself does not otherwise appear to us, for it is affected by this world, as an ought, as a free production of something new. The rational law of universality and necessity can as little be a practical commandment as can the categories, or the unity of apperception, be knowledge. If in accordance with this law of reason Kant assumes the content, "act in such a way that all rational creatures can exist in accordance therewith," then he has thus drawn upon the entire world of appearance, and that which he denied in theoretical philosophy, he acknowledges as true. Because living things, and the fact that they may exist or be annihilated – pure thought knows nothing of them. That a wound yields death, that deprivation of food causes hunger, which one does not have from eternity, in short, continued existence and destruction, all of these are change, already in terms of thought. The highest truth and the summit of the system, the last judgment [das Weltgericht], presupposes that there has been action, and arbitrary action; that there has been alteration, and thus analytically contains that which is categorically denied. How can practical reason, since it must draw upon experience, extend beyond the limits of possible experience, and how can truth arise? But if it does not draw on experience, the law of universality and necessity requires nothing other than that something not cancel itself, and this something is again nothing other than the form of conceptual unity itself, as it also underlies theoretical reason. The only content that the imperative can have is that thought be thought.

If reason is the cause of the practical commandments and therefore determines their content, then they, as shown above, can only make demands on the actions of the individual. Yet in Kant, their object is also the existence of general conditions, for example the state, directly and in its entirety, or punishment as retributive justice. Kant confesses that this contradicts the original essence of reason, but that it is capable of "expanding itself *a priori* by such postulates." But reason is not capable of such an expansion, such a pursuit of the world outside us; only the real drive of the ought within us is capable of this.

Through such expansion, Kant finally also succeeds in deriving theoretical results from practical thought. Namely, God, immortality, the last judgment, regarding which practical reason does not vouchsafe the insight that we effectuate them, or that they *should* exist, but that they really *do* exist, where, therefore, practical reason, contrary to its own concepts, is directed not to the production of objects but to the knowledge of existing ones. In this, Kant is supported by his denial of time and change; for with this the difference between theoretical and practical knowledge is really abolished; future and present, will and being become the same. The act, the choice, which, already in terms of words separates the practical from the theoretical, is precisely what is abandoned as untrue.

Now here as well, the inner contradiction of the system should be most striking. Because reason calls for conditions of a certain sort, Kant recognizes the truth of its requirement (the future, which depends upon choice), but not the fulfillment thereof, for example, that a state should actually exist. But in invoking conditions of another sort, he recognizes not only the requirement but also the fulfillment as being inevitable, e.g., God, immortality, the last judgment. He should have said: Reason demands the state, criminal justice, God, the last judgment; and its requirement, its ought-to-exist is true, and it is so because reason commands it, which can have no other standard of truth; but whether they really exist is a question with which practical reason has nothing to do. Or, he had to say: that which practical reason demands, also exists necessarily – but in that case, not only God and immortality, but also the universal reasonableness of our actions; and this obviously contradicts the facts.

This is Kant's attitude toward rational dogmatism, both the consistent version of Spinoza and the vague arbitrary one of the Wolffian school. The latter deduce the existing world of change from its unchanging laws of thought. Kant shows this to be contradictory, but then he himself makes the same contradiction, by deducing from just such premises a moral world which also includes action and change.

Impetus to Further Development: Transcendental Philosophy, Result of Fichte's and Kant's Standpoints

The essence of Kant's criticism contained the impulse toward a completely new development. The contradiction between pure thought and the real world produced his system, and his activity, therefore, had to be directed toward sharply separating these opposites. Hence, rational philosophy was not merely brought to the consciousness of its enterprise, but also brought to inward awareness, since the separation makes reason an object of its own reflection. Those who preceded him contemplated the world, into which they tacitly transported thought. Kant contemplated thought itself. In technical terms: this is the emergence of transcendental philosophy, the philosophy which observes its own consciousness, while it takes up its objects, looks upon the activity, the means of which it makes use.

This measured separation of the faculty of knowledge from its objects, however, necessarily provokes a new philosophical question, namely, how is not merely the perception of the truth possible, but perceptibility at all? How do the two divorced worlds, reason and the objects outside of reason, unite into one idea, even though it be erroneous? This question is deeply rooted in the essence of abstract philosophy and the subjective principle. The man who breaks away from the world must wonder: how can this world still excite conceptions in me? The investigations of Descartes, Spinoza, and Leibniz on the connection between the body and the soul are already echoes of it. Now, however, the entire fate of philosophy is laid upon its shoulders, and at present it is crowding out everything else which ultimately must be dealt with, which Kant himself pronounced to be the actual tasks, those regarding God, immortality, freedom. The development of philosophy is now continuing on this path, and it is as if humanity will have attained its goal if it could explain how it came to conceptualize anything.

The explanation which first presents itself, of which Kant therefore, as the starting point, avails himself, is this: things make sensory impressions upon us, we lend to these impressions the form of reason, and both together make up conceptualization. But a close inspection reveals the inadequacy of this explanation, and this led to the system of Fichte. The impression on the senses, namely, is quite without reason, it being purely physical; it cannot, therefore, become something intelligible, no matter the elevation; otherwise, one would be able to construct thinking just as well by using physical ingredients. A thing is not a thought and can never become a thought, and the thought form can only be affected by a thought, not by a body and a physical effect. Hence, the connection between the two would be impossible. Kant did not here, in theoretical reason, usurp the *truth* of imagination, as he did in his practical deductions, but rather the *existence* thereof.

But why is it that he cannot establish a connection between reason and things, since, as experience shows, such really exists? The reason for this, as

Fichte demonstrates, [138] is that he contemplates reason as a static form, and consequently as a thing. A thing and another thing that is set over against it, will always remain apart. It was therefore necessary to regard reason as active; not as the determinations of thought and laws, but as the *activity of thought*. This was the precondition for explaining this connection.

In what manner it was to be explained, however, was in turn motivated for Fichte by the stage of the Kantian system. The previous philosophy generally had the conviction that only reason is true. Kant shared this conviction, but at the same time expressed what it entails, namely, that things are untrue. Nevertheless he asserted their truth, but only as a veiled one. But this cannot mean anything other than: if things had been properly recognized, it would have to be understood that they too are nothing but reason, but that means that they are *not* – the *only* thing that is, is *reason*. Kant thus unconsciously asserted it, and Fichte had only to explain it.

But in doing so he completed his explanation of conceptualization. In other words, reason is both the forms of thought and the things, but it is both only by producing them in their activity. If, for example, the relation of cause and effect, which is of reason and not of experience, is analyzed, then there is already in it this, that a thing produces another thing. Hence, pure reason contains objects, and the Kantian distinction cannot be preserved at all; rather, the inevitable spillover from the form of reason to the object outside of it proves that they are not separate things – indeed, they are not things at all – but only products of an undivided activity. Thus one can no longer ask how, by means of matter and the capacity to conceptualize, conceptualization and knowing are possible, for it is not matter, nor the capacity to conceptualize, but merely conceptualization and knowing.

This step was thus inevitable for rationalism, since it insisted that there was no truth outside of reason, and yet had to make comprehensible the possibility of a conceptualization.

---

[138] This transition from Kant to Fichte is manifested most vividly in the essays of the latter in his and Niethammer's *Philosophischen Journal* [Philosophical Journal].

Chapter 4: Kant's Doctrine of Law

Fulfillment of the Rationalistic Character
Kant resolutely extended the rationalistic character of ethics and natural law to its farthest limit, and executed it with deliberation. In the practical field, too, he excluded all that is empirical, all that comes from objects other than the laws of thought, and sought the sum of the ethical only in the latter. This is the position he occupies in the development of moral and legal philosophy.

He confessed without hesitation the assertion of Grotius, and the so-called *perseitas* [perseity] of the good, without making a distinction between *principium cognoscendi* and *principium obligationis*: God can be imagined to be the author of obligation vis-à-vis the law, and furthermore to be the one to whom everyone owes obedience *according to* a law, but not to be the author of the law itself – this is, and can only be, reason; otherwise the law would be contingent.[139] God is so little the author of the law that He himself stands under it. Even God can act in no other way than under a maxim or such-like, may only treat other rational beings as ends, not as means, must conceive of Himself as a participant in the kingdom of ends, even though the chief one, cannot add anything to the content and motive of the moral law,[140] and thus is the constitutional monarch of the kingdom of reason.

Kant also expressly states something that his predecessors only groped after: there is no ethic in the relations and dealings of life (as something made by God and not reason), but only in what remains in our thinking after all abstraction. From here it enters first into actions and then into relations. Hence for Kant it is not a question of the nature of the individual act which interferes with the real world, which either fulfills or abandons its purpose, but only of the general rules which have been formulated without regard for the present, principles for which the goal of all action is not to contradict them. This shows what Grotius

---

[139] Kant, *Metaphysische Anfangsgründe der Rechtslehre*, p. xxviii [p. 19 of *The Metaphysics of Morals*].

[140] Kant, *Grundlegung zur Metaphysik der Sitten* [Foundation of the Metaphysics of Morals], pp. 74, 75, 85.

and Pufendorf were after when the former[141] asserted that the moral laws do not have the certainty of geometry because they cannot be separated from matter, while the latter asserted the mathematical certainty thereof, and writes of the necessary instability of relations in such a way that the moral law is by no means affected by them. [142] He was impelled, although less clearly, by the idea that the ethic exists only as a rule, and not as an act.

In the same sense Kant separates the motives of the will. Nothing in which the will is determined by an object outside of thought – pleasure, desire, affection, love – is an ethical motive. The only ethical motive is respect for the law, and indeed, the law of reason. Laudable acts out of the love of God or man are as little moral as are laudable acts out of ambition and selfishness. Inclination and love, far from increasing the ethical quality of the act, rather detract from it, as Schiller's epigram justly brings out:

> Willingly serve I my friends;
> but, alas, I do it with pleasure;
> Therefore I often am vex'd
> that no true virtue I have. [143]

Finally, for Kant the content of all ethics is solely the law of thought, consistency. His predecessors, even philosophers like Leibniz, had everything that should exist be a requirement of reason, and suddenly the content of the good for them is again love, humanity, equal rewards and punishments, without their being aware of and explaining how these are required by the laws of thought, or even connected with them. But Kant accepts nothing as ethical of which he is not at least convinced that thought itself contains it inevitably, and therefore ruthlessly eliminates everything regarding which he is consciously aware that such a proof is impossible. For Kant, the moral law must be *categorical*, not hypothetical (valid only under certain conditions of experience). It must therefore be *merely formal*, that is, have no object, no content, no material. As such, the moral law is nothing other than the law of thought: universality and non-

---

[141] Grotius, *De Jure Belli ac Pacis*, Book II, ch. 23, §. 1.

[142] Pufendorf, *De Jure Naturæ et Gentium*, Book I, ch. 2, §. 9.

[143] *The Poems of Schiller*, trans. E.A. Bowring (New York: John B. Alden, 1883), p. 268.

contradiction. It reads: act according to a maxim which, made into a universal law, does not contradict itself (actually, which made into a universal law does not destroy the social state of the world of experience). Or, according to a different expression: act according to a categorical purpose, that is, not according to something that you posit arbitrarily, but something that every rational being must posit. Nevertheless, there is only one such purpose: reason or the rational being itself, and therefore: you must have the rational being, both yourself and other rational beings besides you, as an end (here Kant unknowingly confuses reason/the law of thought/consistency and the rational being/personality/the real subject).

From here he constructs the moral world; for him, it is a kingdom of ends, inasmuch as all the rational beings set themselves the purpose of treating themselves and one another simply as ends. According to all of this, the good, as Kant himself emphatically emphasizes, is not an original concept which thought discovers; rather, it follows from the law of thought, as derivative.

In the same manner, in the theory of law, external freedom is first shown to be contained in the essence of reason, in the notion of the absolute, of universality and necessity. It goes like this: the nature of reason is that it itself, i.e., its law of necessity, is the original and solely effectuating factor in action. For this it is necessary that the will *really* not be determined by impressions of the outer world (which implies as a postulate that it must have the *possibility* of not being determined thereby – freedom of the will). Such impressions of the world are twofold: desires aroused from within, and force from without. Thought must surmount both in order to be the absolute. By requiring the first, it is the moral, by the second, it is the juridical law. Morality is therefore internal legislation, self-compulsion; juridical law is outward legislation, removal of outward force, coercion of others.[144]

But because the concept of external freedom has been gained from reason,

---

[144] Hence, it is not the subject aiming at this rational, that is, aprioristic action, who is coerced by juridical law, as with morality; rather, it is others who are so coerced. In this manner reason, because it dictates moral and juridical law, secretly switches the subjects to whom it speaks. This follows from the inconsistency criticized above, that Kant allows reason to dictate objective conditions. Its command here is really this: on the one hand, *you shall* overcome your desire, on the other, *it shall not be* that you be coerced!

it everywhere becomes a subject of investigation as to whether the opposite of a given institution [Anstalt] would contradict this concept – for only then is it recognized. For example: "It is possible to have each external object of my will as my own. Suppose there to be a maxim entailing that such an object of the will must remain ownerless. If this were made into a law, it would be *repugnant* to law."[145] In this manner, Kant stands on the same level as his time, which tore apart everything that was not necessary in this manner. Institutions [Institute] of feudal law, the church, which claimed their place in the natural law of the older protagonists, are expelled from it. The national economy collapses, and taxation falls only under the purview of the protection of rights. Kant was the first theoretically to derive institutions which do not follow from freedom but which nevertheless cannot be done away with in any actual state, as means for those that do – such as maintenance of the poor, education, the prohibition of public immorality, public health, contributions to the church. He has been followed in this expedient of his by the entire mass of modern proponents of constitutional law, as well as the natural-law textbooks.

Recognizing the world of phenomena alongside reason, Kant found the laws by subsuming the various materials under the general rule of reason. He thus fell into the same necessity as the others, not merely of subsuming objects of experience, but taking the ordinary effects of them as [if they were] premises of the rule itself. Yet Kant was the first to realize that this does not accord with the philosophy of reason; he knew what *continuo ratiocinationis filo deducere* [continuous deduction of the thread of reasoning] means. He tried to prove that he did not discover the state through this observation, but without much success.[146]

This finalization of the abstract character therefore corresponds to the fact that, since Kant, the philosophy of law changed its name. The earlier prac-

---

[145] *Ibid.*, p. 56, §2.

[146] *Metaphysische Anfangsgründe der Rechtslehre*, §. 35, p. 192. [*The Metaphysics of Morals*, pp. 89–90.] Kant here demonstrates *a priori* that people are not simply [the embodiment of] reason, but also at times unjust to each other, as well as aberrant in their judgments. This is something that Pufendorf demonstrates more appropriately from experience: *quis est, qui ignoret?* in *De Jure Naturæ et Gentium*, Book VII, ch. 1, §. 10. Cf. pp. 134ff. above.

titioners, as shown above, had some empirical drive as principle, and only the inference from this was purely rational. For them, therefore, the expression inherited from the Romans, *natural law*, was still appropriate. But the principle of Kant being consistency, thought-necessity itself, the only characteristic name now is the *law of reason*.

Restriction of the Subjective Character

But if Kant in one fell swoop finalized the rationalism of ethical laws, by comparison he comported himself toward the subjective principle in such a way as partly not to favor it, and partly even to prevent its development. For the acting man and his freedom belong to the world, a world which Kant maintains is untrue, and although Kant necessarily tolerates him, like he does this world generally, he subordinates him to his higher world, the law of reason. This manifests itself both in the scientific deduction of the basic concepts and in the results of his legal doctrine.

Legal freedom is not given for man's sake and does not follow from his living existence, but follows from the existence of the forms of reason, and exists so that one may act *a priori*, that is, so that thereby the logical law is the first cause of an intelligible world. It is not so much the freedom of the individual, as the thought of freedom which is the same to everyone (the maxim of coexistence). Therefore, it is already primordially restricted for each; there is a juridical law (the consequence of that thought) before all agreement (the consequence of individual active freedom). From that idea, the state follows of necessity. It is therefore an imperative, required directly and unconditionally by reason. The civil authority stems from this concept of reason, its sanctity and its power can therefore not be doubted; the people of the world of phenomena cannot decide on it; hence Kant's disgust regarding the judgment of the French people over their king.[147] The freedom (law) of the living man only follows from the idea of the equal freedom of all, which does not consist in the permission [Erlauben], but only in the uniform restriction of each; it follows indirectly, as an emptied sphere ; it is a non-prohibition. Reason here makes the right of man [das Recht des Menschen] into its right, which then follows from it and exists for it, and

---

[147] *Metaphysische Anfangsgründe der Rechtslehre*, pp. 207ff. [pp. 97–98 in *The Metaphysics of Morals*].

therefore for the most part is withdrawn from man's power of disposal, which after all is the only way that it could express itself.

Moreover, reason also directly manifests itself as being invested with rights and prescribes to man enforceable duties which are no longer due to the idea of universal freedom. The subject of these rights Kant calls humanity or man in himself, in opposition to the man of phenomena, thus not the man of action but the one inexorably determined by reason, by the logical law itself. The duties of the family, between the spouses, between parents and children are derived from this right of reason (even though they do not follow from it), and evidently do not stem from the freedom of the individuals, which is why, likewise according to Kant, they cannot be waived by mutual consent. This right of reason demands punishment as retribution. Punishment, then, is not a means of preventing people from being injured in the future, but a necessary consequence of reason, which would be violated immediately by its omission. The law of non-contradiction, of uniformity, has a right to exist, and its existence is just the *talio*. Non-punishment of crime does precisely the same thing against the law of reason that violence does against the living man.[148] Furthermore, the law of reason makes acts into violations of rights which do not infringe the right of any living human being (unnatural sins.) So it is only man as such (reason) who, as a member of the popular assembly, helps to form the court of law and, for example, issues the sentence.

Necessary Progression to Fichte

The existence of two principles of law – reason and the I – appears in Kant's system as perfectly consistent, in that they correspond to its two opposing worlds. His system as a whole justifies the inclusion of the contradictions that

---

[148] This was the least comprehensible thing of all; it made Feuerbach believe that, given this theory of retribution, Kant must have been decrepit when he wrote his doctrine of law. It is natural that the results from Kant's purely objective rational principle would not be understood, given that the whole development could not stand still with him, but aspired to the pure subjectivity of Fichte, to which Feuerbach already most certainly adhered in his view of punishment. Cf. von Linck, *Über das Naturrecht unserer Zeit als Grundlage der Strafrechtstheorien* [Regarding the Natural Law of our Time as the Foundation of Theories of Penal Law], Part II.

permeate the law of nature, and to that extent he can also be called the true representative of it. This explains the general following that he gained at the time, and the authority which he still possesses among all abstract legal philosophers. His doctrine of law resembles the momentary balance of a tipping body that delays its fall, and so seems to be true bearing and consistency. The real change took place only with Fichte, who for that reason also encountered less of a reception.

But being justified in terms of his system is not yet being justified in the thing itself. The right of real people has no association with that of people as such, as little as, in the system as a whole, the world of appearance has with that of reason. Here is no explanation as to why phenomena are there and why everything is not reason, which is why, in our conceptualizations, we cannot determine where the truth ends, and where the deception begins. Thus in ethics it is not evident why freedom of choice [Willkür] (i.e., of people) exists and not merely freedom of the will [Willens] (i.e., of reason), why compulsion, if reason demands it, depends on the pleasure of the claimant, why there is a right of unreasonable people alongside the right of people as such. So then, here too it is not possible to determine with necessity what belongs to one person and what to another, to what degree reason should limit individual freedom or leave it untouched. For there is nothing higher over both, which sets for each its limits; but the right of man in itself, in terms of its concept, excludes all freedom of real human beings, and vice versa.

And so Kant cannot do anything else than attribute, entirely arbitrarily, something to reason here, something to man there. For example, he allows wealth to depend upon the regulation of human beings, while he allows family relations to be governed by reason. He wants the state to be necessary, and yet he cannot give up its contractual formation. In order for the sovereign to have an unlimited right, it is necessary at the same time that everyone who obeys be himself (in his reality) and be a member of the sovereign, and yet it is not the real man at all, but his reasonableness, which votes in the assembly and passes judgment in the court; the one who obeys is something else altogether.[149]

This dualism, this inner, all-pervading contradiction, makes it necessary to

---

[149] Cf. *Metaphysische Anfangsgründe der Rechtslehre*, p. 195 along with p. 320 [pp. 91, 102 in *The Metaphysics of Morals*].

progress towards an undivided principle. But the restriction of personal freedom also pressed in this direction. This alone, as the living mainspring of the
development, could not receive more than an initial impulse from Kant's reaction, who with scientific circumspection submitted it to the law of reason; but
with this impulse it was enabled with equal resolution to rise above that law.

Kant revealed the insoluble difficulties of deriving the juridical law from reason: the impossibility of deriving from it the right and entitlement of the individual; the question as to why reason, if it must compel freedom, cannot compel
other purposes; and why it protects the same actions in one case which it forbids
in another.

It was imperative to give up the law of reason as a basis for legal freedom,
and to locate that basis in the real man in his free activity.

In this specific doctrine as well, the phase of Kant leads to that of Fichte.

Chapter 5: Fichte's System

Personality, not Law of Thought

Reason became something different with Fichte than it was in its earlier development. No longer was it the epitome of thought determinations; instead, it was the thinking being, the person himself, inasmuch as he acts according to those determinations. I myself, self-consciousness, am reason. The highest conviction of rationalism – only reason is true – hereby received a new meaning, one completely different from the old one: only self-consciousness, only the thinking, the personal, is and has reality. That which has no consciousness of itself, a thing (the forms of thought itself as such), is not there at all, "and he who thinks differently does not understand himself" – this is the thesis that Fichte carried through with all his resolve, as the first and last result.

Identity of Consciousness

Right now, our consciousness seems to bear witness to the existence of these unconscious things. But that is deception. Those things are not truly there; they cannot, therefore, be the cause of our conceptions of them; only our consciousness is, and those things are only there because it conceptualizes them to itself, and therefore are there only as conceptualized (for us), not as being (for themselves).

But if you ask: why do we conceptualize things if they do not exist apart from ourselves, and why do we have the consciousness that we of necessity conceptualize them? The answer is: the law of consciousness (or more significantly: the concept thereof) says that objects must be conceptualized. Such is discovered by self-observation, which is the outcome and the precondition of all philosophy. I am not conscious in any other way of myself – hence, I am not there at all – without also setting some object, even if only my own self, over against myself as something distinguished from me. This act is not an affair of pre-existing consciousness; consciousness only arises with it.

Denial of Objects

But I see this act by which I set the object, and distinguish myself, the active (subject), from what I set over against myself (object); even if this opposite is itself nothing else than myself; because it is just my activity. So, the subject and the object are both only the one and the same I in its actions; this is the identity of self-consciousness, which exists only by being active in this opposite way, as a subject-object [Subjektobjekt]. The double series, the activity which posits objects (the real I), and the activity which looks at and differentiates them from itself (the ideal I) in its inseparability (identity), is reason. The objects cannot therefore be anything separated from it, outside of it, because its own concept is just the positing of these objects. I have to posit objects before all experience, because before I posit them, I do not even exist. But this means as much as: there is no experience, that is, no conceptualizing, which is effected by a cause outside conceptualizing. Rather, the activity which, in accordance with its nature, posits and looks at objects – reason – is the only being. It is only to the unphilosophical consciousness that the effects of the law of this activity seem to be experience.

Subjective Idealism

The way in which the I opposes itself to itself and distinguishes itself from itself is manifold, and from this arises the diversity of conceptualizations. Two main types of activity are above all distinguished: in one, the act which posits objects (the not-I) precedes, and the view [Beschauung] is determined by it — *perception* [Erkennen]. In the other, the view, the concept (the original I) precedes, and the positing of the object depends on it — *action*. In the first case, everything is necessary; for the law of the I acts without me knowing how I must set these objects; the real activity is a necessary one. In the second case, the ideal begins in me, pure activity, which, since it has no object, can choose this one or that; hence I am free. The concept of action therefore demands that the pure, free I actually not be determined by an object in any manner, but instead that it determine the object out of itself — this is *the ought*.

Task to Discover Everything a priori

Fichte demonstrated, as was shown, that the positing of objects is contained in the notion of self-consciousness. However, if the viewpoint that there is no object and no experience is to be demonstrated, it must be shown how self-consciousness is compelled by the law of its activity to conceptualize precisely such and such objects, indeed all those which everyone feels bound to conceptualize to himself, which, according to an unphilosophical way of thinking, exist outside of him. The whole world of experience must be discovered from the laws of self-consciousness (*a priori*). This then is the task of the Fichtean system.

Hence, it is not merely the form of perception, but also its substance, the things themselves, which are to be derived from reason; not merely the ethical rules, but also the relationships which they determine. That plants, animals, other people are there outside of myself, that the race is maintained through reproduction, my body by food which the earth vouchsafes me, must as necessarily reside in the concept of self-consciousness as do reciprocal legal restriction, marriage, property; for how else would I know all this, since I do not get any conception of it from the outside, and with the non-existence of things, cannot do so?[150] This task, which cannot be ignored in the Fichtean system, has aroused the greatest astonishment and, through its clash with all ordinary thinking, and certainly with the actual existence of things, has hindered its spread. But as ridiculous as the enterprise seems and as unfeasible for the unbedazzled, it contains the truth that the substance of things and their restriction, the ethical rules and the relations for which they exist, cannot be separated from one another; the one has no existence apart from the other; they are the product of *one* act. The fallacy is only to consider this act to be one of human consciousness. But Fichte not only *a priori* derives external objects, but also the forms of thought themselves. While Kant only comes across the categories and tabulates

---

[150] This alone can be the criterion of reality even according to those presuppositions. If we distinguish the conceptions of real objects (horses, lions) from fantastic (dragons, gnomes) by the fact that the former exist in the outside world, the latter only in our conceptualizations, then with Fichte the difference cannot lie here, because for him *everything* exists only in conceptualization, with the difference being that the former are conceptualized according to the law of self-consciousness, thus in a necessary manner, while the latter are conceptualized apart from this law, in arbitrary acts of conceptualization. The further question of how it comes about that, among these objects which of necessity form the perimeter of our entire conceptualizing, I also at any moment in time necessarily conceptualize just those of which the empirical consciousness says that they surround me right at this moment (e.g., the house, the street in which I live, the people who just then walk across the street), this question, to which his system peremptorily leads, Fichte does not even raise.

them and arranges them schematically, Fichte undertakes to demonstrate their necessity, to have them emerge from the one supreme assumption of his system, that of the actuality of self-consciousness according to the law of I-not-I. In this as well, he is the forerunner of Hegel, who likewise does not submit to the categories as given, but undertakes to generate them by the dialectical movement.

Real Principle in Fichte's Doctrine and Its Consequences

Fichte incorporated the real, which remains after all abstraction has been accomplished, the self-conscious acting I, into his system, which from this receives a livelier character.

The previous method was subsumption, which was used by the Wolffian school, the natural-law doctors, and Kant. It is based on there being, apart from the rational rule, which is the major premise, also matter separate from it, as the minor premise. Scientific activity brings both together and draws a conclusion. Fichte does not have two such halves and can spare them, because his living principle produces something besides himself. His scientific activity does not bring together what is separated, but pursues that indivisible production. For him, the essential organ of philosophical perception is the vision [die Anschauung]: it envisions the activity of the I in itself; only then does the abstracting mind derive characteristics from it, and retain its contents as something static, no longer alive – as a concept. It is demonstrated here that wherever there is only a spark of life and action, the forms of reason no longer attain to perception, but rather a capacity is required which does not separate relations, but is all-encompassing, which we call vision.

Furthermore, with Kant the content of the ethic is the law of reason; the freedom of man to be determined by this law is just the precondition of fulfilling it. With Fichte, this freedom of the I to be determined by reason – i.e., in this case the concept of its own existence – is itself the content: "the ought is the *drive* of absolute self-*activity*." Thus, legal freedom is not a consequence of the commands of reason, but a direct act through which the I posits itself as free. Accordingly, with Kant the band that holds together the different spheres is a logical one: the law of reason contains the forms of perception, the prescriptions of action, and the imperative of legal freedom. In Fichte, it is a real one: the active I perceives, is driven by itself to the ethic, posits itself as free.

Satisfaction of the Interests of Recent Philosophy by Fichte

This system corresponds to the innermost interest of the new philosophy. The world no longer lays down a necessity for man to conceive specific objects and recognize laws; necessity lies only within him and the nature of his consciousness. He does this all for no other reason than because that is what he is; it obligates him to nothing than his own existence (equal to God). On the other hand, the logical interest of rationalism is also satisfied by the fact that everything that exists is already posited with the concept of self-consciousness, in such a way that it cannot be thought away. But that is why, in principle, the first satisfaction is undone; for man, although free from all the outside world, has an inexorable ruler in the laws of logic of his consciousness. In terms of the same *a priori*, he can be told which objects he should conceptualize, which requirements he should set for himself. And yet he is not himself this law; for although it may be his nature, it is not his will. He gains nothing in the exchange. Nevertheless, this is the most that could be done for human freedom; for man to make all objects and moral laws at will, so that his free will is the cause of conceptions and ethics, cannot be asserted because it contradicts the undeniable facts. The best that could be done was to posit the necessary law of his consciousness as the cause, and this is only an apparent satisfaction, an unproductive gain.

That is why in this system, the life spark that wishes to flare up is repeatedly suppressed, like the Greek god who devours his children at birth. The universal act of consciousness is observed through vision and is a matter of empirics, so that only its *existence* is *exhibited*, not its *necessity demonstrated*. But this act is at once comprehended in a concept, and now, as in the other systems, deduction from the impossibility of the opposite takes its place.

Relation to Spinoza

Hence, Spinoza's rules are paid full homage. The I is the substance, the world its necessary consequences. With Fichte, it is not that the world is *produced* by the *activity* of the I – as appears to be the case – but rather, that the world is *contained* in the *concept* of self-consciousness, and it is given as something that is.

Yet as far as the *content* of Spinoza's doctrine is concerned, Fichte is precisely opposed to him. He makes the inconceivability of objective rationalism clear. There is no impersonal world-law or universal existence such as Spinoza would have it, since there is only what is self-conscious. The career of the entirety of abstract philosophy can be summarized as follows: Spinoza's assertion of logical pantheism, and the procedure of the Wolffian school to demonstrate everything from the laws of thought, challenged Kant to investigate whether the coherence of things corresponded to the coherence of reason, thus to a separation of thought and its objects, leading straight to the question of knowability. And with Fichte this led to the insight that there is only actual thought, only personality, and thereby to the rejection of logical pantheism of the Spinozan sort. So it strode in the opposite direction, with Fichte bringing subjective rationalism to completion in the place of objective rationalism. As did the Wolffian school before him, Kant proceeded from himself, the thinker, and to this degree, the unity of apperception is for him the focus of reason; but he then detached reason from himself and treated it as an independent objective power. But with Fichte, reason exists only as the I; this is therefore actually and generally the principle, it is God and the world, as substance is with Spinoza, and it cannot really be distinguished as the one or the other; for it is first itself when it imagines the world to itself (in both meanings of the word[151]), and the world is only there while imagined by it.

Untenability of the Fichtean Standpoint

Yet this, when it becomes clear, entails the fearful thought: only I, the individual, the I known as so and so, am; and I am the entire world, and if I cease acting, I die, there is nothing more. Fichte could not bring himself to admit that other self-conscious beings could exist, for how should these various I's come to each other, affect each other, and impart the consciousness of their existences? Every not-I is only my I. My conception of other people, like anything else, cannot be brought about by their existence, for it is the product of my own thought activity, which is sufficient to engender it, and nothing outside of it is capable of this. These other people with whom I interact, strangers, friends, relations, are not truly self-conscious acting beings, but are only conceptualized as such by me in a necessary manner, like the beings of dreams. The same is true of God, should a follower of Fichte's believe in Him. He could only be the creation of his intelligence, his I, which he sets over against himself, not something else;

---

[151] ["imagines" – *sich einbilden* – can also have the meaning of a false impression.]

only for him, not for Himself, only something conceptualized, not something existing.

To think in this manner is insanity, and Fichte does not admit that his system promotes such thinking. He deceives himself by conceiving the I not as the existing, but as one of the existing, or as rational being in general. But such an I fills the entire world, and it is not evident how another such I can exist alongside him. So then, if Fichte wished to make a universal I into God, which only individualizes Himself into many people and separates them from Himself, then this was the step which Schelling took immediately after him, but which also abolishes Fichte's system. For according to Fichte, the I is not there at all prior to its positing itself over against itself, in so doing coming to awareness,[152] but this is to consider an individual I, Fichte or any one of his readers, as the only one; the universal I would not be conscious of one of himself. This individual I runs through the entire system. Should the universal I be the principle of law [Recht], positing itself as free, then there would be posited as free a necessary law [Gesetz] like the Kantian man as such, or even Spinoza's nature; that you or I are free is not thereby stated, but denied. And upon this latter is what Fichte's natural law is based. When furthermore it is demonstrated with natural law that the I must see other I's opposite him, then this only makes sense with the individual.

Nevertheless, in his later writings (which certainly were not true to his earlier ones) Fichte did involve the universal I, although he did not make proper use of it. But only the system of "My I" influenced the progress of philosophy and his own doctrine of law.[153] Fichte thus conducted the isolation of persons

---

[152] *Grundlage des Naturrechts nach Principien der Wissenschaftslehre*, p. 11.

[153] Fichte's I is, however, equal to Kant's unity of apperception (of which it is merely the more vivid expression), pure I, not the empirical I; in itself it is abstracted from every material determination that I perceive in myself, and the mere pure thought-activity conceived with it. But just because it is *pure* I, it is by no means yet *objective* I. Just as is that unity of apperception, it ever remains subjective thought-activity, positing objects for a (subjective) consciousness, just as the characterization "I" indicates. For this reason it is necessarily individual, albeit not individual A or individual B, but individual as such. Fichte speaks precisely in this manner in his *Das System der Sittenlehre* [Science

to the extreme. He who philosophizes, views himself as the midpoint and, as follows of necessity, as the cause of the world. But this position also makes clear that he cannot get back to those from whom he has freed himself, given that every bond with a real world and with real people has been severed. Man and his thought cannot be the midpoint of things or the knowledge of them.

———————————————

of Ethics]: "Now it is certainly, as we have seen, involved in Egohood [i.e., I-ness], that each Ego [I] should be an individual, but only an individual in general, and not this particular individual A, B, C, &c.... Hence since it is accidental to the Egohood in general, that I, the individual A, am precisely this A, and since the drive of self-sufficiency is to be a drive of the Egohood in general, as such, this drive certainly does not crave the self-sufficiency of the particular individual A, but of reason in general. The self-sufficiency of reason as such, is our ultimate purpose; and hence not the self-sufficiency of our reason, in so far as it is an individual reason" [*The Science of Ethics as based on the Science of Knowledge*, p. 243]. Fichte's I can therefore be conceptualized at most as the general law of subjective consciousness, not however as something objective, separated from this consciousness (similar to Schelling's absolute I). But then it is something abstract like Kant's reason; if it is to be real, then it is just the thinking of the individual. Even when Fichte later (not perhaps without being instigated by Schelling) progresses to the fact that one must conclude from the I (actually real subjective thinking) to a basis thereof, and the basis of that existence is God, this god may not be so construed as a reality but merely as a picture, a silhouette, from which the activity of the I, which consists precisely in depiction, image-making, proceeds. That archetype, the god, is not on behalf of itself and in itself, but merely the source or the law of the conceptualizing and acting activity of the I, and accordingly the world is not immediately produced by this god but rather is conceived by the subjective I (consciousness) in accordance with that image or law. Among all the shapes it takes, Fichte's doctrine therefore remains pure idealism, pure subjectivism and pure movement without contentual being. It is nothing other than Kant's system of categories set in motion.

Chapter 6: Fichte's Doctrine of Law

Abstract Character of Ethics

In the practical field as in the theoretical, Fichte only furnishes a modification to Kant's system, whereby what with Kant is a static thought-form, with Fichte becomes the activity of the I. The entire outline of the system remains the same; only the lines shift in terms of this differing viewpoint. In this manner, Kant's doctrine of the ethic, which consists in nothing else than *a priori* action, is maintained. But with Kant, *a priori* action is that in which action is undertaken in accordance with the logical law of universality and non-contradiction, thus according to a maxim which does not contradict itself when executed; with Fichte, on the other hand, *a priori* action takes place when the I acts out of itself, thus in terms of its conviction, which it recognizes as duty. Here and there, action is considered in terms of the effect of external objects and the pleasure and pain they excite – empirical action – as something opposed to the ethical, and the ethical is nothing else than being free from this; or, as Fichte expresses it: thou shalt use nature as the means for reason (i.e., the law of the actively thinking I), not vice versa. But for Kant, action coming from inside is conformity with the laws of logic, hence the universally possible maxim, while with Fichte it is the actuality of the I as such. Action from enthusiasm [Begeisterung] is therefore the final solution of Fichte's ethics.

Resultant Oppositions to Kant

And so, Fichte's principle of enthusiasm has as little content as does Kant's law of universality and non-contradiction. For Kant, the ethic is a formal (abstract, contentless) law; for Fichte, it is formal (abstract, contentless) enthusiasm. The charge that he puts to the ethical world (the community of rational being), to encourage one another to act from *conviction*, obviously provides no content to the conviction. According to that modification of Kant's point of view, Kant's two postulates – recompense in accordance with desert, and God as Judge – take on a different shape with Fichte; or rather, after having become shadowy figures with Kant, they drop off entirely (as do all parts of the object). Recompense, or salvation, as the case may be, is not to be sought in an enjoyment of a sort of "liberation from all dependence" but only in a complete such liberation, i.e., it is not to be sought in a good apart from extrasensory (rational) action, but only in such action, and it is the moral world order, although incomprehensible (actually quite easily comprehensible), that such action in accordance with reason (i.e., in accordance with freedom from the senses) also leads to this liberation. Nor is there any external (in the objective world) consequence attached to the action, as Kant postulates beyond temporality. For this reason there is no need of judges and executioners who distribute these consequences, no God, for God is nothing other than the epitome of the relations of this extrasensory order on my moral action.[154] For this reason, religion itself is nothing else with Fichte than this purely formal, non-empirical action being willed and believed as religion; salvation, i.e., freedom from all dependence is tied to this, whatever its consequences may be in the empirical world. This faith is religion.

Finalization of the Subjective Character

Accordingly, religion has absolutely no object, no God outside of us, no world beyond this life, no special commandment; it is nothing else than the consciousness of the moral, i.e., unempirical action of its unempirical nature. Moral community and the church therefore entirely coincide. They are just the endeavor of mutual encouragement to such aprioristic action.[155]

This abstract enthusiasm, enormously stimulated and exalted above external goods but completely devoid of content, runs through Fichte's *Reden an die Deutsche Nation* [Speeches to the German Nation]. Among all the German philosophers, it is precisely Fichte who is celebrated as the philosopher of practical

---

[154] "Man summarizes and establishes the relations of that order on himself and his action, when he discusses them with others, in the concept of an existing being *which he perhaps calls God*. This is the consequence of the finitude of his spirit, but it is benign if he does not use that concept any further for anything." *J. G. Fichte's ... Appellation an das Publikum über die durch ein Kurf. Sächs. Confiscationsrescript ihm beigemessenen atheistischen Aeusserungen* [Fichte's Appeal to the public regarding the Elector of Saxony's decree to confiscate alleged atheistic statements made by him], p. 38. Indeed, it is quite naïve to offer such a confession as a *justification* against the charge of atheism, and yet it is even more an imposition on the part of philosophers that we are supposed to accept this confession as such.

[155] Cf. regarding all of this *Das System der Sittenlehre*, pp. 304ff.

morality. He merits this because he animated the nation to elevate itself above material conditions and interests and its selfishness (over possession and enjoyment), to pure enthusiasm and self-sacrifice for an idea. Certainly this forms part of true ethics (formal); but that merit was likewise due to the contribution of a fortuitous provision of life – the liberation of the Fatherland. At the time, it was a call to powerful spiritual elevation in the face of external force and internal weakening. But Fichte's doctrine can never serve as an enduring example, as a proclaimer of true and complete ethics, either from the practical or the scientific side. In the latter character, it would signify the ruin of true ethics. That nation which had the mere act of enthusiasm, the surrender to any idea regardless of moral content or commandment for human life-relations, as the sole bond of its moral community would wear down or disintegrate. Any goal undertaken with enthusiasm and with elevation above the material condition [die Sinnlichkeit] would then be considered moral, even if the most sacred commandments of the objective moral order were left unpursued or even violated. Where only the grandeur and self-satisfaction of the subject has validity, rather than the ethical order grounded in itself, there the extreme of the subjective orientation is the basis. The untruth of this doctrine later manifested itself in the most tangible aberrations both in literature and in life. Fichte introduced the same notion of content-less I-activity into pedagogy, whereby the main content of his speeches to the German nation was geared to eliminating all positive knowledge and learning from education and nurture – burdening the pupil with the production of the entire future fund of knowledge from out of his own pure thought-activity.

Deduction of Law

With regard to the doctrine of law, the first thing to consider is that Fichte not only finds the ethical rules *a priori* but also the relations and objects thereof, the existence of desire, the earth, other people, my own body, etc. I must ascribe to myself a body, accept the existence of other beings, etc., not because I find them outside of myself but because of reason in me, and indeed these external objects are deduced in a peculiar way, not from ideas of nature but from the ethical ideas. As such, natural philosophy drops out entirely; everything is ethics. In fact, in terms of Fichte's standpoint nature has no significance of its own as an expression of thought, but is only there for reasonable beings to have as the object of their reasonable actions, namely their mutual self-restriction. The world is only "the sensory material of our duty; duty is what is actually real in things, it is the true ground of all appearance."[156] Its meaning is therefore that it be something shared, regardless of what it actually is. All of this only follows from his view of perception and concerns his method in general, without having a particular significant influence on the content of the doctrine of law. What is essential to his doctrine of law is that it finalized the subjective character of natural law, as Kant finalized its rationalistic character.

For Fichte, legal freedom does not follow from the ethic (practical reason) but from the real existence of the I. From the start, then, legal freedom is the freedom of the individual, not the notion of general freedom and equality. It does not have the ethic as its goal; it is its own goal. It is not something that has to be realized, an object of the ought; it is something already existing. Through its real power, the I posits itself as free, and when it observes itself, it can only find itself to be free. "Freedom is philosophically, not ethically necessary." Coercion is already given in its concept, and thus does not follow from the ethic. With Kant, the freedom of individual persons is already originally restricted because it first proceeds from general freedom, which itself furnishes measure and boundaries when it distributes freedom to them. With Fichte, it has no measure or restriction because the I itself posits it immediately. It consists "in the right of reasonable beings to be the sole cause in the world of sense." The power of coercion contained in it must of course be as free of restriction as it itself is. This, *my* immediately existing and therefore initially unrestricted freedom and possibility to exercise coercion, is the principle of the doctrine of law.

The law of self-consciousness requires that the I accept other thinking beings; this must be demonstrated in theoretical philosophy; individuality, self-consciousness only arises through this opposition. If other thinking beings place themselves in opposition, one must ascribe to them the same unrestricted power as one does to oneself. But furthermore, he cannot give up his own initially-posited freedom as the only reasonable being, and must also require the recognition of this from those posited over against him. To this end it is necessary, first, that he restrict himself freely; otherwise, he would not be a reasonable being standing in opposition to them, because the criterion of a reasonable

---

[156] *Appellation an das Publikum,* pp. 46–47.

being is its own restraint. Secondly, others must restrict themselves in the same act of mutual conditionality. In order to maintain everything as initially posited – my rationality and freedom, and the freedom of others which is deduced from it, including their action – and not to annul one of them and thereby to commit a contradiction — the *community of law* is necessary. Its content is the juridical law, which thus follows consequentially from the concept of the free individual.

Separation of Law and Morality

In this manner, Fichte attained what natural law was after: he provided to law a unique principle separate from morality, without forfeiting the scientific connection; and this was possible only through the standpoint of his system. It would appear that this was already discovered by the earlier theorists, above all Kant: morality is the inner legislation (self-coercion), law the outward (coercion of others); hence, entirely different legislations (!), with the unity of these two being practical reason, the law of universality and necessity. Yet precisely because the unity of both lies in a law or concept, the separation is entirely useless; it does not accomplish what is sought from it. Both legislations, namely, need to function in concordant manner in terms of that concept, and when they take on an opposite character, as is actually the case, this manifests itself as a contradiction of practical reason in itself.

Fichte, on the other hand, secured for his separation the achievement of a living unity of self-conscious being, rather than a logical one. Every living creature can be active in various ways in terms of its nature; the concept, the law cannot. The I contains on the one hand a drive to a certain activity – this is how morality is generated; on the other hand, it is already an existence, a power, something freely willing, acting – this is how the law arises. In terms of their essence, drive and power have an opposite effect, and the I, which they both are, nevertheless remains one and the same. In this way, Fichte could say "as the moral frame of mind is love of duty for the sake of duty, so on the contrary the political frame of mind is love of self for the sake of self... love yourself above all things, and your fellow citizen for your sake!"[157] Kant's law of reason, by contrast, can only have as goal the rational necessity of all action everywhere.

---

[157] *Grundlage des Naturrechts nach Principien der Wissenschaftslehre*, Vol. II, p. 114.

Solution to the Earlier Contradictions

By means of this separation, consisting not merely in words and appearances [Dekorum] but in result, Fichte is able to solve the problem that prior to him was vainly grappled with. It is no contradiction of reason that coercion take place in the sphere of law [Rechtsgebiete] even though legal obligations are also required by morality. For it is not the I as my drive (as ethic) that coerces here, but the I as existence and power, mine that coerces others, and others' that coerce mine. It is no contradiction that the same actions that are forbidden here are protected there. Law could only consistently command and prohibit them in one and the same way: "it is impossible to understand how it is that a law of permission can be derived from an unconditionally commanding moral law which thereby extends over all things."[158] Namely, that it uses something as means (permission) which initially and immediately annuls its goal, in order perhaps to get to it indirectly, contradicts the nature of a law. But the I, which here protects free action, is no law, it is immediate existence itself. It is quite removed from the contradiction involved in competence following from the law. For it does not follow from the law, but is already there before the law, from the I, and the law itself is first derived from it and only contains restriction, not freedom – as must be the case for law.

The Contradictions Return by the Back Door

Fichte's predecessors had already sought to remove these contradictions; but the point of view by which Fichte alone was able to remove them leads at the same time to other consequences which at the least were not cultivated in natural law. In terms of its nature, my drive (morality) is binding, unconditionally commanding. But this is by no means the case with my unbounded power (basis of juridical law); on the contrary, in terms of its nature this excludes every law [Gesetz]. Putting into action that which rationally follows from it cannot be unconditionally commanded, precisely because it is freedom. Whether it will submit to this depends on itself: "because they (people) are set free, such a boundary cannot lie outside freedom, as something by which freedom is annulled; but this is by no means the case if freedom is restricted; rather, through

---

[158] *Grundlage des Naturrechts nach Principien der Wissenschaftslehre*, Vol. I, Introduction, III.

freedom everyone should set these boundaries themselves, i.e., everyone should *make* themselves into law, in order not to disturb the freedom of those with whom they stand in mutual interaction."[159] The consequence from the concept of my freedom, the legal community, is therefore by no means practically necessary but only advisory, as to how to establish it in case I wish to correspond with the consequences of that concept, "in case I *wish* to be consistent." "Law is not practical, but technical-practical."

The necessary following step is: rights to specific objects, in the manner of property or family rights, are not immediately given, in the way Kant derived them from the law of reason. For anyone, when he does not freely restrict himself, is entitled to everything unlimitedly, so that restrictions arise first through arbitrary agreement. "All rights to something are based in a contract."[160] The primordial right [Urrecht] of man, which he had prior to civil society, is not, as in the past, freedom restricted in accordance with the maxim of coexistence, which in this restriction is also ethically secured. Rather, it is the unlimited power with which one threateningly opposes another, and there is no other safeguard than the possibility of uniting and establishing a state. The state here truly arises from a contract, because its construction is arbitrary, and so is its design. Now the law prescribes both tentatively, in the event that one wishes to be consistent. It may be repealed and rebuilt at any moment; this explains Fichte's decisive approval of the French Revolution. It is true that Fichte, like Kant, also allows the compulsion that forces the rebel to enter into the state.[161] With Kant, this compulsion is the consequence of rational necessity, which commands the state unconditionally; with Fichte, however, it is only the consequence of the unrestricted arbitrary will of those already united. With equal justification they could have coerced the recalcitrant to dance a minuet; and he has the same freedom to reciprocate their coercion, should he be the stronger, for what requires him to be consistent? In any case, it is not a rational necessary coercion, for his freedom is not restricted by itself, nor is it annulled. What is

---

[159] *Grundlage des Naturrechts nach Principien der Wissenschaftslehre*, Vol. I, Introduction, II.

[160] *Grundlage des Naturrechts nach Principien der Wissenschaftslehre*, Vol. II, p. 266.

[161] *Grundlage des Naturrechts nach Principien der Wissenschaftslehre*, Vol. I, Introduction, II.

here proven, as has been said above, is that subjective rationalism makes the thinking individual into God, just as objective rationalism does with impersonal reason. The free I as the absolute beginning of jurisprudence can as little be bound as can Spinoza's world law. With the latter, all actions are lawful because nature effects them; with the former, they are lawful because the I effects them.

The first character trait of Fichte's doctrine of law is therefore: Law has no power over people; its realization depends on their arbitrary will. The question then becomes, what is its content in case someone actually wishes to comply with it? For this also characterizes the system. The law [Recht] of the law of reason [Vernunftgesetzes], of the Kantian man as such, must succumb: *only the personal is entitled*. The freedom of living people is the exclusive cause of coercion. In this manner, the law of marriage is removed while adultery is freed: "the state can neither issue laws nor establish punishments against it, nor against whatever sort of extramarital satisfaction of the sex drive. Whose rights would be violated by this offense?"[162] In this manner, punishment cannot be retribution, for the notion of correspondence has no rights, and whose (which person's) right would be satisfied by retribution? The law of uniformity, which with Kant is reason, is with Fichte a mere thing without self. Fichte has to ask: what is this marriage, or this retributive justice, that it should exercise compulsion over me? Can it conceptualize, distinguish objects from itself, set goals for itself? Is it an active self-conscious being like me? And if not, then it does not exist at all; it is merely my production. How could I as a free and entitled person think of this as capable, as cause in the world of sense, which is not even capable of positing a world of sense?

Just as with the first relation, in which we say freedom may only be restricted *by freedom*, so with the second, we say freedom should only be restricted *for the sake of freedom*. Hereby in the first place, man in his personality is the exclusive principle of law. I may be subjected to coercion only when I will it, and when I subject myself to it; I only do so for my own security in accordance with reason. "Love yourself, and your neighbor for your self's sake!"

On this point, natural law is necessarily pushed into a corner, and on this highest point its untenability once again manifests itself. To wit:

---

[162] *Grundlage des Naturrechts nach Principien der Wissenschaftslehre*, Vol. II, p. 201.

Only the separation of the self into drive and freedom makes it possible to alleviate the earlier contradictions. But with that, the mutual penetration of both is also abandoned. Freedom *can* and *should* be subject to drive, but that is the manner of the ethic generally; the peculiar thing about the sphere of law, that freedom must be subjected to it, is no longer attainable. The living self, which recognizes an ideal ought, but really is independent of it, can only be bound if the cause of the ought also has a real power. With each of the problems that Fichte solves, a new difficulty arises precisely opposed to the previous one. It used to be impossible for natural law to gain freedom from the binding force of reason, from which it proceeded; now Fichte cannot go from freedom, which he makes into a principle, to a binding force. The law of *reason* indeed ceases, leaving a completely lawless arbitrariness behind.

While Fichte justifies the coercion of law by deriving it from the original freedom of the I rather than the ethic, in exchange he forfeited the ethical significance of coercion. What remains is merely factual power, and he can only incite the feeling of an accidental defeat on the part of the coerced. It is similar to the so-called law of necessity of the earlier doctors and Kant. He who is pushed off of the plank because someone else has the power and there is no law above them, will not consider this to be what was owed to him, as for example a debtor would consider being forced to pay what he owes. Even in the state, law has no ethical guarantee. The state is based on contract, but on what is contract itself based? In terms of the legal concept of the state, I need to keep the contract only if I wish to, including the contract which contains the community of law, the state itself. Only the strength of the united persons binds me, as with Spinoza, and could just as well force me to do something else than this consequence of my freedom. The coercion exerted by the entirety of the citizens against an offender is thus no different than the violence unleashed by the offender in the transgression.

If it is consistent that the law permits what morality prohibits, because permission and law are based on freedom, then everything becomes permission and nothing remains of law. To the degree that the concept of law as inner drive truly obligates, there is nothing else than morality, as Fichte himself claims; as such, its separation from morality and its actual treatment by Fichte is far less grounded than it is with the other writers. To the degree, however, that it does not inwardly demand, and thus is something else than morality, to that degree there is *no demand at all;* it is a game, instructions on how to rigorously set up something of complete indifference, for which you happen to be in the mood.

All of this was no secret to Fichte, but he nevertheless considered his doctrine of law to be well-founded. Yet the nerve itself, apart from which no law of reason and indeed no law at all can exist, is diseased. This is the restriction on behalf of others, even if merely uncertain. Here Fichte obscured the consequences of his principle, because if he acknowledged them, he would have to give up the principle, which he cannot do if he does not wish to fall back into the old contradictions. To wit, Fichte gained the concept of competence, of positive entitlement, not by deriving it from the restricted law of reason but by positing it as the originating thing. But it is simply impossible in terms of consistency to get from it to restriction, leaving entirely to one side whether it must subject itself to this consistency, or only should do so, or merely do so as a matter of entire indifference. By contrast, consistency requires that I not restrict myself but that I subject others to myself. "Love yourself above everything" follows from my unrestricted freedom, but "and your neighbor for your own sake" does not. Fichte arrives at restriction and legal community only through a twofold deception. The reason by which he expressed it positively is this: "As I, the reasonable being, have established myself as free and others as free, I must also wish for them to recognize me as a reasonable (free) being; I can only achieve this if I restrain myself." The actual restriction (indeed its possibility) does not, however, lie in the essence of freedom but in the essence of the ethical drive, and it is as free that I have made myself the basis of law, not as impelled by reason. If the latter were the case, my freedom could not even emerge alongside it, it would already be determined through and through; I must act perfectly to be recognized by others as reasonable, and we find ourselves precisely in the same place as those who discover law from the ethic.

But Fichte seeks to distance himself from the obvious inconsistency that I commit here when I first posit myself as infinitely free and then restrict myself, by claiming that the restriction exists only for the sake of freedom. But that is only the confusion of *my* freedom with *universal* freedom or the freedom of others, the distinction of which is the basis of the system. As the first principle was: my freedom can only be restricted by *my* freedom (not by others or the notion of freedom), or else it is not restricted but abolished as freedom, so must the second be: in accordance with consistency, my freedom should be restricted only for *my* freedom (not for others' or universal freedom), otherwise....

The one position requires the other. If Fichte withdraws the first statement, then he has a different principle than the free I, which exercises coercion, and has returned to the Kantian standpoint. If he insists on it, then he must also stand on the second, in which consistency requires first from my freedom: maintain yourself, do not enter into slavery, be prudent and restrict yourself where you might otherwise lose, dissemble, keep your word when necessary! in the way that Machiavelli implemented this system. And then, secondly, positive: make your freedom, which you first posit as limitless, against which you have placed others only in order to gain consciousness through the opposition – now make your freedom really limitless, by subjugating those who are endowed with freedom and capable of resistance, and by receiving them in submission. If you can, make yourself into the ruler of the world. Freedom of the individual as the principle of the doctrine of law necessarily leads to this end.

Parallel of Natural Law and the French Revolution in Both Stages

Life is everywhere more consistent than science. While the rationalist orientation in German science does not consistently keep both principles – thought-necessity [Denknotwendigkeit] and the real I – separate, but, as was shown, trembles for the latter largely for its consequences and festoons it with the results of the former, the history of France placed each alongside each other in their total finality. It is the parallel between natural law and the French Revolution, which immediately meets the eye and has long been recognized. Nevertheless, the parallel exists not only in general, but even in the gradations. The Republic (of course, not in its origin by executing the king, but in the principles of its existence) accords with the Kantian standpoint. Here everything which did not follow from the concept of freedom was destroyed; but the notion of freedom and equality is still a necessity which stands over every individual, from which each first receives his right. Reason, the impersonal, holds the scepter, but as with the Kantian version, it has no real power to maintain itself. Living persons do not follow its mathematical lines; it wishes to rule over the personal, but the personal is stronger.

There then arises the system of the real personal I, of Napoleon, who has no other notion over him than his *own* freedom, which he restricts when he wants to, and only for *his power*. He is bound by the rational consequence from his own will, and this distinguishes him from other conquerors. For this reason he does not digress in random ventures, in useless inclinations. It is as if the calculated execution of power delights him more than its actual arbitrary use. But *only this* consequence binds him.

> Ideas live easily alongside each other,
> But things in space bump up against each other.

Fichte could deceive himself and deduce a restriction for his original freed I. But the living I, which does not owe its freedom to the laws of the republic and its equality, but to its own real power, could not commit the inconsistency and impose a restriction on itself for others. And when it is consistent, the world only has room for one such I.

Chapter 7: Summary of Results: Natural Law in Its Final Form

The Character of Natural Law as the Combination of Kant and Fichte, and Completed in the General State of Scholarship

Natural law as founded by Grotius was brought to its scientific conclusion with Kant. The subsequent treatment by Fichte by no means superseded and displaced Kant's standpoint; he only exercised criticism of it which Kant could turn around and exercise against him. For their oppositional relation is only this: of the two poles between which natural law swings, the free self and the logically necessary law, of which it is not possible to stand on both at the same time, Fichte takes his position on the former, Kant on the latter.

Taken in its entirety, Fichte's doctrine hereby appears to be extreme by contrast with Kant's moderation. The shape in which natural law lately has come to be completed in German science is therefore predominantly Kantian. The entire edifice of natural law is taken from him; tendencies toward Fichte only crop up in details, in those instances in which the general superficial conception of man's arbitrary will (the empirical I) is more satisfactory than Kant's categorically necessary commandment (*homo noumenon*).

Here is how the relationship is presented in the most popular and most often consulted textbook of the time, that of Gros.

Outline of the Textbook Doctrine of Natural Law

The content of natural law, loosed from a connection with any particular system of philosophy as the general scientific manner of understanding, can be summarized as follows:

The doctrine of "natural law" or "the law of reason" must proceed from the *state of nature* by contrast with the civil condition, i.e., a condition of natural arbitrary will, without law and the state. Not that such a condition need have existed; but it must be assumed in thought, it must be abstracted in thought from the existing law and state, in order to derive the necessity of law and the state, the rule by which they are to exist and the degree to which they are obligatory, purely from the nature or the reason of man (the individual).

It now arises from the nature or reason of man that man as a sensory-reasonable being must have *freedom*, both internal freedom, i.e. to be determined only by reason (the logical law) independently of outward impressions, and external freedom, in accordance with which he can be active in the world of sense as a rational being (i.e., in accordance with that logical law). The laws that follow from internal freedom and on behalf of it, form the sphere of morality, while the laws that follow from external freedom and on behalf of it, form the sphere of law.

The external freedom accruing to man as reasonable being is in itself unrestricted. But because such unrestricted freedom is due to every person, and the freedom of everyone is oriented toward one and the same object, the world of sense, the freedom of all would mutually nullify itself. Hence there follows from reason, as the law of non-contradiction, the basic principle: each must restrict his freedom to the degree necessary to allow others to exist alongside him. This is the *maxim of coexistence*. It is the supreme, indeed the only principle of natural law. All others (regarding property, marriage, the state) are not self-existing legal principles, but only applications of this one principle to various factual relations, and what does not follow from this maxim, hence what does not have as goal the mutual recognition and self-restriction of freedom, could possibly pertain to the moral sphere but not to the legal sphere, and therefore cannot be prescribed coercively. It is precisely this infinite freedom with the restriction by the equal freedom of the others that is the *primordial right of man*. (The primordial right is only the subjective expression of that which is expressed objectively by the maxim of coexistence). The primordial right therefore characterizes the right of man not to be obligated to others for anything other than that for which they can be obligated to him.[163] It also entails that man not become a mere means for others, and so cease to be an end.

This is the deduction of the legal principle, the first and chief work of natural law; there now follows the second, the subsumption of relations under this principle.

First, the coexistence of freedom implies the mutual non-injury of the person – bodily existence, free spatial movement, honor – these being *innate rights* (not to be confused with the primordial right). Directly following from this is *property*: for external freedom and absolute efficacy ("causality") of people in

---

[163] In this concept of primordial right as given by Kant, the influence of Rousseau's notion that freedom is based on mutual reciprocity is nowhere to be seen.

the world of sense requires that any particular thing be able to be subjected to his will, and the coexistence of freedom requires that one person not disturb another's such relation to a thing. The act of such subjection is occupation. Finally, there follows from this the *binding nature of contracts;* for by virtue of that absolute efficacy in the world of sense, one must also be able to subject the actions of others to his will, since they also belong to the world of sense (his "arbitrary will as the determining basis of actions in taking possession"); nevertheless, by virtue of the concurrently existing freedom of others, it extends only as far as others agree to. But the latter have the possibility of agreeing to this because the capacity freely to restrict oneself also pertains to the essence of external freedom. The act of such permission, thus the expansion of freedom on the one side and self-restriction on the other, is contract. (If this agreement alone is the basis for the binding nature of contracts, it follows that the content of the contract is legally indifferent, and that any contract, whatever its nature, is equally binding; nevertheless, natural law doctors list only those species of contracts which they find in common law.)

Anything beyond this can hardly be directly inferred from the maxim of coexistence. Whatever is held to be a legal institution therefore has validity only by means of contract. Marriage is a contract for the mutual use of the sexual functions. A different goal, namely life community, does not lie in the legal nature of the marriage contract, unless through an accessory agreement, and all content of the marriage contract (temporary marriage, polygamy, incest) is legally admissible and valid by virtue of the both parties' agreement. This according to, e.g., Gros, following Fichte. For his part, Kant sought to demonstrate exclusive sexual community as the necessary content of the marriage contract and indeed directly from the maxim of coexistence and the primordial right of man, by reasoning that the opposite turns the other party into a mere means. With regard to the education of children, there is no legal obligation upon parents (not merely according to the original practitioners, such as Grotius and Thomasius, but also Gros and others), although Gros gave everyone (not only the parents) the right to educate minors, they being legally incapable. But Kant here asserted a natural-law obligation on parents to educate their children on the basis that whoever brings a person into the world *"without his consent"* (in a sense violating the person's will) is bound to reconcile him to his condition. The law of inheritance is likewise a contract, but with the modification that a

moment of limbo enters between the tender (which only upon death is an irrevocable and thus actual tender) and acceptance, during which time the community [die Gesammtheit] safeguards the matter for the heir (Kant). Intestate
succession of course is held to be presumptively testamentary. In this manner,
family relations rest entirely on arbitrary contract or, in the view of most doctors of natural law, drop entirely out of the legal sphere.

One species of contract is the *social contract*, i.e., the voluntary association
of several persons for a common purpose, for which rights and obligations of
the participants are established. Such societies include the business corporation,
marriage, the church, and preeminently the state. Every other association is legally indifferent, i.e., in terms of legal principle it is a matter of indifference
whether they are entered into or not. This is the case with the trading company,
marriage, the church. Only one association is legally necessary, the state. To wit,
the supreme principle of the law of reason commands the mutual recognition
of freedom (inviolability of the person, of property, of contract); but people individually do not fulfill it, by virtue of their sensory composition; its fulfillment
can only be attained when people join forces to establish a power which coerces
every individual should he refuse it. The association to this end is the state. For
this reason, it and it alone is the postulate of the legal principle.

Accordingly, the state is the association for the coercive realization of the
maxim of coexistence. Its purpose is the protection of individuals' rights as they
follow from this maxim. What therefore does not follow from this maxim and
serve it cannot rationally be an object of the state association, state laws, in
short, state coercion, e.g., public education, public mores, public welfare. The
exercise of coercion in these matters violates the legal principle. (The many institutions in actual states for which such coercion exists are by some rejected in
terms of rigid consistency, by others rescued by detours: they either indirectly
serve the protection of rights, by reducing the risk to life and property of the
well-bred, well-educated, and well-to-do, or, in addition to the actual state contract, the members of the state also established an implied contract for these
other purposes.)

Now then, if the state in general is a postulate of the legal principle, then it
can only come into existence among a specific set of people, by virtue of the
freedom of rational beings, though their own agreement, thus *by means of contract*. Whether states actually arose through contract is a matter of indifference;

but legally the power of states and the duty of obedience on the part of subjects is based on an implicit contract and can only be assessed in terms of the consequences of such.

This is the entire content of the doctrine that goes under the names "natural law" or "law of reason," after the material drawn from elsewhere has been eliminated and its own structure is showcased in its purity. Its particular treatment is the derivation of law and the state from the nature or reason of (individual) persons. Its characteristic doctrine is firstly the restriction of coercible commands and state purposes to the protection of the rights of individual persons, secondly the denial of all self-existing power and the exclusive justification of power in the consent and mandate of the underlings. Law and the state accordingly exist only via individual freedom and only for its purpose.

PART IV: ASSESSMENT OF ABSTRACT LEGAL PHILOSOPHY

Abstract legal philosophy must be regarded as culminating with Fichte, even though rationalism still rules in later systems and in a certain sense first received its completion through Hegel. For the latter system merely complied with procedural requirements, while the orientation's interest, to the degree capable of attainment, was satisfied by Fichte. At this juncture, at least initially, it stepped away from the events of the world and from the aspirations of science to make way for a new one, which initially even contradicted it. Hence it is that in the later systems, in which the abstract character – and thus indisputably the mainspring of human isolation – prevails, there is no desire to admit it; furthermore, the results of legal philosophy, which to this point pursued individual freedom, from this time forward took the opposite tack and therefore, although established by abstraction, nevertheless violated the interest which leads only to abstraction, as is decisively the case with Hegel. From Fichte onward, the desire completely to accommodate rationalism is accompanied, even unawares, by the opposite, to be freed from it.

As long as the principle of rationalism was still the principle of life, it was allowed to show itself as such, and could find general recognition. Now it has become a mere principle of a school; it is opposed to the times, to which it must accommodate itself, not entirely successfully.

For this reason Hegel's system was not allotted the same glorious lot as previous systems. For these had gripped the entire age as if with a giddiness, whereby the luminaries of each discipline willingly gave themselves over to carry them out and seek their glory in them, while even the lesser circles of the educated world were soon filled with the new conception or mindset. This latest system, on the other hand, is both limited to the narrow circle of the school, and finds no support, and even the most determined reluctance, among the leading men.

With Schelling it was precisely the antirationalistic characteristic that initially and especially took hold of the most quick-witted, which with the sense that this had not yet penetrated [the broader culture], subsequently inhibited its spread. The further presentation will confirm all of this. Here this provisional remark was necessary in order to justify the assessment that natural law maintained its place even with Fichte, and the later systems were sometimes affected by it as well, as far as the general traits recurring in them are concerned.

Chapter 1: Logical Examination of Natural Law

Logical Contradiction in the Rationalistic Procedure

It is easy to claim *in abstracto:* "Everything is the production of a necessarily working law. This (God) contains the world by its very nature, and it could become nothing but what is; but what is, had to be." This idea appears to be the simplest, the one most in agreement with itself, the only one capable of fully satisfying the thinker by the unity which it extends across all of existence. But whether this law truly expresses and makes comprehensible how all things derive from it, is something that can be put to the test. The bulk of those who seek salvation in such philosophy neglect to penetrate that far. They content themselves with that assumption, believing it *without* thinking, as such demonstrating most precisely the eternal saying: half a philosophy distances one from God, true philosophy returns to Him.

Indeed, whoever would discover that law and the way in which it produces things, would have to be capable of discovering, from out of himself, the whole existing world without having experienced anything of it, since only such things exist which, according to that law, could not be omitted. Such a person would have to know the future; he would have to be a prophet in much greater degree than those of the primordial world. He would be illuminated not merely by individual rays of light communicated by another being: the entire future until the end of the world must be revealed to him. And he could not generate such knowledge otherwise than from his own thinking, which must know best of all, it being the god that brought forth the present, and will complete the future. After centuries of trying to get to know the simple law and the way of its production, after having had such a large quantity of its products made available, it should finally have succeeded!

But no system can yet boast of this discovery. Spinoza stopped at the assurance that things are only the necessary forms of expression of a substance: he did not demonstrate why the substance had to take on precisely these forms, or even could do so. Fichte in his earlier period, Schelling, Hegel sought to provide this demonstration, and it is not difficult to show that they did not succeed. In principle, Kant positively gave up on this. Nevertheless, there is no need here to turn to the invariable experience of failed systems; the demonstration failed because the proceedings it presupposes are contradictory in themselves and therefore in any case impossible – this being a bare negative assertion, it can be proved from the selfsame concept of these required proceedings.

As little as unity can be abandoned by science, so little can multiplicity, which is a circumstance requiring irrefutable explanation. The question is, how can this multiplicity exist along with that rational unity? There are two paths here: either it emerges from simplicity itself – this is decisive, self-evident rationalism. Exemplars are Spinoza, Fichte, and Hegel. Or it assumes a manifold matter outside of reason, through which reason expresses itself multifariously in addition to simply. This is the case with Kant and the school preceding him.

The first path immediately reveals its contradiction. The simple, the undifferentiated, which works only according to a necessary law which is always the same, cannot bring forth a variety. Why do I derive from the absolute (whether the general substance as per Spinoza, or the concept of self-consciousness as with Fichte) a plant here, an animal there, and not always one and the same thing? When I proceed from *as-yet indeterminate* substance or intelligence, it is impossible for me to do so. I must therefore assume to this end a multiplicity of various determinations in the absolute, prior to my deduction. But then unity itself is given up, which consists precisely in there not being anything differentiated prior to the deduction, and the differentiated emerging only through this movement, despite its being uniform.

The other path, which allows multiplicity to exist in matter, which itself gains unity only through reason, is incapable of establishing a connection between the two. The simple law of thought and manifold matter are entirely heterogenous and cannot bring about anything in common. To become connected to variety in a necessary manner, there must already be various relations corresponding to matter in thought itself, hence a multiplicity must be given. Nevertheless, various conclusions thought to be necessary were derived from simple, pure laws of reason and from this matter. Such was the procedure of dogmatic philosophy prior to Kant, and Kant as well in the practical portions of his work.

Here, however, the conclusion is usurped, just as in the first path the minor premise was. Both are attained by assuming various differentiations as an undifferentiated postulated principle prior to all deduction, while thinking them to have been gained by deduction. If one is consistent in the second path, then the multiplicity of things and rules is not derived from reason but is ready-made and given prior to reason and has no portion with reason. But then the unity that is predicated is only a unity of thought itself; matter, from which reason stands apart without any necessary connection, cannot thereby attain unity.

Hence, here as well either the unity that is the scientific requirement must be given up, or a midpoint outside of thought must be sought from which actual multiplicity could emerge, i.e., rationalist philosophy must be abandoned. Kant recognized this inadequacy of reason most deeply. If we do not assume any matter (things outside of our reason), then we cannot give a reason for the various conceptualizations we have; but if we assume this manifold matter, then reason, which allows of no multiplicity in the true sense, is not the principle or origin of things and cannot find anything outside of itself. This is the narrowness of Kant's system. He therefore had to give up the derivation of the world from pure thought and *a priori* knowledge not merely in theoretical but also in practical philosophy, and not only provisionally and relatively, because of the way we conceive change, but definitively and absolutely. Instead, he sought to satisfy the contradictory requirements by postulating a contradictory condition: synthetic knowledge without change, i.e., a multiplicity which is not manifold.

Application to Natural Law

Natural law therefore exhibits both of these attempts, and the impossibility of implementing them. From their simple premise, Fichte and Hegel wished to derive by this same logical process not only legal rules but the various human relations themselves. This is especially the case with Hegel. As simple premise, Fichte had the concept of self-consciousness without any other content as the characteristic of the opposition of a not-I to the I. This opposition is the concept of self-consciousness, and it is such even without any particular thing having to be the object of opposition. Why should the ever-uniform concept of self-consciousness demand the opposition of an organized body, or of other people, or the need for food, housing, education, etc., from which the majority of legal institutes arise, in terms of a necessary conclusion, and not arbitrarily but just exactly as the particular manifestations that crop up? The answer Fichte had prepared for this is the additional ground of determination for the second, by which the one had to turn out differently than the other; for example, if I first recognized reasonable people besides myself directly from the law of self-consciousness as necessary, then I now, but even only just now, must conclude that it is possible for me to have an effect on them, and so I must have a body. The untruth is firstly, that the abstract influence – the specific body had to be; but then it is already entailed that the first conclusion gave a certain result. The concept of consciousness, when it truly clothes itself with the opposition of the not-I, when something truly is, can by no law of thought produce a *specific* not-I, whether it be a body, other people, or whatever. There is an unbridgeable gap between the abstract and the concrete of any sort.

The natural law doctors as a whole and Kant, on the other hand, presupposed the manifold relations outside of reason; but what is just in them would always be the simple law of reason. Only insofar as a proposition necessarily has arisen by subsuming the ethically indifferent relationship under this rule, is it just. The only hindrance standing in the way of this is that such necessary propositions do not arise. The law of reason ever remains what it is, the immaterial, while the relations ever remain what they are, ethically indifferent. The rule takes up the material that is subordinated to it, but it might just as well take up another; the two do not combine to form an indivisible product. In the logical law of non-contradiction, which Kant, under the names universality and necessity, made into the principle of morality as pure law of reason, the consistent morality of a Franz Moor[164] would be just as appropriate as the Kantian, should one not assume a purpose for humanity [menschlichen Wesens] and relations in the world lying outside that law, which indeed contradicts such a morality. In that case, though, this purpose, not that law of reason, is the positive principle of morality which generates the multiplicity and specific nature of the laws.

Just as little does the abstract concept of freedom, and the uniform restriction thereof for others, generate a specific legal institution. In this freedom, a right over one's own life or over things, etc., cannot be accepted prior to subsumption. The mere restriction to equal protection for others has first to produce the *specific objects* of freedom from out of the infinite freedom comprising all objects. Therefore, in the same way that we deduce from this a right to things that excludes the right of someone else, we could deduce a right to conduct vendettas [Fehderecht] in terms of specific equal norms. For in what closer relationship does the empty concept of infinite freedom stand to someone else's

---

[164] [A character in Friedrich Schiller's play *Die Räuber* [The Robbers], cold, calculating, and without conscience.]

members than it does to things, all of which, in terms of this same concept, pertain to it in the same way that those members do? Contracts are by no means necessary, even if we assume a historical connection between the moment of promise and the subsequent ones: is freedom not violated if I lie assertorically? Why then if I do so promissorily? Why does Kant consider it a violation of the freedom of the intelligible man, which lowers him to a means, if his spouse does not have him exclusively as her spouse; why is this not also the case in other relationships, e.g., in which more than one person are employed at the same time, as with domestics?

If one sets human relations under the concept of equal freedom for all, then one set of relations could just as well flow from it as another, and either without contradiction. What impels the right choice is only the divine vocation, to which freedom is given in actuality, the content of which *is* given, instead of which *must be* given according to the laws of thought. It is the vocation of man to maintain himself through commerce, to be bound by contracts, to live in exclusive marriage. Only the purpose of things, the way in which and the purpose for which they are used, decides whether they should be *res communes*, communal property or private.

Relations have thus already produced a multiplicity of ethical determinations prior to the deduction of reason. Reason only recognizes these, it does not produce them; and if these relations had not produced them, reason would not be able to. Thought is not the effectuator of the ethic, and science must seek a different principle than reason in order both to recognize specific ethical requirements and to maintain unity in them. Certainly, the true cannot anywhere contradict thought, and those logical rules or the concepts abstracted from the given institutes must be found in all ethics. A provision that contradicts itself would not be a just one, because it never existed. Freedom and restriction are the ineradicable features of all law, and the eternal just law is therefore inconceivable without them; but they are not yet themselves a law, and they cannot produce one, regardless of what material is provided to them, not only a just one, but none at all. They are merely the restrictions of the same, which can tolerate the most opposed content. *From Spinoza to Hegel, this is the untruth which always recurs in changing forms, the eternal self-deception of the rationalist way of thinking: it borrows from reality things, ethical requirements, and assumes their development; and anything which does not* contradict *a form of thought is then passed off as* required *by it.*

Everything that is necessary is of an analytical character. With all deduction and movement, it can only posit that which was there prior to the deduction, and what necessarily pertains to the concept prior to the deduction. If Spinoza's statement, the nerve of rationalism, is adhered to: "the effect is given inexorably with the cause," then everything is analysis, there is only monism [Eines]. This is either simple, undistinguished – for in that case, with all conceivable lawful development, nothing can be produced from it but the simple, the undistinguished – or it is assumed up front to be a manifold determinate; in that case one begins with a composite concept, precisely what human thought cannot bear. The requirement of science, the requirement of people, that unity exist in the many things and ethical requirements, would not be satisfied through abstract procedure seeking this unity in reason. For if it was contained in this, no multiplicity would exist. On the contrary, if the multiplicity which undeniably is present is to be produced by unity, then the world and the ethic cannot have a necessary law as cause.

This is not to deny that all the knowledge, including that of the just, is only gained through our capacity to perceive, which after all may be called reason. But static thought determinations, which is what abstract philosophy understands to be reason, are only capable of grasping in its determinacy a content that we already possess, and of hindering its loss or the confusion caused by its shading into something else – a mere negative use. Even active thought and knowledge (reason in a higher and richer sense), which does not exist in these hollow, isolated forms, is after all only a means of knowledge, not the object of it. This latter lies outside of us: the divine Spirit and His free acts, nature that He created, history that He directs, the Word that He proclaims, the goal that He sets for the world. The true, the just are therefore that at which reason in its activity arrives, not what it is; they are what is discovered *through it*, not *from it*. It sees the light and testifies of the light, but it is not the light and did not make the light. This is precisely what is wrong with rationalism: it turns the organ of truth into truth itself, and because of this, it thinks that by dismantling and examining this organ it has obtained the content of the true, which this organ was supposed to convey. Even Fichte, although apparently conceiving reason as active, creative, nevertheless seeks all knowledge in what it is, what the concept of self-consciousness abstracted from action contains as necessary characteristic. No one is so foolish as to believe that the corporeal instruments through which we receive and distribute food, actually *are* our food. Such a conception corresponds with rationalism's procedure. Reason ignores everything worthy of knowledge outside of itself and considers only itself as active in knowledge. It disdains the nourishment offered to it in order – as the result of all areas of science has shown – to shrivel up in itself.

Lack of Certainty for Pure Rational Proof

Reason as a principle of science, as was shown, does not contain unity, but neither does it contain any assurance of truth, and thus does not satisfy any of the general scientific interests. Kant shows the inadequacy of the ontological proof on which all systems of reason [Vernunftsysteme] are built. Namely, the concept of absolute being, whether thought of as a personal God or empty existence, does not yet contain the necessity of actual existence. It is not a contradiction with the notion of being that there be no being. Because he makes the mere law of thought into a standard, Kant here, in accordance with his general character as sketched above, overlooks the actual guarantee of this proof, which is the existence of he who philosophizes, and who, in accordance with the law of non-contradiction, indeed postulates existence generally. One could otherwise go even farther than Kant and ask: who guarantees the proposition of non-contradiction itself, which is intended to guarantee or not guarantee the ontological proof? Only someone real, existing, united with knowledge and thus knowing, could contain the proof for himself and for the existence of others.

Fichte brought this assurance, which everywhere is the basis, to awareness, in that he deals with it right at the start of his scientific doctrine. In this manner, the same progress is found in the relation to the guarantee of the assumptions as to the assumptions themselves. But if existence itself, which is to extend this guarantee, is also taken as principle, then it cannot guarantee the same. "As true as I am!" is a poor guarantee coming from a finite being. For there is no certainty with regard to the "I am;" it is not in my power whether or not I will be in the next moment. But everything that is built on this consciousness of existence as consequence, expires with it as well. In one of Homer's most famous statements, the truth of which impresses us above and beyond many others, Hector is horrified of the slavery that awaits Andromache after his death, but he comforts himself: this fate will not be – certain though it will occur – because he himself,

Hector, will no longer be. Abstract substance, logically postulated with my existence, cannot be *causa sui*, in that I myself am not *causa mei*. My life itself is only a thing of experience; it is mutable, passing; it requires the eternal for its foundation. Thought cannot be such, for it itself is a consequence of my being, not a mere deduction from it. I am its real presupposition, for which reason it cannot be my presupposition. A real existence outside of myself must therefore be assumed as the eternal, which grants the eternal guarantee to what is mine, and thus to the reality of my thought. Not that which logically follows from the concept of my existence as foundation is what is persuasive to me, but that which my entire being (as effect) professes in a real manner. A greater test and confirmation is not required by any human mind.

The method of natural law therefore runs as follows: precisely while I am a thinking being, such and such is eternally absolutely just. It can be argued against this, *firstly*, that if there is no other source of judgment [Entscheidung] than that you are and that you think, then one thing is as just as another. *Secondly*, even if certain results present themselves, they still would not have any guarantee of their eternal absolute truth. For in itself your thought has no reality, and you yourself possess only a passing, relative reality.

Contradiction of Content: The Basic Concept Required by Natural Law

This shows that the method of natural law which recognizes a multiplicity of ethical prescriptions and nevertheless derives them from reason, thereby contradicts itself. The same contradiction is involved in the *content* of natural law, which was already depicted and here can only be summarized.

Abstraction must adhere to two postulates as the bases of law: freedom of the individual, and a law of pure reason which restricts that freedom. These bases are, however, irreconcilable. If the law of reason is the principle of deduction, then it excludes freedom; if individual freedom is that principle, it suffers no restriction. There remains only the choice between logical despotism and individual arbitrary will. Both of these principles in their decisive opposition are demonstrated by Kant's and Fichte's systems. And the result was confirmed already by the basic conceptions: Kant, starting with logical necessity, was only able to deduce a non-prohibition, not an entitlement; Fichte, on the other hand, proceeding from the real I, only attained anarchy.

But apart from these all-round philosophers, the entirety of natural law doctors formed a third party consisting in unconsciously making either one or the other of these contradictory things into a principle. The contradiction in this is obvious and everywhere encountered. In this manner, Wolff, proceeding from the principle of freedom, maintained that there is no *societas* and no *imperium* without voluntary agreement. On the other hand, he derives the parental association from the rational prescription of childrearing, and the same with countless others.

The representative of this party is Feuerbach. He stands out among all other practitioners by his acuity, precision, and prudence; with him, natural law insofar as it is determined by a universal system of philosophy and therefore likewise determined by juristic requirement and judgment, attained the completion of its basic concepts. In the deduction itself, he everywhere remains true to himself, and when despite this he arrives at contradictions, these can only be rooted in the points of departure. His confession of faith in his critique of natural law therefore contains the mixture of Kantian and Fichtean standpoints (for the doctrine of law cannot do without both principles, even if pure speculation had the courage to give one up), and their irreconcilability is demonstrated precisely through the sureness of his train of thought.

Like Fichte, Feuerbach wishes to have the right of individuals as the principle of law, thereby separating this from morality; this is to be no mere negative permission but rather a "positively sanctioned" entitlement, a "legal capacity" [juristisches Vermögen]. But like Kant, he also wants to have practical reason as the principle of law; for legal capacity to be ethically sanctified and restricted, it must follow from practical reason and exist for the purpose of practical reason (morality). Both are undeniably demonstrated. But it is precisely through this that Feuerbach finds himself cornered at the decisive point: how can positive entitlement be derived from practical reason? Unable to hide the fact that such is impossible, he nevertheless takes refuge in the Kantian unknowability of things: certainly it must follow from reason, but the "how?" of it cannot be understood.[165] This is obviously an entirely false usage of the thing-in-itself. For how something that truly follows from reason follows from it is considered by

---

[165] *Kritik des natürlichen rechts als propädeutik zu einer wissenschaft der natürlichen rechte* [Criticism of Natural Law as a Propaedeutic to a Science of the Natural Law], p. 265.

Kant to be knowable, otherwise all cognition would have to be abandoned. With him, the incomprehensibility of the "how?" relates only to our real impression of the ought, not to what the object of the ought is, and in what manner reason holds it to be necessary. Nor should a withdrawal behind Kantian unknowability be able to provide any protection at the present time.

And so, Feuerbach's critique – the culmination of natural law – has no other result than what was expressed above: *natural law demands the positive entitlement of the individual, and demands that this follow from a law of reason; but how this is possible cannot be understood.*

The Institutions that Arise from this Contradiction

This contradiction in the derivation of general concepts might be acceptable, since this derivation is only of scientific interest. The problem is, those contradictory principles lead to contradictory results in specific institutions, and the statesman who pays homage to natural rights sees himself challenged everywhere by conflicting institutions. If one follows the freedom of the acting person, then such a person must be given the opportunity to bring about change, and the results of this action, which is to say, the inequality of the legal condition, have to be recognized: property, guild rights, political privileges, in short, all acquired rights of whatever kind. But in that case the unchanging equality of the law of reason has been violated. On the other hand, to satisfy the law of reason, every historically generated advantage must be abolished, not merely prerogatives of occupational group [Standes] or commerce [Gewerbs] but also unequal property and claims acquired through contract. For either nowhere or everywhere is the original equal opportunity of each to obtain the same rights as others a justification of the inequality that now exists.

Therefore natural law's watchwords, "freedom and equality," are a logical contradiction. They nowhere provide a positive decision; but it is certain that the one will repeal the other, simply in terms of the concepts. Freedom demands action, which is change, inequality. Equality for its part continually demands immutability, and excludes freedom and action. When one principle is followed this time and another is followed that time, then at least such a procedure ought not be passed off as being necessarily guided by reason.

Chapter 2: Real Examination of Natural Law

In an investigation which looks for its standard not exclusively in logic but likewise in human interests and their satisfaction, it is permitted to conduct a critique simply by highlighting the results which are decisive in this respect; and as we logically inferred the unsustainability of the results from the unsustainability of the principles, so now conversely, we may prove the untruth of the foundations from the repulsiveness of the results.

Dissolution of Morality into Mere Correct Thought

The ethic itself, not merely its specific content, is here derived only from thought, either from my concept as thinking being (subjective rationalism) or from thought as cause of the world (objective rationalism). Hereby the particular character of the ethic, which exists in an original real relation, is abolished. Morality can have no other value than consistency, and immorality is only a form of inconsistency, to wit, the logical contradiction between thought and action. This is clear to both Kant and Fichte, although the ethicists who do not follow a comprehensive system still consider the morality of their theory to be what their immediate consciousness considers it, something independent and unique. The source of the ethic – thought – is therefore violated much more directly by a false chain of reasoning than by an act that runs afoul of it; the former would be a much greater sin. One is reluctant to accept such a result, however surely it results from the foundation; yet a trace of this is found in Hegel's contention that it is mortal sin to view our knowledge as limited.[166] It can only follow from my concept that I *am* something, not that I *ought* [to do] something. For my thought has no real power over me; a drive such as contained in the ought is incomprehensible as a product of thought, just as is the trepidation that is linked to the ethic. Conscience is only comprehensible when two real beings are assumed, not merely ones that act but also ones that prescribe. It is even more obvious that thought-necessity as the general cause of the world excludes the ought entirely. For the ought consists in the one demanding while the other is capable of refraining; but what the law of necessity entails in every

---

[166] Hegel, *Enzyklopädie der philosophischen Wissenschaften im Grundrisse* [Encyclopedia of the Philosophical Sciences in Outline], §. 386.

specific case is unavoidable; otherwise, it would not be the consequence of a necessary law. Spinoza therefore openly and dauntlessly abandons the concept of the ought, of good and evil. And with Hegel, as will be shown, this philosophy actually makes a comeback.

Negativity of Ethics, Morality as well as Natural Law

But the content of the ethic which is derived from reason can have no other nature than a negative one. Reason cannot generate anything; it can only exclude. Regardless of whether its commandment prescribes actions or omissions, it is only oriented to the avoidance of what should not be done or what should not be omitted. The ethic is ready from the outset with a concept, and what is required is not that something arise and occur, but that the concept not be eliminated. What is to be done is what would be unreasonable not to do. All virtue is fulfillment of duty – non-transgression. Hence, the original independent value of the act receives no recognition; this is only derived from the consistency, the decisive thing being the agreement of maxims in accordance with which one acts, not the act itself. Every true positive virtue – love, faith – is an act and it is uninterrupted; it cannot be thought of as inactive. Fulfillment of duty, on the other hand, is in itself without action, for when no demand is made, this virtue is not for that reason suspended; and so when action is undertaken, because action is not its core, then the principle is the main affair, for the act is only the means of preventing its own non-existence. The ethic must therefore be solved as a mathematical example: it must be able to prove what is duty and what is not, and everywhere the duty is either fulfilled or not. After all, the fulfillment of duty, which lacks all positive intensive content, is not capable of augmentation.

Relation of Negative and Positive Freedom and Equality

But what every unbiased mind reveres as the pinnacle are positive virtues, which originally and in terms of their essence consist in action, endlessly striving and creating, which therefore cannot be found and exhausted by any finished concept. Who could find the essence of love, for example, from the concept of thought, or of ought? What are the actions that necessarily arise from the concept of love, or will real true love be content with these actions deduced from their concept? Where it exists, it always leaves thought far behind, and no moral philosophy should dare to dictate or even wish to know in advance what it achieves.

Every great act, every manifestation of the sense of heroism, of the truly God-filled mind, comes therefore as a surprise, and is accompanied by the feeling that it was not to be found *a priori*. For it is a new creation, as wonderful as creation in general. The slightest object outside of us, when we look at it seriously, fills us with the feeling of incomprehensibility. A wonderful sensation is contained in the "It is!" — "This is your father, your friend; this is what got you into this situation;" why this one? yes, why are you who you are now? And such incomprehensibility consists in the fact that being cannot be dissolved in thought, that it is not logically necessary, but its reason is in a higher free power. How incomprehensible must this power itself be, God, and the positive virtues that He wills, that are like His essence! They are of unfathomable depth.

It cannot be said of the personal God what Spinoza said: I know Him, or I know Him not; but rather, I know Him, but I could know Him infinitely more. So it is with the Christian virtues; one can practice them here, but one can practice them even more, they demand this, but infinitely more is not beyond their requirements. There is no limit to how much they can be augmented. Love and faith can always grow in warmth, in strength, in excitement, because life and act are not mere elements of their expression, but their actual essence, what is elevated in them.

But rationalism only wishes for what it can master. It therefore makes God into an abstraction of being, which cannot be lacking, and virtue into fulfillment of duty, the ethical value of which consists in the fact that its opposite would abolish thought. It can deal with this abstraction just as it wishes, it can fully comprehend it, dissolve it in its thinking, in that it made it from that; they are less mysterious and wonderful than a grass flower.

In this manner, all positive virtues must disappear from modern [der neueren] ethics. Love is reproached by Kant precisely as a motive contrary to reason (morality). Hegel tolerates it as a lower stage in which reason is interwoven with matter; the uppermost here as well is fulfillment of duty, unavoidably demanded by the logical process and which only occurs in its consciousness.[167]

Above all, *faith* must lose the acknowledgement that it pertains to the ethic.

---

[167] Hegel, *Enzyklopädie der philosophischen Wissenschaften im Grundrisse*, §. 447.

For it is positive in the highest sense, a positing, a synthesis, and the polar opposite of analytical thought. It looks nowhere to the mere exclusion of the possibility of another, in the way that analytical thought does, and thus in the mere positing of what one already had. Which, after all, makes it possible, even probable, that things should be different, for example, that Christ rose again, that we will rise again, is made into an object of knowledge, the purest act of will, with the power of freedom – thus not contained in what preceded, but primordial – with a creative act. Just as what gives and authenticates freedom is courage alone, not the anxiously calculated security which only recognizes a good outcome when a bad one is unthinkable, so also is faith, and not the logically necessary deduction. As positive as faith itself is, just as positively it is an ethical requirement. Only a free act could establish this requirement. It cannot be derived from any necessary law, in that such a law does not require any faith for its existence, and thus cannot require it, indeed makes it impossible, because in the end it is necessary to know what it contains and what it excludes. The ethical meaning of faith stands and falls with the God of Christianity. He can require it because He could also refrain from doing what He does, for which reason creatures cannot know, but can only believe that He will do this. But it is because He requires it, because He *wished* to require it, not because it was necessarily required by His existence and His concept, apart from His act.

So then, the excellence of natural law consists in excluding what contradicts the concept of law. This makes it the completed, absolutely just law. It is thus enduring when it can lack nothing, when it contains nothing else than the determinations without which law is inconceivable; whereas all positive legal constructions, from the highest to the lowest, contain much extraneous material which can change without the legal concept ceasing. The highest condition containing nothing but the eternal therefore has no other virtue than this: not having what changes or could change. As if, since the uppermost is eternal and unchangeable, everything that is unchangeable must be the uppermost.

This concept of law, the characteristics of freedom (*in abstracto*) and their restriction are finished and given from the start of human relations; nothing but them is needed to recognize and establish the highest legal condition. Nothing new, nothing higher is to be formed, only that which lies beyond this concept shall be removed, and not much insight is needed to complete for eternity the construction of the legal world, which after this cleansing is no longer capable of improvement. This doctrine of justice certainly excludes what contradicts the legal concept, such as true lawlessness of a person or anarchy, but no less so all the great, all the unexpected, which have as little to do with those two characteristics as love and enthusiasm have with the concept of duty. In the same way that positive virtues are banned from morality, everything is banned from law which cannot be found by assuming it away, which a living drive for noble designs produces. In this manner, the entire state edifice of the Middle Ages, this positive elevated work of art, is rejected *in toto,* without any further examination of its content regarding what might have been lacking here or there, but simply because it all could be imagined otherwise than how it existed here, without causing the concept of law to cease – because it is the product of a force which is able to form something new, and which reason cannot emulate.

The highest destiny of mankind at which Kant arrives is eternal peace, i.e., that there be non-war, non-disturbance. This is all that reason has to offer in place of a positive condition, the kind to which the Republic of Plato and the true Christian writers refer, even if only in isolated strokes.

Nevertheless, these purely negative requirements, when contrasted with mutable, incomplete conditions, have an affinity precisely with the highest positive ones. Because of this, at first glance and by the sound of it, opinion is disposed to agree with them. But regardless, they are absolutely opposed to these positive requirements.

By means of such an affinity, the notion of the *equality before the law* aroused general enthusiasm, and even now, after the extinguishment of this fire, no one would dare to conceal the fact that only this equality of men truly satisfies, and that the opposite of it surely arouses opposition. But it is not because this equality before the law is contained in the concept of man that it is obvious to all, but because the idea of man, his divine purpose, intends the same thing; and only in this way of requiring equality, not in the other way, does it possess this power of conviction.

Freedom issuing from the concept is only equal for all because it determines none; it is an equality of empty possibility. Where it is filled with content, acquires certain rights, becomes a specific freedom, it also becomes unequal. But the freedom to which end man is purposed by God [i.e., freedom according to the ideal] is positive, and in its reality and its content, which alone is its value, it is the same for all. It does not tolerate, the way the other does, differences in possession, enjoyment, spiritual knowledge, etc. The freedom of the Platonic nobility, burdened with no earthly care so as to pursue the divine – this positive freedom is the destiny of every person. The mass of people, occupied by worries about where the next meal will be coming from, directing their labor to common things – this is as contrary to equality in terms of the idea as the inability of a class of persons to acquire possessions, is contrary to equality in terms of the concept. This is only one example of positive freedom, which according to the idea is equal to all, because the full content of it cannot be described and exhausted before the fact, as the negative can, but is an affair of the future, an augmentation, the end of which is hidden from us.

One could argue that this positive equality does not lie in eternal justice: what do you care if alongside you a higher life develops, a higher happiness exists? It is enough that you have the right to be who you are. Can the perennial complain that it is not the fruit tree, or the pebble that it is not a diamond? But this argument is flawed. For no man is allowed to be what he is as long as he is not allowed to be what his idea is, and this is the same for one person as for another: to be the image of God. But in terms of this purpose, everyone must also have the highest right, and there is nothing higher than the highest. For this reason, the inequality which cannot be avoided in actual conditions, is justified in terms of the same idea that the positive equality of man requires as end. For neither mankind as a whole nor the individual corresponds to it, but one more so than another. For this reason it is fair for the perennial to be left to itself and the fruit tree tended, for the pebble to lie in the alley while the diamond graces the king's crown. The man must have a different right than the woman and the child, the uneducated worker in his humble activity a different right than the leisured landowner, to the degree that the vocation of sex, age, status or class entails it.

For its part, negative freedom is already a finished product, which every moment requires the concept of the thinking being to be in all human beings; whereas the ideal of man must first be cultivated, and elevated by God. So then, in terms of the concept, faith must already be removed from law, for the concept contains no specific religion and only entitles each equally because it entitles none. On the other hand, man in terms of the idea is a Christian. If this is truly achieved, then there is no difference in entitlement by virtue of faith, and each is entitled in the specific elevated manner that Christianity entails. But as long as mankind has not arrived at this, the unequal entitlement of religious parties is justified precisely by the equality of destiny. Maintaining positive equality will not be achieved by abolishing differences, because to do so would also destroy the content, the specificity of which is only given in such interconnection with the present unequal vocation. But the freedom and equality which requires no specific content only needs to eliminate this inequality to be established.

In terms of this negative principle, every variation in law either shows itself *justified* because it lies outside the sphere of equality, or else it must be rejected as *injustice.* The standard of the positive principle, for its part, stands between two extremes – the *imperfection* which is relatively justified in terms of time and relation, but relatively unjustified in terms of the end of things. It also distinguishes between such advantages which, according to the concept, can only be gained through the disadvantaging of another, which, depending on circumstances, are considered imperfect or unjust, and those which either do not shortchange others or do so only because of the limitations of given conditions, as for example the protection of landholding families to keep them from losing their luster or fortune, and to maintain an uninterrupted bond of memory over generations, or the right of the spiritual estate not to have to gain a living otherwise than by performing ecclesiastical activities. The former view now considers advantages of the latter sort with an envious eye and seeks to erase them as contrary to the concept. But the latter view sees in them the content of the positive, prospective equal freedom for all; even if it does not approve of one particular iteration, whether generally or in a specific instance. It does not aim to eradicate them, but rather to elevate the others to them. It does not aim to turn the nobility into citizens, but to make the citizens noble.

Thus, as a whole, the positive just law (as far as law can be spoken of in the consummated human condition) makes a claim to eternity, just as abstract law does. But it does not consider itself to be the uppermost because it is unchangeable, like abstract law; it considers itself unchangeable because it is the uppermost. It is itself a specific legal construction and its elevation is seen in its content, in the forces it generates, in the appropriateness to higher natures, to specific living beings. It declares the legal constructions of experience to be mutable, not because every specific legal construction must be mutable by its nature, but because all those specific constructions are not yet what they should be.

The distinguishing feature of the historical view of the ethic, therefore, is by no means proclivity for relative judgment or the past for the past's sake, but that its absolute is a future, a goal of things yet to come.

Destruction of Public Law

These are the consequences of the abstract character, in accordance with which only what is logically necessary has validity. Therefore they are unavoidable in every system of reason, regardless of their form and the more or less hidden manner in which they may be manifested. It is now necessary to give an overview of the consequences as they are evoked by the subjective principle in its immediate effect; for they are what distinguishes the development up until Fichte from what follows thereafter.

The subjective mainspring affected the moral view less in science than in life. In life, namely, the violation of the holiest relations began to be considered minor missteps; indeed, they even came to be considered permissible, if only they did no immediate harm. Science, however, did not wish to renounce moral dignity, and found a shield in logical necessity, which it set above man, under which, in this time of need, those relations could find shelter, even though only via arbitrary assumption; for the unconditional prohibition of divorce and incest, for instance, can as little be demonstrated by logic as by the well-being of others.

In the legal view, on the other hand, philosophy did not shy away from the results, if only freedom and the right of man were carried out as a principle of the laws. In its morality it had something to fall back on, and whatever it destroyed that was holy in law, it could always resort to the excuse that this was only removed from coercive institutions, not repealed entirely. Thus, consideration for the dignity and beauty of the state in its outward manifestation was consistently banished from the laws of its institution – blasphemy, suicide, perjury, where it did not endanger specific persons, even the murder of someone sentenced to death, who himself had no more right to his life, could not be considered a crime – marriage must be able to be dissolved arbitrarily, violation of marriage be thrown open. Every restriction in the disposition over things (even if intended by nature for generations, e.g., forests) or in the operation of trades for the purpose of general prosperity was inadmissible as such, regardless of accomplishment. The concept of the fatherland, the nation, in which people appear in non-voluntary association, has no place in this doctrine of law. Any aggregate of people can make itself into a nation [Volke] and no nation is a nation when they do not will it. The core of natural law as philosophical doctrine is not so much popular sovereignty as the sovereignty of individuals, and the sovereignty of the people as a whole over them has thereby ceased. No one is obligated by anything to which he has not freely subjected himself. Only what everyone happens to want is law, and if they do not agree, there can be no law.

This sovereignty of every individual *establishes* the state in terms of a contract, the existence and content of which requires unanimity. This sovereignty *rules* over it continually, for all power is valid only as the product of that unanimous decision, whether it is the power of a monarch, a representation, or merely the power of a majority vote. The king, the representation, even the entire people, to the degree that it makes decisions in accordance with a law of suffrage, are only delegates and officers of that original people, i.e., disunited individual persons. In the church, this view leads to the consummation of the collegial system, according to which the members' will is the law for the church rather than the church and its immutable content being the law for the members. These results, as already the principle, completely abolish the concept of public law. There is no more state, no church, no family, the law of which is valid; only the right of individuals, separately and in aggregate; there is nothing but private law. People are in the state, not to form unity but to secure their separate existences. Where, driven by necessity, those relations are recognized, it is not for their sake but because people come to an understanding about them. What looks like public law is only a voluntary transfer, and therefore a revocable one – private law. In this manner the ethic of the world perishes and the divine disappears from the earth. People are left with the burden of having to cultivate this on their own, while the sacred archetypes and the desire in their breasts may *never* correspond to an outward formation expressing them and lending visibility to their meaning. No human disposition could endure a world created in terms of such a doctrine. Those called to sanctification would have to rub shoulders with profanity; the living, with the emptiness and the negativity. And death from the non-satisfaction of yearning or from the boredom of monotony, is the punishment which the law of reason unavoidably imposes on itself, should it be in a condition to implement what it demands, and to maintain it for the duration.

The innermost untruth of natural law, which must strike every unprejudiced observer as soon as it is stated, is that it completely disregards the *inherent purpose of life relations*. Every human life relation bears within it its own particular purpose and thereby lays upon people a vocation to fulfill it accordingly, to give shape to it. This is the basis for the moral requirements that pertain to it, and also the requirements of its legal arrangement. For instance, the inherent purpose of marriage (the union of spouses for full life community), and not the reciprocal relinquishment of freedom among spouses, is that from which the entire legal formation of marriage proceeds: the obligation of faithfulness and community for better or worse, the prohibition on polygamy, incest, arbitrary divorce; the purpose of parental relations from which proceeds on the one hand paternal power, on the other the sustentation of children. The same holds true for every other human relation: property transactions, occupational groups, political groups, local community, state, church. This purpose of life relations is the principle of both ethics and law. All actual law indeed aims for this, and law is rational to the degree that it is shaped in accordance with these relations.

For natural law, however, this inner purpose of life relations does not exist, for it takes bare freedom and reciprocal recognition of the freedom of men as its standard. In that way, however, the true requirements of a rational law or a law answering to nature by necessity escape it. What God or nature wish to attain in and through every relation is not pursued; rather, only the uniform in everything, in order for men to maintain their freedom, with no one forced to do something he does not wish to do. For this reason, natural law is *destructive* in all spheres of life; for "destructive" means nothing other than the ruination of the order required by the nature of a relation. It is destructive to the family, for in accordance with its doctrine incest, polygamy, arbitrary divorce are liberalized; destructive to the social group, for the determining consideration is not the assured preservation of all but merely free laissez-faire. It is especially destructive to the state. It does not recognize the tasks which lie in the purpose of the state, to maintain a higher order over men, nor the organic distribution of position for its fulfillment, nor the authority and power which accrue to it automatically and originally precisely for this purpose; rather, it considers the state to be an arbitrary meeting of men for the mere protection of their freedom along with their necessary equal status, without any sort of power than what men freely establish in it. The entire business of natural law is indeed none other than to ignore the true objective life order, which lies precisely in the purpose of life relations, and to derive such an order simply from nature, or more accurately, from the freedom of man; the result can therefore be none other than the destruction of this order.

This purpose of life relations is the ground on which true legal philosophy takes its stand in opposition to the false philosophy of natural law.[168]

The Truth in the Motive of Rationalism and the Law of Reason

In his state, Plato violates the right of individuals; this kept him from attaining the ideal of beauty for which he sacrificed them. Here we see the opposite. Everything is sacrificed to human independence, and it destroys itself precisely through its exclusivity. For in this exclusivity it cannot acknowledge a free existence above it, and falls under the rigid necessity of its own forms of thought, which do not tolerate personality and freedom. Expressed in the language of the school: subjectivity as a principle necessarily leads to abstraction, and this in turn erases subjectivity. A motive that destroys itself cannot be the true one, at least in this form. On the other hand, a motive cannot be without truth which for several centuries held the faith of the best and brightest, and set the most outstanding minds in motion. This truth is now to be sought out.

What prompts man to resort to abstraction is the non-conscious and therefore haphazard character of the world around him. Awareness of the dependence of created existence is not lacking to man, but he cannot consider himself the creature of this motley being, lacking control of itself, as the world manifests itself. So Spinoza sees the unity and intelligence in his mind, and stands in amazement of and reverence for it, as if confronted with another being higher than himself. He must find it expressed in the world if he is not to despise that world. Because in actuality he possesses no power to change the world's manifestations, he considers the static, the immutable in his understanding, to be what has created and joined them. The course of development elevated this static intelligence into an active one. The result gained by the scientifically logical progression up until Fichte, is: *only the self-conscious is. Everything impersonal only has a purely derived existence and requires personality as cause. Only the personal is entitled and can be an end.* This philosophically establishes the right of the living over the dead, of those with understanding over those lacking

---

[168] Cf. Stahl, *Principles of Law*, § 5.

insight and consciousness; it brings the true pure motive of rationalism to its final end.

But the mistake here is that it is still human personality – as with Spinoza it was the static law of reason – which is regarded as the sole existing and therefore as the absolute, or even the mere concept of personality, which then always leads back to what is human. From this comes the absurd result: the world – of which it is now understood that it is inconceivable except as the work of a self-conscious originator – can only be the product of *our* self-consciousness. In this way our faculty of thought, which is imparted and therefore only capable of registering, must assume the place of an original and creative faculty. The world itself – in that its shape is truly necessary and immutable *on our behalf* – ceases to be the product of a *free* intelligence *at all;* it must be asserted that the creation compels the creator. This is the negative gain of the orientation, the truth that results from the inability to implement the opposed attempt: the world cannot be derived from human intelligence, and another cause for it must be sought. In terms of the positive gain of this orientation, however, the cause can only be personal since nothing unconscious has causal existence. The deeper insight in the course of the newer philosophy therefore ensures against the divinization of matter, but no less against the divinization of the impersonal law of reason, with which it, misunderstanding itself, began, and from which the principle of acting reason cannot free itself, as long as it conceived as merely human or as reason *in abstracto.* This insight is the end of rationalism outside itself, at which point it must be abandoned, which therefore is not to be expected from its own process.

No less, however, did rationalism have a true motivation in the endeavor to comprehend the world in terms of the inherent, highly pronounced intelligence in it. God as the absolute intelligence built His creation not by accident but by intelligence, and should man, who is the image of God, even in the most degraded condition, not recognize this intelligence, even if only as a premonition and by approximation? The error lies in considering mere reason – formal thought determinations – to be this active creative intelligence, the product and expression of which is the world.

In the ethic, too, liberation from all created things, which as such are not self-conscious and not powerful, is the true motive of abstraction. Man cannot be the mere means for the state, as little as he can be the product of nature; through the dignity of personality, he stands over both. His happiness, his freedom, his act is what he should be, and the most perfected edifice of the state carried out without the knowledge and will of individuals has no ethical value. But over him is a personality whose purpose it is to fulfill his goal, whether it is aimed at individual actions or at the maintenance of enduring relations. Accordingly, instead of the rigid political virtue of the ancient world and the superficial profane virtue of most recent times – in terms of which one man is a god to another – the original virtue which has the fear of God as its center must take over.

But in ethics, as in theoretical philosophy, only human personality is laid at the foundation, and this rupture has brought about the horrors and emptiness of recent times. On the other hand, this liberation from the impersonal is behind the great political results, the enduring benefits and the ornaments of the age, which gloriously distinguish it above all others. Its epitome is humanity in the noblest sense of the word. It abolished torture and serfdom; it grants freedom of investigation and communication, freedom of aspiration to the highest as well as the lowest; it therefore guarantees the freedom of departure from church and state and the protection at least of private rights for every creed. It creates the tolerance which allows man to be accepted on his own merits, which recognizes his will, measures his capacity and therefore is mindful of the blindness of individuals or entire peoples in faith and deed. By contrast, how entirely separated by religion, state, class, was one person from another in ancient and medieval times, so that the one ceased being human to the other! And what outward persecution and inward contempt did the purest, most noble efforts meet with from those who thought differently! These gains are no longer contemplated with satisfaction because people became accustomed to them, and received them in the wake of great troubles; and indeed, there is no shortage of attempts recklessly to abandon them and to extinguish them. We see many taking serfdom under wing in order to be historical, and preaching fanaticism in order to be religious. The Christian religious parties, freed from previous partitions, prompted by self-interest to rapprochement, begin to do the opposite, to shut out one another in antagonism. Instead of free education, which favors open manly independence, people believe they need to reintroduce slavish discipline. But these efforts at reaction are by their very nature ephemeral and without consequence; public opinion opposes them; humanity will not allow what was purchased with such great sacrifices to be snatched away again. The fact that such humanity is a noble fruit of modern science in the manner of thinking as well as in public institutions will not be denied by anyone who is unbiased. In it can be seen the enduring value of the now-discredited subjectivity viewpoint, and if the destruction caused by the noted mistake forces us to seek a new doctrine which restores the ruined glory, then we only have to recognize such a one that at the same time secures that achievement.

The liberation of man from nature and the unconscious constructs of the ethical world therefore is the gain of Fichte's stage. The absence of something higher, such as human personality and the knowledge of it as something personal, is that to which this stage necessarily points, even though from this point philosophy took different paths, and in doing so left no stone unturned.

PART V: THE REVOLUTION AS THE FINALIZATION OF NATURAL LAW

Chapter 1: The Doctrine of Popular Sovereignty until Rousseau

The Relation of Liberalism and the Revolution to Natural Law

The great world-historical significance of the events in France at the end of the previous century, which we call *the Revolution*, lay not in the mere act of revolt, but in the coherent doctrine which was realized through that revolt. The Revolution is no mere act of violence and overthrow; it is a system of principles and institutions, a political and constitutional system. Indeed, for this system it is indifferent whether it is attained by "peaceful development" or by the spilling of blood, for the system itself remains the same. Even what is called *liberalism* in the technical, historically established meaning of the word – as opposed to what is understood in a mere linguistic sense as being the liberal manner of thinking and liberal institutions – is nothing other than this system of Revolution, either in its full energetic implementation or in a dilution that natural living conditions, external resistance, or its own sloth tend to bring on.

Liberalism, or Revolution in this sense, is the product of the principles upon which "natural law" is based. In the Revolution they appear in their final consistent accomplished manifestation, as in natural law they appear in their most subterranean foundation; in the former from their practical side, in the latter from their theoretical side. Natural law seeks the aprioristic explanation and justification of the state, while the Revolution seeks the aprioristic establishment and formation of the state. That is to say: the former makes the attempt to do away with the state in thought and deduce it purely from reason, while the latter makes the attempt to do away with the state in actuality and found a new one purely from reason, although both enact the rational state merely from the notion of freedom or the will of men. This explains why natural law is so compliant when it is confronted with reality; it can reconcile itself with any condition, and seeks to justify it by assuming a tacit agreement, in so doing satisfying its theoretical interest; the Revolution, by contrast, aims to break the power of reality, and destroys any institution that does not follow from its concepts of pure reason. For every constitution, the former provides the fiction that it was willed in order for it to consider itself free; the latter tolerates no constitution that was not willed and as such is not truly free.

The most eminent of liberalism's authors is Rousseau. With him the principle of older natural law is conducted consequentially to the point at which it issued forth in the complete doctrine of Revolution, needing only to be consummated. It therefore precedes the French Revolution, in the same manner that a physicist's explanation preceded the experiment. Nevertheless, he showed himself to be a poor physicist, for the experiment failed.

But natural law by no means developed into the teachings of Rousseau and the Revolution on its own; the practical turn and energy come from another source, the flow of which courses through modern history; its confluence with natural law first gave rise to the doctrine of the Revolution. This other train of thought is to be shown here.

The Defense of Rebellion in Consequence of Church Movements (Buchanan, Milton, Languet)[169]

The ecclesiastical reformation of the 16th century also took on a decisive political character, both with the Roman peoples and the Reformed bloc. In the first place it was taught regarding the constitution of the church that according to immutable divine order (*jure divino*) the Christian congregation, as the community of the saints, must have the supreme authority in ecclesiastical matters. In many countries, especially those in which state power resisted the Reformation or at least ecclesiastical autonomy, this was then extended to the point that the community of the saints, the people of God, was considered to have the supreme authority from God generally and therefore also for the civil condition, and therefore is authorized and even obligated to depose and even punish kings who resist God's commandment. This doctrine spawned powerful movements in Scotland and England, and in fact preceded the overthrow of the state in England. Despite deep-seated differences, this overthrow rightfully has been called the harbinger of the French Revolution. In this shape, in which the movement is fulfilled as a theocratic conception of the reign of the saints based on the inspiration of the Holy Spirit, on parallels with the Old Testament, it has yet to receive a scientific explanation. But from this movement there came, usually in defense of such explanations, an attempt to justify, by other means within the scope of the scientific learning of that time, that which the specifically theocratic conception had attained in life. These are the writers in the age of these

---

[169] [See footnote 3 on p. xvii for comments on Stahl's treatment.]

religious-political wars and uprisings, usually characterized as *"king opponents"* [Königtumsbekämpfer] (Monarchomachs), in particular Languet, [170] Buchanan, Milton.[171]

These writers have the same motivations of the mind, and their writings have similar demands and purposes. Languet as a French Huguenot wrote in opposition to the royal power that suppresses the Protestant faith;[172] Buchanan justified the cause of the Scots against the Catholic Mary Stuart; Milton conducted the famed defense of the English people against the accusation of Salmasius with regard to the execution of Charles I. But they also largely share the entire body of thoughts and rationales, except that Milton exceeds the others both in democratic coloring and in wealth of thoughts and mastery of depiction.

They initially combat the doctrine "that the prince is not bound by the laws," taken from later Roman law and used against the movement in a servile or slavish sense. Their own doctrine elevates the peoples over the princes: all power proceeds from the people and is transferred from the people to the king; therefore the people is higher and more powerful (*superior et potentior*) than the king; that is, when rule is exercised badly, power can be demanded again for the goal for which it was transferred, so that the people ends up with penal power over the king. They prove this first *by the nature of the case* (*lex naturae*), since power only exists for the purpose of the people, since a people is possible

---

[170] [Stahl credits Hubert Languet with authorship of the *Vindiciae contra Tyrannos* (see following footnote). Modern scholarship attributes this to Philippe du Plessis-Mornay: see the discussion in Franklin, *Constitutionalism and Resistance in the Sixteenth Century: Three Treatises by Hotman, Beza, & Mornay*.]

[171] Junius Brutus (Hubert Languet, †1581), *Vindiciae contra Tyrannos* [English translation: Mornay, *A Defence of Liberty against Tyrants*]; George Buchanan (†1582), *De Jure Regni Apud Scotos, Or a Dialogue, Concerning the Due Priviledge of Government in the Kingdom of Scotland;* John Milton (†1674), *Defensio pro Populo Anglicano*, 1651 [English translation: *A Defence of the People of England by John Milton; in Answer to Salmasius's Defence of the King*].

[172] Languet's liveliest thought is that when the king suppresses the true church, introduces "idolatry," the people are required to resist and punish the king, because God says, "whoever does not call upon the name of the Lord shall die the death" (quaest. II).

without a king but not vice versa, since the people precedes the king (so they all thought); then *from Holy Scripture*, the dicta that those who rule should be servants, that he who does not call upon the name of the Lord (even the king) shall die the death, likewise the Old Testament series of events, namely the election of Saul by the people; then the *example of the Romans* (especially with Milton), partly the dicta of famous men such as Cicero, Tiberius, partly the laws, namely the *lex regia*, by which the people transfer power to Caesar; finally from *the analogy with ecclesiastical relations* (with Buchanan and Languet) while already in the Catholic church a powerful party was of the opinion that the entire church (the episcopate) stood over the Pope, that a distinction needed to be made between the papacy and the person installed in the papacy, etc.

The notion that all power and majesty is originally held by the people and only derivative with the king is therefore already developed here.[173] But this notion is manifested in isolation, without connection to a general scientific conception of the state such as is the case with the natural law doctrine of Grotius and Hobbes. To wit, with all these writers the notion is lacking which attends Grotius' natural law, of the foundation of the state by contract, which first places human will principially above all authority. They do sometimes conceive of the relation between prince and people as a contract or covenant, but they do not derive the unification of the people, and their being constituted to form the state, from contract. Hence the basic idea of the higher power of the people over the king is not used to present the people's rule as a necessary and permanent constitutional condition, but merely to justify the isolated act of revolt. There is no question as to whether the people should retain and transfer power, and the recovery of power is everywhere referred only to the case in which the

---

[173] "Ut potestatem sic majestatem etiam populo adimere et in regem conferre studes, vicariam si vis et translatitiam, primariam certe non potes uti nec potestatem" Milton, *Pro Populo Anglicano Defensio, contra Claudii Anonymi, aliàs Salmasii, Defensionem Regiam*, ch. 7, p. 199. ["As you have endeavoured to take all Power out of the Peoples hands, and vest it in the King, so you would all Majesty too: A delegated, translatitious Majesty we allow, but that Majesty does chiefly and primarily reside in him, you can no more prove, than you can, that Power and Authority does." *A Defence of the People of England*, p. 168.]

king is at fault,[174] apart from which he is not denied a real and hereditary right of dominion. On the same basis, by the people who are to judge the king they understand the ordered arranged people, thus the lordships, governments, royal officials, in short the magnates[175] (the majesty [Ansehen] of which itself is referred back to a popular mandate), or the people in its naturally given unity, without being derived from the consent of individuals.

Connection of Natural Law to the Doctrines of Revolt (Sidney, Locke)

Hence natural law existed as a scientific theory of the state which undertook to change nothing in life, in particular not to unsettle the existing supreme power. And there existed likewise this doctrine of revolt, which proceeded merely in terms of a practical goal, to make the people judge over the king and an avenger of tyranny, without a scientific conception of the state. It was first Sidney and then Locke who joined together this practical doctrine of revolt and the scientific political doctrine of natural law, and thereby founded the system of Revolution which Rousseau brought to completion.

Sidney follows in the footsteps of those writers, in particular Milton, and combats the doctrine of a lawless royal power and unconditional obedience, in particular against [Sir Robert] Filmer, demonstrating from the nature of the case the superiority of the people to the prince, the freedom of men to establish their constitution and elect their ruler. To do this he appropriates the natural-

---

[174] Even with Milton, chs. 6 and 7.

[175] Hubert Languet, namely at the end of quæst. III: „Hujus vero foederis seu pacti (i.e., between prince and people) regni officiarii vindices et custodes sunt." ["The officers of the kingdom are the guardians and protectors of these covenants and contracts." Mornay, *A Defence of Liberty Against Tyrants,* p. 212.] As such, "those who have generally undertaken the protection of the kingdom; as the constable, marshals, peers, palatines, and the rest, every one of whom, although all the rest do either connive or consort with the tyranny, are bound to oppose and repress the tyrant; and those who have undertaken the government of any province, city, or part of the kingdom, as dukes, marquesses, earls, consuls, mayors, sheriffs, etc." *Ibid.,* pp. 212–213. Likewise quaest. II: "qui universum populi coetum repraesentant" ["represent the whole body of the people," p. 97]. Milton vindicated for England, in accordance with the existing constitution, the supreme authority of the plebs without special voting rights for the optimates.

legal deduction of the state and precisely in the form given it by his countryman Hobbes: how people are originally in a natural state of complete independence, and out of mutual fear erect the civil state, by contract.[176] But in terms of that living mainspring of kingship bowing to the people, he modifies this natural law theory and converts if from a contemplative to a revolutionary one. This occurs most decisively through his elimination of the tacit contract, which until then natural law had generally assumed for the existence of states. He accepts the first thesis of natural law, that the subjects of state power cannot be bound otherwise than by their consent; but he denies the second, that everywhere, and especially under a despotic constitution, this consent is granted or anticipated, and denies that the subjects are truly bound.

> Tho the right of magistrates do essentially depend upon the consent of those they govern, it is hardly worth our pains to examine, Whether the silent acceptation of a governor by part of the people be an argument of their concurring in the election of him; or by the same reason the tacit consent of the whole commonwealth may be maintained: for when the question is concerning right, fraudulent surmises are of no value; much less will it from thence follow, that a prince commanding by succession, conquest, or usurpation, may be said to be elected by the people; for evident marks of dissent are often given: Some declare their hatred; others murmur more privately; many oppose the governour or government, and succeed according to the measure of their strength, virtue, or fortune. Many would resist, but cannot; and it were ridiculous to say, that the inhabitants of Greece, the kingdom of Naples, or duchy of Tuscany, do *tacitly assent* to the government of the Great Turk, king of Spain, or duke of Florence; when nothing is more certain than that those miserable nations abhor the tyrannies they are under; and if they were not mastered by a power that is much too great for them, they would soon free themselves. And those who are under such governments do no more assent to them, tho they may be silent, than a man approves of being robbed, when, without saying a word, he delivers his purse to a thief that he knows to be too strong for him.[177]

---

[176] Sidney, *Discourses concerning Government*, ch. 2, section 1.

[177] *Discourses Concerning Government*, ch. 2, section 6.

With this train of thought, natural law, which is to say, Grotius' doctrine of the state contract, steps off of the stage of contemplation and onto the stage of action. It is not to be found in Grotius, Hobbes, Pufendorf, Thomasius, Wolff, Kant, nor even in Fichte. But it is to be found in Sidney and following him, Locke and Rousseau. The two main phases of modern legal philosophy can be distinguished as the natural law system and the revolutionary system.

Locke,[178] who through his doctrine of the separation of powers broke new ground in another direction, namely that of the construction of the constitutional system, in this respect only stands on the same ground as Sidney, albeit perhaps with a more refined execution. Like Sidney and in the same manner, he marries natural law theory (the "perfect freedom" of the state of nature and the establishment of the state on contract) with the ideas of combatting kingship. In this, though, he takes a step toward Rousseau, in that he expresses the notions which otherwise dawn already with Milton in a more specific fashion: royal power is nowhere actual sovereignty (supreme power), or could only be considered as such in a certain sense.[179] In the meantime, his entire conception is based on the notion that the king acquires a true right (even if not sovereignty in the strict sense) through contract and transfer, and therefore devotes an entire section, just as his predecessors did, to the justification of revolt against tyrants; that is the demonstration that in the case of abuse, the king can have the (thus truly) transferred power revoked again.

But in order to complete the doctrine of popular sovereignty, the step still needed to be taken by which the people does not transfer its power at all, the king does not acquire any right; that accordingly the entire concept of a revolt

---

[178] *Two Treatises of Government.* The peculiarity of Locke's natural law theory itself, based on his empirical standpoint, is of no influence in this regard. This will be discussed in more detail in the appendix to Book III [pp. 259ff.].

[179] To wit, the people as legislator is the "supreme power," but because the legislating assembly is not always active, the executive which likewise has a share in legislation may be called the supreme power, but only as the executor of the laws, § 149. In this way, Milton said of the English king (*op. cit.*, ch. 8), "neque enim ad leges ferendas sed ad custodiendas à populo latas constitutus erat" ["a King of England can of himself make no Law: For he was not constituted to make Laws, but to see those Laws kept, which the People made," *A Defence of the People of England*, p. 182].

drops out, since the dethronement of the king, even without a reason, is nothing other than the ever-authorized competence of the ever-legitimate sovereign, the people. Rousseau took this step.

The Jesuitical Doctrine

At the same time the doctrine of revolt was developed by the Jesuits, albeit from an entirely different standpoint. They taught, in the interest of the papacy, that the secular power is not from God, like the ecclesiastical power is, but in its specific form (*formaliter*), i.e., as regards the specific form of government and specific rulers, is from the people or the community (*a populo vel communitate*), and thus is not a matter of divine but human law.[180] It is the same notion as was expressed earlier by Milton and later by Rousseau. The former wrote, "power (*potestas*), not princes (*principes*), is from God," while the latter wrote, "it is not clear whether God wills that this form of government be preferred to that one, or that one should obey Peter rather than Paul, and this is what matters."

The conclusion is obvious: when people do not abolish the ruling authority in its entirety but only remove a particular king, who indeed as such derives his power from them, then they do not sin against a divine institution. In this self-same spirit, in certain degree the Spanish Jesuit Juan de Mariana in the early 17th century went farther than even the French Revolution. He sanctioned the revolt not merely of the people, as decided in an assembly, but also when such an assembly is not possible (*si publici conventus facultas erit sublata*), in which case every individual is required to murder the tyrant, for where the possibility for citizens to gather is taken away, the will still exists to destroy tyrants, to punish the infringements of princes, etc. But this is not to take place by poisoning, partly because execution by poison is not a punishment practiced in Christendom, partly because this poses a threat to others besides the tyrant. In particular, the assassination of Henry III by a monk is praised.[181] To the degree that the doctrine of revolt was praised by the defenders of the papal system, it was

---

[180] Suarez, *Tractatus de Legibus ac Deo Legislatore* [Of the Laws and God the Lawgiver], book III, ch. 4. Cf. Stahl, *Der Protestantismus als politisches Princip* [Protestantism as a Political Principle].

[181] Mariana, *De Rege et Regis Institutione* [Of Kingship and its Institution], book I, chs. 6 and 7.

combatted by the representatives of Gallican episcopalism.[182]

Without a doubt, in this manner the Jesuits made an essential contribution to the undermining of royal majesty and prepared public opinion for the subsequent overthrow of the state. Nevertheless, their doctrine in itself had nothing in common with that of natural law and the Revolution, even though it corresponded with it in certain results and even in the manner of argumentation. For the latter put kingship under the pure human will of the people, while the former combatted it for the benefit of a theocratic power to which the people likewise is unconditionally subjected, just as princes are.

---

[182] Petrus de Marca, *De Concordia Sacerdotii et Imperii, seu de libertatibus ecclesiæ Gallicanæ* [Of the Concord of Priesthood and Empire, or the Liberty of the Gallican Church], book II, ch. 2.

Chapter 2: Rousseau

Inclusion of Doctrines Developed to this Point
With Rousseau[183] we find the gamut of notions as they developed up until him: the natural law doctors (Grotius and Hobbes), the defenders of revolt (Languet, Buchanan, Milton), finally those who drew upon both (Sidney and Locke): that men are free and independent by nature, and through contract establish the state for their protection and utility; that majesty and power are based solely on transfer, because no one in himself has them over his equals; that the people can reclaim the power that it has transferred, and may judge its king. All of this is only the inheritance that Rousseau received from his predecessors. If we inquire into what sets him apart, into the new and powerful principle that appears through him as the fulfiller of this development of thought, as representative of the world-historical catastrophe of the Revolution, then this can be stated in one word: the *inalienability of freedom*. Freedom was already the principle of development up until Rousseau; he was the first to make its absolute inalienability into a principle, and to implement it as such. This is the character and the epitome of his doctrine.

Accordingly, he first refutes Grotius' contention that a people can subject itself to princes by contract, indeed unconditionally, in the way that a man contractually can enter into slavery. To renounce freedom, he responds, is to renounce one's status as a man, to renounce the right of humanity, indeed its duties, and no alienation is permitted where no compensation or any equivalent is possible. With Grotius, the contract establishing the state had a civil-legal and therefore accidental nature; with Rousseau, by contrast, it receives a public and necessary character. It is the duty of men and of peoples to stay free; preservation of freedom is therefore a public necessity, in accordance with which the validity of the state contract is oriented.

Rousseau's Doctrine
The problem, however, arises from this principle: to find such a form of state association ("forme d'association") that *really does not alienate* freedom, but in

---

[183] *Du Contrat Social* [Regarding the Social Contract], 1762.

which everyone, by obeying the state, only obeys himself, and therefore remains as free as before. This form of government is then the one necessarily offered by nature, the only permissible one; any other is void, even for the slightest deviation ("moindre modification"). While Rousseau's predecessors considered a multiplicity of legal relations to be possible depending on the specific constitution, only one is manifested here as lawful and valid for all existing states. According to Rousseau, this form ("les clauses de ce contrat"), i.e., the solution to the problem, is now *the complete alienation of each member of society with all his rights to the whole community*. Rousseau's opinion that this truly solves the problem is based on the following:

First, the alienation must be done to *all*, to the whole community, not to a subject different from these "all," a king, a senate, a representative assembly; for in that case one does not alienate oneself with the alienation, because one remains an equal part of these "all" and gains as much as he gives up, or to use another expression, it is the *absolute reciprocity* through which freedom remains unalienated despite the alienation, for which reason social obligations are binding only for the sake of this reciprocity.

Second, it must be a *total* alienation without reserve ("sans reserve"), because the condition of equality ("condition égale") is achieved when each surrenders with all his rights, and only then does absolute reciprocity truly manifest itself. If a member of society retains something, an acquired right, he would stand over against others with it, and they would have divested themselves for the protection of that right while not receiving it back, in so doing truly relinquishing part of their freedom. Accordingly, the inalienability of freedom in this sense includes equality, and it is thus the *principle of equality,* which was lacking in Rousseau's predecessors, which he was the first to draw up and scientifically implement.

In this way freedom is not abandoned, and the coercion which is applied by the state contract is none other than the association *forcing the member to be free* ("on le forcera d'être libre").

Doctrine regarding the Basic Relation of the State Association and its Correlates

Through this complete alienation of all to all, a will of the whole association as a unity arises. This is the *general will* ("volonté générale") in which all individuals equally concur, but which stands above all individuals, as unity. It is the *sovereign*. Which is to say, power can befit no other subject than this will, which is the constant result of the collective wills as equally entitled and equally contributing. Sovereignty is inalienable from the collective whole; in this way, the inalienability of freedom is realized. People, state, sovereign, general will are therefore entirely the same thing.

Any other state constitution is therefore inadmissible. It is not admissible for a prince, an aristocratic body, a popular assembly ordered by census, to have sovereignty. Only the collective will of all is sovereign. And this means not merely that "it shall be, we must strive for it," but rather, "*it is*." This is the legal relation everywhere. What is different is invalid, is unjust. The general will is always and everywhere competent and is called upon to exercise its legitimate sovereignty against such usurped sovereignty.

Accordingly, the basic idea, and indeed the overall content of Rousseau's doctrine, is the inalienable and non-transferrable power or sovereignty of the people, i.e., the collective whole or the collective will. The correlates thereof are the indivisibility, unrepresentability, and unrestrictedness of this power to which the people are entitled.

The people have power which is *indivisible*. A branch of power, namely the executive, cannot be separated and transferred to the prince (in opposition to Montesquieu and Locke). For this would engender a subject of power; a will would obtain, even if only in a specific sphere, which is not the general will.[184]

The people have power which is *unrepresentable*. Delegates of the people cannot issue any laws, for they form something else than the general will, a will in which not everyone concurs equally. Laws which are not issued or approved by the people itself are not laws, and have no validity. There are therefore few states with true laws. The English people believes that it is free, but it is actually only free at the moments of parliamentary elections; when these are over, "it is a slave, it is nothing."[185] To this end, meetings of the whole people must be regularly held, called not by magistrates but by the power of the people, and as soon as the people is assembled, all majesty of the magistrate gives way, for when the

---

[184] *Du Contrat Social,* Book II, ch. 2.

[185] *Du Contrat Social,* Book III, ch. 15.

represented appear, the representative has no more meaning.[186]

The people have power which is *unrestricted*. It cannot be bound by basic laws ("loix fundamentals") for such restriction can only be based on contract, but the people (the sovereign) cannot contract with itself, obligate itself to itself contractually. It cannot be restricted by acquired rights, for everyone alienated those rights unconditionally. It can err about what is best for it, but it can do no wrong, for there can be no wrong that it does against itself.[187]

The thesis that the sovereignty of the people is non-transferable, indivisible, unamenable to representation, incapable of restriction, only provides various aspects of the single notion of inalienable freedom of men in Rousseau's sense. It is this which characterizes the basic relation of the state association.

Doctrine regarding the relation of government

But even in the further development of the state constitution, Rousseau's doctrine has no other leading motive and purpose, not for example the excellence of elements of government and the like, but simply and solely the preservation of the inalienable power of the people. That the mass cannot of itself and directly govern is a factual necessity that one cannot evade. Rousseau admits this: the sovereign people cannot be represented in legislation as the supreme deciding power (which establishes general rules for objects), but it can be represented by the government. This is the "gouvernement" and it can be a prince, a senate, aristocracy, national representation, etc. *Sovereign* and *government* are therefore two entirely different things. What is decisive for the inalienable power of the people is the relation between sovereign (people) and government (prince, senate), and on this basis Rousseau teaches that there is no contractual transfer of power, indeed no contract at all, but it rather must be viewed as the people, as sovereign, determining by a law the form of government, designating

---

[186] *Du Contrat Social,* Book III, chs. 13 and 14.

[187] *Du Contrat Social,* Book I, ch. 6. Certainly, Rousseau recognizes limits to sovereign power in the natural rights of citizens, their lives, their freedom. But they must sacrifice everything for what is important ("importe") to the community, and regarding this *importance* only the sovereign decides (Book II, ch. 4). It is not a sum of specified rights which the sovereign may not infringe, but abstract freedom the limits of which he establishes at will. This is the basis of state absolutism.

thereby the persons in a document (act of election). Both the law and the act of election are results of the complete power of the people and nothing else. The "gouvernement" does not hereby gain a power, a right, a contractual position vis-à-vis the people, but merely a task, a service, for which it is applied ("commission," "emploi"). The magistrate (king, senate) are mere servants of the sovereign people ("simples officiers du Souverain") who exercise power in its name, being its mere depositaries. The power can therefore restrict this power, change it, revoke it, whenever it wishes ("quand il lui plaît"), and vice versa, the magistrate (even the king) cannot resign, abdicate, for it is not his right but his duty, an affair of obedience to the sovereign and his law.

In this manner, all existing constitutions are to be accounted and juridically assessed. This is the irrefutable natural law, against which no positive law is valid; it is universal constitutional law. There is therefore no variation in constitutions. Rousseau does distinguish between monarchy, aristocracy, and democracy, but only as various forms of government, not as forms of sovereignty, and therefore not truly as different constitutions. For a true variation in constitution can only have to do with a variety of the subjects of sovereignty, not with a variety of governmental organizations, and least of all if it is revocable, and therefore only *de facto* and not legal. Which form of government will exist is an open question, a question of prudence and efficiency; indeed, Rousseau advises against the democratic form of government because it does not distinguish (*distingé*) between the sovereign and the government as it ought. But among all these forms of government the absolute democracy of the constitution, which the doctrine of the sovereign and irreplaceable people constitutes, remains immovable.[188]

Rousseau, then, distinguishes as do his predecessors (Locke and Montesquieu) between legislation – the affair of the people – and the executive or government – the affair of the "gouvernement" or the king, as the case may be; but in this he differs from all his predecessors in not giving the organ of this executive a real power or any sort of right, but treating it merely as an instrument of the entirety, without will or right. This means that there is no longer any need to justify revolt, as Locke does; the whole concept of revolt drops out. The people everywhere has only its own ministries, which it vests precariously; no legal

---

[188] *Du Contrat Social,* Book III, chs. 1 and 4, chs. 16 and 17.

relation is changed even if it dethrones the king, as little as the king changes a legal relationship when he dismisses his minister.

Doctrine of the Purpose of State Association

Finally, the objective that Rousseau sets for the effectiveness of the state is determined only by the principle of inalienable freedom, i.e. the same condition which is also unalterable in the association. This objective for him is the public good ("bien public"), not in the sense of the well-being of all according to their different situations and circumstances, but only the well-being of all in the condition equal to all; not the satisfaction of all the interests which differ according to the various interests, but only satisfaction of the interests which one citizen has just like another. Accordingly, he distinguishes between a general will ("volonté générale") and a mere will of all ("volonté de tous"). When among a people each, particularly each sphere, pursues its particular will in voting, the joint result is only the will of all; but when the people as a whole pursues the interest which is uniform for all, only then is the result truly (materially) the general will. But Rousseau does not give a guarantee for the latter and not the former, and does not seek one beyond the elimination of differences in legal status (namely all corporate entities), by which he expects to eliminate the diversity of interests.[189]

This is the point from which Rousseau would logically have to continue to communism. For in order to make interests uniform, it is not sufficient merely to eliminate the diversity of *legal* statuses; *any* difference in situation must be eliminated, above all, the diversity of *economic* situations. Moreover, in the general vote, there will always be an interest of the haves against the have-nots, and therefore there will always be only a "will of all," not a "general will."

In the main, then, Rousseau is a member of the school of thought scientifically inspired by Grotius — the system of "natural law" — and indeed, he brings it to finality, and pushes it to its extreme. He also belongs in particular to the Romanist faction of this school of thought, insofar as he conceives of the will of man merely empirically, materially, eliminating every remnant of a higher commandment, a necessity. In Kant's case, it is the freedom of others as a commandment of reason (a commandment of *homo noumenon*) that compels one into

---

[189] *Du Contrat Social,* Book II, chs. 3 and 4.

the state; with Rousseau, it is only the concern for oneself, one's own benefit.[190] Rousseau's own peculiarity consists in making the freedom of man into an absolute law, which does not allow the slightest surrender of freedom by freedom. This is his doctrine of the inalienable freedom of men, the immovable equality of the condition of all, from which is inferred the inalienable, unrepresentable power or sovereignty of the people. While earlier exponents (the defenders of revolt) understood the sovereignty of the people merely as a *potential* (latent) power which, when needed, erupts and puts an end to the tyrannical government, it is, according to Rousseau, a necessary and ever-present *actual* power; the people (the collective) cannot cease for one moment actually and completely to exercise it itself. The will of the people and therefore the will of the collective persons – collectively, but thought of in a thoroughly equal condition – is the source and lord of social order in inexhaustible actuality.

True, it was claimed that Rousseau had a higher principle in his "general will" than the mere collection of individual wills, because he distinguished this from the "will of all" ("volonté de tous"). But this distinction signifies, as already demonstrated, precisely the opposite, that the general will even in terms of its content does not entail a higher harmonic order, but only the abstract equal well-being of individuals, and in any case it refers only to the inner requirement of the voters, not to their constitutional relationship. In this regard, Rousseau speaks everywhere in the most decisive terms that the general will (the sovereign) can be nothing else than the will of all, i.e., in which all individuals concur in entirely equal fashion. Rousseau's concept does not have the least relationship to the general will of Schelling and Hegel. What Rousseau makes into the principle and the power of the social order is therefore only the will of man

---

[190] "Sa (human nature) première loi est de veiller à sa propre conservation, ses premiers soins sont ceux, qu'il se doit à lui-même; livre I, chap. 2" [The first law of human nature is to is to ensure its own conservation, its first care is those, which it owes to itself; Book I, ch. 2]. "Comment les (his strength and freedom) engagera-t-il sans se nuire et sans négliger les soins qu'il se doit? ch. 6" [How will he engage them without harming himself and without neglecting the care he needs?]. If the basis of obligation of the state-establishing "engagements" are specified: "qu'en les remplissant on ne peut travailler pour autres sans travailler aussi pour soi" [that by filling them we cannot work for others without also working for ourselves]. Book II, ch. 4.

without a higher necessity, without a majesty [ein Ansehen] or a command-ment over him, and it is the will of man *par excellence* in his selfishness, detached from every moral goal, from every harmonious life-formation to which he would have to aspire; therefore only human right, without human duty. What remains as content, duty, virtue is then again only man himself: the (sensory) well-being of man, the majesty of man, and accordingly the majesty of the peo-ple. Enthusiasm has no other object than devotion to the majority, recognition of equality, fraternity. The law of God and nature – for individual life, family, state, worship – all of this drops out, and the sanctity of the popular will is ele-vated to absolute power, it is religion, morality, justice. This is the spirit of Rous-seau; it is the spirit of the Revolution.

But if this absence of true ethical content is disregarded, and Rousseau's doc-trine is considered merely as what it pretends to be, a system of equal freedom (right [richtiger] choice) and equal satisfaction of men, which is to be funda-mentally recognized and mechanically guaranteed, even in this character it demonstrates its untenability. Rousseau commits the tangible error where free-dom and satisfaction are concerned, of considering the abstract unity of the col-lective (the mere result of voting) to be equal to the personalities of which it consists. He attaches, as is not otherwise possible, that abstract unity to law and power, for freedom and satisfaction are to be pursued for concrete personalities, and only make sense as the freedom and satisfaction of personalities, not as the freedom and satisfaction of a collectivity. The false calculation of reciprocity rests on this: if I, with an equal share in the vote, submit to a thousand votes, I do not give up my freedom, since arithmetically I made the same number of votes binding upon myself as the number that I made binding upon others; as if only the formal aspect, equal participation in the forms of decision-making, and not the material aspect, the content of the decision, were the decisive factor for my freedom and satisfaction. Likewise the false thesis that the general will can do no injustice while no one can do injustice to himself. If the collective can do no injustice to itself considered as an abstract unity, this is not to say that it cannot do injustice against itself considered as the concrete personalities of which it consists. The actual result of Rousseau's doctrine therefore is not the freedom (choice) and satisfaction of men, nor of the majority of men (for the same ones who, in the majority today, guillotine people, in the minority tomor-row get guillotined); but the freedom and satisfaction of the abstract law of the majority.

If Rousseau now believes that abstract voting must coincide with the interests of the people, at least of the majority, because everyone has the same right and thus the same condition, he should have gone further than he did. Namely, as stated above, he should have equalized economic conditions; but then that would not be enough either, since differences between health, labor power, beauty, intelligence, education, moral conviction, etc. would always remain. But that would also overlook the fact that people even in equal conditions strive to make these conditions unequal, to their own advantage; and equal competition gives no guarantee that what is unfair or unjust will not be implemented in voting.

Rousseau had to grant fully the inalienability of freedom. But true freedom neither includes the condition of immobile equality of condition (the English freeholder is free even though the landlord has a more favorable position, for his livelihood is free even though there are wealthier people) nor is it permissible to conclude that the inalienability of freedom leads to the sovereign power of the people. Sovereignty has never been granted to the people for them to yield it by alienation; from the start it pertains to the ordered state, to the constitutional authority; and sovereignty does not pertain to the "condition as man" as freedom does, nor does it pertain to the rights and duties of humanity.[191]

By the way, if Rousseau combats the irrevocable transfer of power to the king from the side of the popular mass as an inconsistency on the part of Grotius, he himself commits this very inconsistency, since he commits an irrevocable transfer of power to the popular mass from the side of the individual. It is in my "inalienable freedom" that I cannot irrevocably bind myself to the rest of the whole, and as Rousseau himself demands unanimity for the first establishment of the state, he would have to demand it for every future act, otherwise it would leave open the possibility of contract termination. If the ethical form of the community is based only on the will of the individual human beings, they must be able to repeal it when they wish. Popular sovereignty therefore not only leads to anarchy, but is anarchy.

---

[191] See the relevant sections of Volume II of this work for the more detailed elucidation of individual claims.

Verdict

Rousseau's presentation manifests the system of the Revolution in the strictest scientific train of thought. In life it dissolves into a series of individual postulates which nonetheless stand in indissoluble coherence. As is known, they are as follows:

Popular sovereignty – the collective mass of the people or the majority, as the case may be, is continually the supreme authority and power; all governments possess that power only by the authority thereof and therefore can be stripped of it, held to account, and punished according to the will of the people.

Democracy – just for this reason, the collectivity (all individuals) exercises the supreme power (legislation) truly (actually) and immediately (1793).

Freedom – the citizens in their freedom are not restricted except to the degree necessary to the equal freedom of others, hence not for the goal of public welfare, public mores, public faith; that therefore no restriction exist on the breakup of estates, on taking up residence, on commerce, on sects, consequently also on moral offenses (*Declaration of the Rights of Man*). This postulate was defended not so much by Rousseau as by Locke, the North Americans, Turgot and others.

Equality – in all public relations, differences in rights according to objective conditions (e.g., landholding), estate and vocation, corporate affiliation are to be abolished.

Rationality – what is rational, i.e., institutions recognized as rational by the respective majority, are to be established immediately and unconditionally, without regard for historical condition and traditional ways of thinking, without regard for acquired rights, the latter not only having to yield, but having no validity as rights in relation to the rational condition.

The *abolition of state religion* – the state is to be indifferent to religious confession, allow every form of worship, sanction none as public, give shape to life relations (e.g., marriage) without regard to revealed commandments, guarantee fully equal political rights without regard for differences in religious confession. But in this regard, Rousseau's doctrine deviated. On the strength of his deeper view of things, he recognized that the state cannot exist without a religious drive of mind, but, sharing an aversion to Christianity on a par with this entire school of thought, he arrived at the result: a religion must be invented and introduced by the state, which, however, only has the state as its purpose. This religion must be accepted by each on penalty of death or exile, and another may not exist in the state.[192]

These are the postulates that the Revolution undertook to realize; it is these which impel liberalism up to the present hour, even if, in the face of the existing power of kingship, it does not parade the extremes of popular sovereignty and democracy; and the consistent implementation of individual freedom is often abandoned in the face of the force of natural life conditions, especially where material interests demand it.

What has been said about natural law must, of course, apply in this way to this system, which is only the practical implementation of natural law. This system likewise has its being in tearing human freedom away from the higher power and authority over it, in dissolving the organically articulated state into an undifferentiated mass, in refusing to recognize specific differentiated life relations and their inherent purpose. Here as well, in the area of practice, this orientation misses its target. It makes individual freedom into an exclusive principle, but where a sphere once granted – acquired rights – is not protected, and where the sovereign people, or what acts in its name, maintains the requirements of freedom, either true or supposed, with unrestricted power, there individual freedom is not attained. As natural law oscillates between two foundations, individual freedom and laws of logic, without being able to hold a firm position, just so is liberalism as the living system between the two foundations: individual freedom and the common will. It bases itself first on the non-disturbance of the individual, as with Turgot, Bayle and many leaders of 1789, but then arrives at the impotence, even dissolution of the community; it then bases itself on the power of the unified people, on fraternity ("fraternité"), like Rousseau, Robespierre, and today's socialists, and then destroys individual freedom. The articulation of life relations in accordance with a higher order, the beautiful completed edifice of the moral world, eludes it everywhere, as does the internal standard for the freedom of the individual, for state power, for all the various elements of the human condition.

But even the progress of the public condition which we praised above as the consequence of natural law, is attained, as is self-evident, in the practical assertion of its principles, and indeed mainly by them. Indeed, it is the special fruit

---

[192] See the final chapter of the *Contrat Social* [Social Contract].

of liberalism that it not only influences the right and freedom of the individual, as does natural law, but also extends it to the people as a whole. The notion of the inviolability of individual nations [Völkerindividualitäten] is a glorious (even if often inconsistent) product of liberalism, which deduction via natural law would not have attained. The same is true of the requirement that the people itself actually act in the formation of its public condition. Natural law only extends to personal and civil freedom; the form of government by which these are protected, as long as this protection is secure, lies outside its sphere. Liberalism proceeds to political freedom, while the power to establish laws itself is an inalienable right of men. Here, however, we encounter the serious misunderstanding that the true demand of freedom and self-activity of the people, the right to preserve and co-determine its public condition, is converted into the false demand of popular sovereignty, i.e. the right primarily and exclusively to determine its public condition, and that the people themselves are not conceived as an articulated unity but as a mere collection of the masses. When the orientation is cleared of this murky addition, then that which is to be recognized as liberal in the true sense, in which the lasting fruit of this development of thought consists, will become clear.[193]

---

[193] Compare the relevant sections in Volume II of this work.

APPENDIX TO BOOK III: MATERIALISTIC LEGAL PHILOSOPHY

A contrast with the rationalist orientation begun by Descartes and completed by Hegel is formed by the one which is usually called "empirical" and which was exercised in England and France. In this case, "empirical" is used in a different sense than with Aristotle's legal philosophy as discussed above. With Aristotle, the expression refers to the object, the existing world of experience; here, by contrast, it refers to the subjective aspect of the means of recognition, to sensorial perception. With the former, therefore, "empirical" expresses the opposite of the ideal, i.e., of a fulfilled view, the content of which pertains to another, higher world transcending actual limitations; the latter expresses the opposite of rational, pure empty determinations and laws of thought, and thought generally. It indicates an orientation which regards substance and its sensorial impression to be the original and in this respect the only [thing], while the form of reason, indeed all thought, everything intellectual [Geistige] is considered to be the mere effect hereof. It is therefore more correctly characterized as the sensory, or, in its extreme form, the materialistic orientation.

Following the groundwork provided by Bacon, Locke's doctrine of human knowledge[194] laid the foundation for this orientation, albeit still in purely theoretical, contemplative areas. While the rationalistic doctrine derives all knowledge from reason (innate ideas or logical categories), Locke conversely held the view that reason in this sense (as originally innate) makes no contribution to our knowledge, but that all knowledge arises from experience, i.e., the influence of external material objects on our senses. Locke did not deny that we have innate ideas, categories of reason, axioms by which we think, but he considers them only to be an emanation of sense impressions. He considered the human mind or understanding to be a *tabula rasa;* the qualities of external things effectuate sense impressions in us, and these in turn effectuate images in that emptiness of the mind (e.g. tone, color, resistance). By combining these impressions and abstracting from them, the mind forms the concepts of behavior, e.g., from the sense perception of successive impressions, the mind forms

---

[194] *De Intellectu Humano* [*Essay concerning Human Understanding*].

the concept of time, from the sense perception that one impression begins to exist from another, it forms the concept of cause and effect. Thus, while rationalists regard reason apart from all activity as the source of all knowledge, Locke considers reason to be entirely without content, and its activity (abstraction, combination) constructs knowledge, indeed pure concepts of relation, from sense impressions. In this manner all knowledge arises through sensation, and reflection (this activity of understanding) is itself conceived as an inner observation, thus at bottom as itself a sensation, for which reason Kant characteristically said, "Leibniz intellectualized the phenomena, while Locke sensified the concepts of reason."

This function of reason is actually only passive; thought is a material thing that is set in motion by a material impetus. In line with this, the highest certainty for Locke is the certainty of sense impressions and thereby the existence of external things, while vice versa with rationalists these are entirely cast in doubt and only the logical form is considered to be certainly known. The implementation of this notion, the construction of all supreme concepts in terms of them is masterful, but Locke overlooks the fact that sense impressions, as he depicts them, are impossible without pre-existing concepts of reason. For example, to observe the succession of impressions, one must already have the view of time; in order to observe that one impression begins "as a result of" another, one must already have the idea of causality; for which reason, Hume on this basis rightly proceeds to cast doubt on the causal link, since the experience of one *after* the other never proves one *because of* the other. Indeed, this activity of reason – abstraction and combination, reflection – which he allows to proceed without any rational content in sense material, must have a law, and that would be an innate idea, a category independent of sense impression.

In the area of practice, this point of view now necessarily leads to the acceptance of satisfaction and, ultimately, sense satisfaction as the ultimate goal. When sense impression is the source and supreme truth of cognition, then it must also be the source and supreme rule of action. Locke therefore even denied that there are practical ideas that are necessary in themselves; virtue should be praised not because it is innate to us, but because it is useful, and accordingly it is characteristic of the great majority of English moral philosophers and the French who follow in this direction to accept satisfaction, well-being, happiness as an ethical principle, and to relinquish an independent value, an independent necessity of the good. Several of them, especially at the commencement of this theory, with a personally noble way of thinking, tempered the result of the principle so that it does not come clearly to consciousness, by teaching a satisfaction by the good, by charity, etc. But this gradually receded, leaving sense satisfaction as the center of ethics. In the same way, many gradations are conceived as to how one's own satisfaction (egoism) is assumed to be the basis (thus not necessarily goal and content), and to what degree, from the outset, common satisfaction is that basis.[195]

The logical conclusion of the sensorial principle fashioned into a comprehensive world-view is Mirabaud's "system of nature." For him there is no spirit; the universe or nature is only matter which functions according to its necessary laws. This is indeed the inevitable assumption, if Locke's theory of knowledge, according to which knowledge is only the effect of sense impression, is correct. Therefore there is no God, and the idea of such is an invention of fear or ignorance. Man is a totally material being; thinking is an effect of the material movement of the nerves of the brain; every thought arises only through the sense impressions of material objects. With the end of earthly life, human life ends forever, there is no survival except in glory, in the memory of posterity. There is no freedom of action, for every act is a necessary effect of attraction and repulsion. Good or bad depends on whether it leads to happiness, that is, to continuous sensorial pleasure. The most evil thing is religion, which, terrorizing through punishment, disturbs enjoyment in the present by holding out a prospective future.

The parallel in results of this consummately materialistic view with the consummately rationalist, hence logical-pantheistic view is unmistakable. Instead of God, there is a necessary lawful movement of its own unconscious

---

[195] The succession of sensorialist systems of morality and their various fractions, the presentation of which is not our task here, is done well by Erdmann in his *Geschichte der neuern Philosophie* [History of Recent Philosophy]. For the rest, a truth underlies these eudemonistic moral systems, by which in terms of the eternal order, the satisfaction of personality is no less an independent absolute goal as is the fulfilment of the higher (divine) commandment. The error lies in the fact that the latter is here made into a mere means for the former, while satisfaction is usually placed in the well-being of men in accordance with empirical-sensorial existence.

movement, let it be called matter, substance, logical law, idea; there is no freedom of man, no immortality. Even the rejection of religion as something im-
moral has its parallel in the pantheistic system, since Hegel declares Christian
diffidence [Bescheidung] regarding knowledge to be the heighth of immorality.[196] By restricting human enjoyment, Christianity reaches as much into the
heart of materialistic pantheism as it reaches into the heart of rationalist pantheism by restricting human pride of thought. Even so, the content of morality
in rationalism, as is self-evident, is fundamentally opposed to materialism.[197]

As far as legal philosophy is concerned, Locke himself created no particular
legal philosophy corresponding to his empirical point of view; rather, he took
over the entirety of natural law, this result of the rationalist orientation which
filled the minds of his time, and only modified it in certain points in accordance
with his empirical standpoint.[198] Like the other natural law doctors, he made
individuals in their isolation into the principle of the legal order, taught the
original complete freedom and equality of the state of nature and the foundation of the state by means of contract, and restricted the goal of the state to the
protection of individual rights. But in doing so he did not conceive of man ra-
tionalistically from the side of pure will, of abstract freedom, as they do; but
sensorially, from the side of his entire sense existence. Accordingly, for the state
of nature, i.e., prior to the establishment of the state by contract, he taught a law
of nature which, from the outset, contains the entire individual empirical existence of man ("life, freedom, health, property"), not merely a general statement
from which one and the other is gained by inference. In particular, he taught
the immediate validity of property, especially in the state of nature. While all
earlier natural law doctors derived property from contract, and Kant, who de-
viates from this, yet derived it from the mutual recognition of the will, and
therefore also discovered the acquisition thereof in the expression of will (occupation), Locke deduced property from empirical lack, because without it, thus
with common property, things could not be utilized. Accordingly, he attributed

---

[196] *Enzyklopädie*, § 386 and "Vorrede zu Hinrichs Religionsphilosophie" [Prologue to
Hinrich's Philosophy of Religion].

[197] The positive midpoint of truth over these two orientations is discussed in Volume II,
Book I [*Philosophical Presuppositions*], §§ 22, 29, and 37 of this work.

[198] See the *Two Treatises of Government*.

the acquisition of property to labor, as that by which goods are made to serve the needs of human beings, and not to occupation, by which the will merely expresses itself; and also recognized originally a limit to the acquisition of property in the possibility of cultivation and use for one's own needs. Unlimited acquisition of property only has meaning and purpose where trade and commerce, and money as means of exchange, exist; and all of this is first founded by contract.[199]

Finally, Locke taught that already in the state of nature, penal law can be exercised by individuals against those who violate natural law. This as well has immediate validity by virtue of that full empirical existence of men, and for their protection, and does not require initial contractual introduction, which would signify the consent of those who are to be punished. Indeed, the establishment of the state is itself nothing other than the renunciation by individuals of the exercise of this penal law which originally accrued to them, allowing it to be exercised by the community. For this reason, as he explained, state power is basically divided into two functions, the legislative and the executive; the former determines the laws the infringement of which ought to be punished, and the latter inflicts the punishment. Such penal protection for individual rights exercised by the collective instead of the individuals, and nothing else, now comprises the essence and meaning of the state. While the other (rationalistic) natural law doctrines are filled with the *ideal*, that the human will (apart from any content and object) is the sole cause of human conditions, Locke is filled with the *real*, that man in his sensorial existence and, in particular, what is empirically the basis of it, property, is protected. For this reason the chief means for the former is contract, as that in which the pure will, absent any content, proves itself, while with Locke it is property which accrues directly to men, and the right which accrues directly to him to protect his own, by means of punishment and prevention. Locke's empirical point of view is also characterized by the fact that, with regard to the duration of the marital bond, he gave as reason for parents to remain together the education of the children, rather than cohabitation – not the only reason, but still the main one. Nor was he, as were the other natural-law doctors, at a loss to establish paternal power. It is precisely the

---

[199] Both relations (Kant's and Locke's) taken together yield the truth. See Volume II, Book III of this work [*Private Law*], §§. 2 2 and 2 9.

empirical existence of children which requires this power, while it is excluded by the idea of the children's will, which the others make into their principle.

In accordance with this point of view, Locke remained forever and fundamentally distinguished from Rousseau, although with regard to the doctrine of popular sovereignty over royal power, he is the final precursor to him. Locke is always firmly committed to the independence of individual existence within its certain, sensorially given circumference, which the community must serve; while Rousseau allows it to be submerged as an indistinct unit in the general will. The mere abstract (if only selfish) will of the individual can flow together into such an equally contentless general will, whereas the sensorial existence of the individual always remains separate. In Locke's case, then, it is not the common will on which the emphasis is placed, but the common law, the rule (standing rule) which protects individual rights, and the impartial "judge on earth" which in the event of a dispute decides on the application. This forms the contrast with the state of nature, according to which each individual gives the rule to himself, and also against the absolutism of the king, according to which he alone gives and applies the rule. It is a feature that very characteristically distinguishes the English from the French. Although philosophical abstraction kept Locke from defending the old laws and acquired rights as Burke did, he nevertheless advocated certain unbreakable laws and the safeguarding of a certain legal existence, not an imaginary share in a sovereign lawless collective will.

To this extent, the influence of the sensorialist point of view is expressed in legal philosophy as put forward by Locke. A logical and radical implementation of the same, in terms of its extreme form as materialism, is provided in the system of Bentham, which stands in isolation as an individual conception (particularly remarkable in its rejection of human rights and the other purely formal teachings of the rationalist system, to which he contrasts material well-being, utility), and furthermore the more recent French socialistic theories in all their factions: communism, St. Simonism, socialism.

The innermost focal point of these theories is none other than enjoyment as the highest and ultimate purpose of human life, and thus human community which has no other task and guideline than to provide the same, and the highest possible enjoyment to everyone. Rationalist philosophy of law accomplished the feat of juxtaposing human beings not under an ethical order commanded by God, but in terms of inalienably equal claims. But it only considered abstract freedom to be the content of these claims, be it free movement in the individual sphere as natural right, be it the equal participation in common rule, as is the case with Rousseau's liberalism. With complete truth it could be objected that little is done with this abstract freedom and abstract equality if, because of the inequality of possessions, the real situation of people differs: for the one, abundance, happiness, freedom, for the other, want, distress, dependence. The appropriate response is that if, because of the same nature of man, no one should be able to advance beyond the other in terms of power and influence, then no one should have any advantage in enjoyment of life, possessions, and education.

In the first edition of this book (1830), when we did not yet know anything in Germany about these socialistic theories, I made the same response to natural law.[200] If sense satisfaction is now regarded with clear awareness as the ultimate goal of things, a doctrine of the human community necessarily arises by which there is no other task for it than to provide means of pleasure by labor, and to distribute them in such a way as to make the pleasure equal. Pleasure-providing labor is the highest employment of people, and manual labor holds the highest rank. Pleasure is the fulfillment of the purpose of our existence, and what remains as morality, or rather as the appearance of morality, is the pursuit of pleasure without prejudice to the pleasure of all. Enthusiasm for equal pleasure is the only interesting factor in this materialistic doctrine, just as enthusiasm for equal participation in supreme power is the interesting factor in rationalist revolutionary doctrine. On the other hand, everything that constitutes the fulfillment of a higher commandment over man, the holiness of marriage, the administration of justice, the gathering and upliftment of the human mind for a kingdom beyond earthly pleasures, together with the preservation of the institutions of religion and education which lead to this, the attachment of a regard and a power which, as an organ of this higher order, of royalty or other authority, is to be revered for itself – none of this has any place in such an organization of pleasure.

What in the rationalist point of view is bare law stripped of its purpose in the moral world-whole, in the materialistic point of view is pleasure.

The socialism of Fourier and the distributism of St. Simon are not entirely logical, in that fortune [Schicksal], i.e., the greater talent for work of one person

---

[200] See p. 197 of that edition.

over another, or even justice, the greater effort being rewarded with greater enjoyment, leaves a field of unequalization which does not agree with their supreme axiom, the equal claim to pleasure of human nature. The same is true of Proudhon's doctrine which, while retaining separate ownership and acquisition, states that wages should be determined neither by the value of the product nor by the workmanship, but by the time spent on them. The consequential implementation of the standpoint leads to communism. Indeed, animosity to property must be the end-result of the materialistic orientation which began to germinate with Locke. For property is just a notion, a rational rather than sensorial phenomenon. If one removes the rational admixture from the property relation, nothing remains but pleasure. Consequently, in communism the whole idea of law is fundamentally abandoned. Not even the prudential justice of socialistic theory, stipulating that the more skillful and hard-working worker should have more, remains.

So these are the four slogans – down with Christianity, kingship, marriage, property – which the materialistic worldview has logically fulfilled in the practical fields of our day. The socialistic theories, and in particular communism, have gotten serious with materialistic philosophy (Locke, Helvétius, etc.), in the same way that the Sidney-Rousseau theory of the Revolution got serious with rationalistic philosophy (Descartes, Grotius, etc.).

However, this is only to mark this orientation in terms of its destructiveness — which undeniably, incomparably, is its dominant aspect. It destroys the kingdom of God, the moral order of life. But it also has a seed of growth, similar to the system of the Revolution. Freedom, the egalitarian freedom of men, is also a part of the ethical order, albeit not the only one, and its assertion was required in the face of the presumption of a single class and the oppression, even degrading oppression, of a numerous portion of the people. In the same way, material satisfaction and the distribution of necessary satisfaction for every person is likewise a part of the ethical order, and its assertion is also required, in particular in conditions of excessive abundance on the one hand and extreme deficiency on the other, even if it is not asserted here in the proper manner. Liberalism enabled the self-reliant, the propertied, to gain the recognition of their dignity and their due share in the shaping of the community; the socialistic theory aims at least to be a spur for the non-propertied to achieve the measure of life satisfaction that they deserve. In the same way that it is impossible now for the nobility to assume the position vis-à-vis the citizenry that it enjoyed before the Revolution, it will be impossible one day to waste children in factories, to let workers be worn down by overburdening them, or to leave free labor to its fate, without any public welfare provision.

For this reason, although the rationalist theory of natural rights and revolution, as well as materialistic social theory as a whole, must be confronted as a perverse and perishable doctrine, one may not deny the important aspects of truth, or indeed the true motives that they contain. It is necessary to seek to appropriate these traits into a truth-based comprehensive view of the human community. The positive gain brought by rationalist ethics and legal philosophy has been highlighted everywhere in previous chapters of this book. In relation to the socialistic theories, I have attempted this in the second volume, in which they are characterized and assessed in more detail. The significance and therefore also the elements of truth of the socialistic theories are however by the nature of the case less ethical and legal-philosophical than they are national-economic. Because of this, a history of legal philosophy is not the place for a more detailed presentation. It is justifiably reserved for a dedicated investigation and implementation.[201]

---

[201] See Volume II, Part I, Book III of this work [*Private Law*], §§ 3 1ff., and Part II [*The Doctrine of State & the Principles of State Law*], §§ 2 2ff. (Note to the 4th edition: a yet more thorough presentation of the social theories is now provided in *Die gegenwärtigen Parteien in Staat und Kirche* [The Contemporary Parties in Church and State].)

WORKS CITED

Alvarado, Ruben. *Calvin and the Whigs: A Study in Historical Political Theology.* Aalten: Pantocrator Press, 2017.

—. *The Debate that Changed the West: Grotius versus Althusius.* Aalten: Pantocrator Press, 2018.

Andlo, Petrus de. *De imperio romano Regis et Augusti creatione ... : libri duo.* Argentoratum: Rikel, 1603 [1460].

Aquinas, Thomas. *De regimine principum: libri quatuor.* Lugduni Batavorum [Leyden]: Ex officina Joannis Maire, 1630.

—. *Summa Theologica.* Trans. Fathers of the English Dominican Province. New York: Benziger Bros., 1947.

Bacon, Francis. *De dignitate & augmentis scientiarum libri IX.* London: In officina Ioannis Hauiland, 1623.

Bodin, Jean. *Les Six Livres de la République.* Paris: Jacques du Puis, 1576.

Brutus, Stephanus Junius. *Vindiciae contra Tyrannos: sive, De principis in populum, populique in principem, legitima potestate.* Edinburgh, 1579.

Coccejus, Henricus. *Disputatio Juridica Inauguralis de Principio Juris Naturalis Unico, Vero, et Adaequato.* Francofurti ad Viadrum: Christophori Zeitleri, 1699.

—. *Positiones pauculae & generalissimae loco quasi postulatorum explicationi juris gentium & praelectionibus Grotianis praemissae.* Nova editio, revisa & aucta. Francofurti ad Viadrum: Joh. Godofredum Conradi, 1719.

Dante. *De Monarchia of Dante Alighieri.* Trans. Aurelia Henry. Boston and New York: Houghton Mifflin and Company, 1904.

Erdmann, Johann Eduard. *Einleitung in eine wissenschaftliche Darstellung der Geschichte der neuern Philosophie.* Riga und Dorpat: Eduard Frantzen's Buchhandlung, 1834.

Feuerbach, Paul Johann Anselm, Ritter von. *Kritik des natürlichen rechts als propädeutik zu einer wissenschaft der natürlichen rechte.* Altona: Bei der

Verlagsgesellschaft, 1796.

—. *Lehrbuch des gemeinen in Deutschland geltenden peinlichen Rechts.* Giessen: Georg Friedrich Heyer, 1801.

—. *Revision der Grundsätze und Grundbegriffe des positiven peinlichen Rechts.* 2 vols. Chemnitz: Georg Friedrich Tasché, 1800.

Fichte, Johann Gottlieb. *Beitrag zur Berichtigung der Urtheile des Publikums über die französische Revolution.* 2nd ed. [Danzig]: [Verlag Ferdinand Troschel], 1795.

—. *Das System der Sittenlehre nach den Principien der Wissenschaftslehre.* Jena und Leipzig: Christian Ernst Gabler, 1798.

—. *Foundations of Natural Right According to the Principles of the Wissenschaftslehre.* Ed. Frederick Neuhouser. Trans. Michael Baur. Cambridge: Cambridge University Press, 2000.

—. *Grundlage des Naturrechts nach Principien der Wissenschaftslehre.* 2 vols. Iena und Leipzig: Christian Ernst Gabler, 1796–1797.

—. *J. G. Fichte's ... Appellation an das Publikum über die durch ein Kurf. Sächs. Confiscationsrescript ihm beigemessenen atheistischen Aeusserungen.* Jena und Leipzig; Tübingen: Christian Ernst Gabler; J. G. Cottaischen Buchhandlung, 1799.

—. *The Science of Ethics as based on the Science of Knowledge.* Trans. A. E. Kroeger. London: Kegan Paul, 1897.

Franklin, Julian H. *Constitutionalism and Resistance in the Sixteenth Century: Three Treatises by Hotman, Beza, & Mornay.* New York: Pegasus, 1969.

Goldast, Melchior. *Monarchia s. romani Imperii, sive Tractatus de jurisdictione imperiali seu regia et pontificia seu sacerdotali... studio... Melchioris Goldasti Haiminsfeldii,...* Vol. II. Francofurti: Apud Joann-Davidem Zunnerum, 1668.

Grotius, Hugo. *De Jure Belli ac Pacis Libri Tres.* Trans. Francis W. Kelsey. Oxford: At the Clarendon Press, 1925.

—. *Rights of War and Peace.* Ed. Jean Barbeyrac and Richard Tuck. 3 vols. Indianapolis: Liberty Fund, 2005.

Hegel, Georg Wilhelm Friedrich. *Enzyklopädie der philosophischen Wissen-*

schaften im Grundrisse. III vols. Heidelberg: Oßwald, 1830 [1817].

Hegel, Georg Wilhelm Friedrich. "Vorrede zu Hinrichs' Religionsphilosophie." *Vollständige Ausgabe durch einen Verein von Freunden des verewigten: D. Ph. Marheineke, D. J. Schulze, D. Ed. Gans, D. Lp. v. Henning, D. H. Hotho, D. C. Michelet, D. F. Förster, Volume 17.* Berlin: Duncker und Humblot, 1835. 280–304.

Hobbes, Thomas. *Elementa Philosophica de Cive.* Amsterdam: Elsevier, 1647 [1642].

—. *Leviathan, or the Matter, Forme, & Power of a Common-Wealth Ecclesiastical and Civill.* London: Andrew Crooke, 1651.

Hoffbauer, Johan Christoph. *Untersuchungen über die wichtigsten Gegenstände des Naturrechts. Nebst einer Censur der verdienstlichsten Bemühungen um diese Wissenschaft...* Halle: Carl August Kümmel, 1795.

Kant, Immanuel. *Critik der reinen Vernunft.* 2nd. Riga: Johann Friedrich Hartknoch, 1787.

—. *Critik der Urtheilskraft.* Frankfurt und Leipzig: n. p., 1792.

—. *Critik der praktischen Vernunft.* Riga: Johann Friedrich Hartknoch, 1788.

—. *Grundlegung zur Metaphysik der Sitten.* Riga: Johann Friedrich Hartknoch, 1785.

—. *Metaphysische Anfangsgründe der Rechtslehre. Erster Theil von die Metaphysik der Sitten.* 2nd ed. Königsberg: Friedrich Nicolovius, 1798.

—. *The Metaphysics of Morals.* Trans. Mary Gregor. Cambridge: Cambridge University Press, 1996.

Linck, Anton Arnold von. *Über das Naturrecht unserer Zeit als Grundlage der Strafrechtstheorien.* Munich: Anton Weber, 1829.

Locke, John. *De Intellectu Humano Inquator Libris.* London: Impensis Aunshami & Johan. Churchill, 1701.

—. *Two Treatises of Government.* Ed. Peter Laslett. New York: New American Library, 1965 [1960]. First edition 1689.

Marca, Petrus de. *De Concordia Sacerdotii et Imperii, seu de libertatibus ecclesiæ Gallicanæ dissertationum libri quatuor.* Paris: Sumptibus Viduae Ioannis Camusat, 1641.

Mariana, Juan de. *De Rege et regis institutione Libri tres.* Toleti: Apud Petrum

Rodericum typo. Regium, 1599.

Milton, John. *A Defence of the People of England by John Milton ; in answer to Salmasius's Defence of the king.* Trans. Joseph Washington. [Amsterdam], 1692.

—. *Pro Populo Anglicano Defensio, contra Claudii Anonymi, aliàs Salmasii, Defensionem Regiam.* London: Typis du Gardianis, 1651.

More, Thomas. *De Optimo Reipublicae Statu deque Nova Insula Utopia.* Louvain: Dirk Martens, 1516.

Mornay, Philippe du Plessis. *A Defence of Liberty Against Tyrants: A Translation of the Vindiciae Contra Tyrannos by Junius Brutus.* London: G. Bell and Sons, Ltd., 1924.

Nettelbladt, Daniel. *Systema elementare universae Jurisprudentiae naturalis.* 3rd. Halae Magdeburgicae: In Officina Libraria Rengeriana, 1767.

Oldendorp, Johannes. *Iuris Naturalis Civilis et Gentium Isagoge.* Cologne: Ioannes Gymnicus, 1539.

Pufendorf, Samuel. *De Jure Naturæ et Gentium: Libri Octo.* Londini Scanorum: Sumtibus Adami Junghaus, 1672.

—. *De Officio Hominis & Civis Juxta Legem Naturalem Libri Duo.* Londini Scanorum: Sumtibus Adami Junghans, 1673.

—. *Elementorum Iurisprudentiae Universalis libri duo.* Hagae-Comitis: Adriani Vlacq, 1660.

—. *Of the Law of Nature and Nations: Eight Books.* London: Printed for J. Walthoe, R. Wilkin, J. and J. Bonwicke, S. Birt, T. Ward, and T. Osborne, 1729.

—. *The Whole Duty of Man according to the Law of Nature.* Indianapolis: Liberty Fund, 2003.

—. *Two Books of the Elements of Universal Jurisprudence.* Trans. William Abbott Oldfather. Indianapolis: Liberty Fund, 2009 [1931].

Rousseau, Jean-Jacques. *Du contrat social, ou Principes du droit politique.* Amsterdam: Marc-Michel Rey, 1762.

Selden, John. *De Jure Naturali et Gentium juxta Disciplinam Ebraeorum Libri VII.* London: Richardus Bishopius, 1640.

Sidney, Algernon. *Discourses Concerning Government.* London: [John Toland],

1698.

Stahl, Friedrich Julius. *Der Protestantismus als politisches Princip*. Berlin: Verlag von Wilhelm Schultze, 1853.

—. *Die gegenwärtigen Parteien in Staat und Kirche. Neunundzwanzig akademische Vorlesungen*. Berlin: Verlag von Wilhelm Hertz, 1863.

—. *Die Kirchenverfassung nach Lehre und Recht der Protestanten*. Erlangen: Theodor Bläsing, 1840.

—. *Philosophical Presuppositions*. Aalten: WordBridge Publishing, forthcoming.

—. *Principles of Law*. Aalten: WordBridge Publishing, 2007.

—. *Private Law*. Aalten: WordBridge, 2007.

—. *The Doctrine of State and the Principles of State Law*. Aalten: WordBridge, 2009.

Suarez, Francisco. *Tractatus de Legibus ac Deo Legislatore*. Coimbra: Didacum Gomez de Loureyro, 1612.

Thomasius, Christian. "Die Grund-Lehren des Natur- und Völker-rechts, nach dem sinnlichen Begriff aller Menschen vorgestellet." *Herrn Christian Thomasii Drey Bücher der Göttlichen Rechtsgelahrheit*. Hall im Magdeburgischen: Zufinden in der Rengerischen Buchhandlung, 1709.

—. *Fundamenta juris naturae et gentium ex sensu communi deducta*. Halae & Lipsiae: Typus & Sumtibus Viduae Christophori Salfeldii, 1705.

—. *Institutes of Divine Jurisprudence. With Selections from Foundations of the Law of Nature and Nations*. Indianapolis: Liberty Fund, 2011.

—. *Institutiones iurisprudentiae divinae*. Halae Magdeburgicae: Sumtibus Christophori Salfeldii, 1694.

Warnkönig, Leopold August. *Rechtsphilosophie als Naturlehre des Rechts*. Freiburg im Breisgau: Wagner, 1839.

Wolff, Christian. *Institutiones Iuris Naturae et Gentium*. Halae Magdeburgicae: Prostat in Officina Rengeriana, 1750.

—. *Jus Naturae Methodo Scientifica Pertractatum*. VIII vols. Francofurti & Lipsiae; Halae Magdeburgicae: Prostat in Officina Libraria Rengeriana, 1740–1748.

—. *Vernünfftige Gedancken von Gott, Der Welt und der Seele des Menschen, auch allen Dingen überhaupt.* Halle: Rengerischen Buchhandel, 1722.

INDEX

38, 105

separation from God, 32

human, 48, 244

in subjective slsense. *See* subjective
right

Jewish view of
based on charity, 31–35

jus naturale, 139

lex aeterna, 39, 47, 96, 97
root of autonomous natural law,
94

lex humana, 48

lex naturalis, 47, 49, 95

lex permissiva, 112

moral, 39, 48, 110, 170, 175, 176,
196

natural. *passim*
binds God, 154
detachment from the will of
God as prerequisite, 95
dissolves the bond between the
world and God, 160
each system derived from an
individual drive, 98
ignores the purpose of life
relations, 229–31
modern, founded by Grotius,
146
reason as all-sufficient cause of,
96
root of its erroneous
conceptualization, 47–48
subordinate role of God in, 97
transformed into law of reason,
179

nature of the case, 49, 239

of nations, 139, 146

permissive, 112, 113, 160

positive, 40, 48, 49, 121, 134, 140,
146, 251

theology as (Leibniz), 106

will of God as, 95

principle of
freedom as exclusive, 125
Germanic, 121
personal will of God as, 59
purpose of life relations as, 229–
31

reason, law of, 82, 112, 114, 117,
171, 176, 179, 180, 182, 186,
195, 197, 198, 199, 200, 203,
206, 207, 214, 218, 220, 229,
232

natural law changed into, 179

Roman
abstract character, 121
and subjective right, 39
commitment to existing
institutions, 122
comparison with natural law,
120–23
separation from morality, 39

legitimacy, 65, 66

Leibniz, Gottfried Wilhelm, 94, 95,
97, 106, 158, 173, 176, 260

liberalism, 237, 258, 266
does not recognize purpose of life
relations, 257
implementation of the Revolution,
237
positive and negative effects of,
257–58, 267

Linck, Anton Arnold von, 180

Locke, John, 69, 241, 243, 247, 249,
251, 256, 259–64, 266
adaptation of English liberties, 264
adapted rationalist natural law to
empiricist framework, 262

Louis of Bavaria, 54

Luther, Martin, 64

Machiavelli, Niccolo, 201

man
concept versus ideal of, 117

www.ingramcontent.com/pod-product-compliance
Lightning Source LLC
Chambersburg PA
CBHW071408090426
42737CB00011B/1395